BAPTIST
DISTINCTIVES
AND NEW TESTAMENT CHURCH ORDER

BAPTIST
DISTINCTIVES
AND NEW TESTAMENT CHURCH ORDER

Kevin Bauder

Regular Baptist Books
Arlington Heights, Illinois

Baptist Distinctives and New Testament Church Order
© 2012 Regular Baptist Press • Arlington Heights, Illinois.
www.RegularBaptistPress.org • 1-800-727-4440
Cloth: RBP5125 • ISBN: 978-1-60776-652-0
Paper: RBP5118 • ISBN: 978-1-60776-583-7

Second Printing—2019

Contents

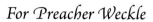

For Preacher Weckle

Preface

THE VISION FOR THIS BOOK grew over time. It was originally conceived as a short booklet-length explanation of Baptist principles. Early drafts of the first chapters were written as much as two decades ago. While I was in the process of writing and thinking, however, it seemed useful to include a slightly fuller exposition of the reasons for the unique positions Baptists hold. While the volume is still meant as explanation and not polemic, it now investigates at least the principal evidences and arguments for the Baptist distinctives.

The range of content has also been expanded. When I first outlined the book, I foresaw a format in which a single chapter would be devoted to each of the six distinctives. As these chapters began to unfold, I became aware that certain aspects of Baptist theology would likely be omitted if I consistently followed the original approach. At first, I attempted to correct this deficiency by simply adding discussions to each chapter. For instance, the examination of the Lord's Table became part of the chapter on pure church membership.

Even this approach left some important topics largely unaddressed. One example is the network of problems connected with Landmarkism. Friends who regularly encountered Landmark views encouraged me to provide them with some help by incorporating at least a cursory response. Other practical matters such as interchurch cooperation merited elaboration, but they really deserved chapters of their own.

These considerations were becoming weightier at the very time when Regular Baptist Press agreed to publish the volume. As it happened, Regular Baptist Press wanted a longer work than I had first envisioned. Consequently, I was able to incorporate several chapters that deal with practical questions that confront Baptists.

While I am glad for the expansion that occurred in the process of writing the book, I recognize that there remain in these pages rather more gaps than I would have preferred. As it goes to press, I can already think of ways in which the discussion could be improved. These will have to await a second and expanded edition that, Lord willing, I will have the opportunity to publish in future years.

I frankly acknowledge that this book would be far less useful if not for the generous criticism of friends and colleagues. Drafts of these chapters have, of course, been read by my fellow professors on the faculty of Central Baptist Theological Seminary of Minneapolis. I am especially grateful to Jeff Straub for his helpful interaction. The entire first draft was also read by Pastor Ralph Warren of Lake County Baptist Church in Waukegan, Illinois, who provided much useful advice. I am particularly grateful for Grant Bird, my assistant, who has edited the drafts, checked the citations, and done much else to improve the quality of this presentation.

The board of Central Seminary took a bold step when they placed me in a professorship that would be devoted largely to writing. I am grateful for their vision and for the strength of their faith. The arrangement that they created has, from a human perspective, made this book possible.

My first lessons in Baptist distinctives and polity were learned as a boy in a small church plant (First Baptist Church) in Freeland, Michigan. The Fellowship of Baptists for Home Missions provided a man of God, Robert Weckle, as a pastor and church planter. His teaching and ministry were irreplaceable in shaping my understanding of the ideas in this book. Equally important was the instruction of my father, Thomas D. Bauder, who became a Baptist pastor during my high school years. His patient explanations of Baptist ideas are still ringing in my ears. Later professors (George Houghton in college and Robert Delnay in seminary) did much to confirm and build upon the ideas that I learned in my youth.

The above individuals have all contributed to this book, either directly or indirectly. I am more grateful to them than I can say. They have headed off some bad thinking and helped me to repair some broken sections. The remaining flaws, however, are my responsibility alone.

Plymouth, Minnesota
March 20, 2012

Introduction

DENOMINATIONAL LABELS are going out of style. I think that is unfortunate. Those labels are a kind of shorthand. They stand for sets of ideas. When people say, "I am a Lutheran," or "I am a Presbyterian," they are not just identifying themselves with an organization or a social group. They are identifying themselves with a combination of convictions. Each of the major denominational labels stands for a set of ideas. At one time, Christians thought that these ideas were so important that they deserved labels. They used the labels to distinguish one set of convictions from another. They wore their labels as the badge that identified their distinctive beliefs.

I am a Baptist. Unlike some denominations, Baptists did not choose their own label. Their opponents gave it to them as shorthand for the doctrines and practices that distinguished Baptists from other Christians. Because Baptists were strongly committed to these ideas, they embraced the label. They were pleased to accept a name that stood for important teachings. Since I agree with those teachings, and since I also think that they are important, I am happy to share the label.

What I have discovered is that most people who wear the name *Baptist* no longer know the ideas it stands for. If asked to name the characteristic teachings of their group, most merely observe that their churches perform baptisms by immersing rather than sprinkling or pouring. Increasingly, church members display an astonishing lack of knowledge about just what Baptists believe.

Sadly, that ignorance is too often shared by Baptist leaders. It is not difficult to find lists of Baptist distinctives, but such lists are often marred by one of two faults. The first fault is that many of the lists were compiled by writers who really did not know what Baptists believe. Consequently, their lists either omit important teachings, or they add teachings upon which Baptists have never agreed. Sometimes they do both.

The second and more serious fault is that some lists have been compiled by people with theological axes to grind. Some groups would like to claim to be the only true Baptists. They attempt to bolster their claim by trying to define all other Baptists out of existence. Their lists are little more than propaganda tools.

This point was brought home to me when a friend asked me to recommend a current, nontechnical work that would explain what a Baptist is. I teach Baptist polity in a seminary. I ought to know where to find such a work. As I pondered the question, however, I could not think of a single work that I could heartily recommend. Every pamphlet or book that came to mind was one that required, at best, a guarded endorsement.

This came as a surprise to me. Baptists used to publish many good statements of their beliefs. I can think of older works that I could recommend virtually without reservation. But I cannot think of anything that is available now that does not require further qualification or explanation.

A need exists for a short book that will explain Baptist thought and practice to ordinary church members and, perhaps, to those who are training for ministry. The present book undertakes this task. It will answer the question, What is a Baptist? for people who are not theological experts. It will not, however, try to defend all of the distinctive Baptist beliefs in detail, though it will usually indicate where the main proofs lie.

In this book, I wish to explain which ideas and practices set Baptists apart from other Christians. I am addressing this explanation primarily to those who have either grown up in or entered Baptist circles without understanding the beliefs that shape the Baptist mind and heart. Secondarily, I am also offering an explanation to non-Baptists who are curious about Baptist beliefs. I do not, however, intend this volume to be a polemic to answer all the arguments of those who disagree. Neither do I intend to treat exhaustively every aspect of Baptist theology. This book is an overview, not for the theological professional, but for the thoughtful inquirer.

The Baptist Distinctives

Baptists are defined by their characteristic beliefs. Taken together, these beliefs are called the *Baptist distinctives*. Before we actually begin to explore these distinctive teachings, I need to say a word about how they function.

The distinctives, taken together, are what set Baptists apart from other Christians. Therefore, no belief that is held universally by Christians can qualify as a Baptist distinctive. Some teachings set all Christians apart from other religious people. These "Christian distinctives" are known as essentials, or fundamentals. All true Christians affirm the fundamentals. Because Baptists are Christians, they also believe the fundamentals. A person who denies one of the fundamentals cannot be a Baptist because that person is not a Christian (though too often such persons dishonestly continue to call themselves Christians and even Baptists). By the same token, Methodists and Presbyterians affirm the fundamentals, for they, too, are Christians. A person who denies a fundamental doctrine cannot rightly be called a Methodist or a Presbyterian. The fundamentals are the common property of all true Christians, whether Baptist, Lutheran, Calvinist, or Wesleyan. Therefore, a fundamental doctrine is not really a Baptist distinctive, even though all genuine Baptists believe it.

On the other hand, we must not say that *only* Baptists hold *any* of the Baptist distinctives. Baptists are characterized by several beliefs. Not one of those beliefs is absolutely unique to Baptists. No matter which one you choose, you can find other Christians who acknowledge it. No single distinctive *by itself* is sufficient to distinguish Baptists from all other groups of Christians.

What makes Baptists different is that they alone hold the combination of beliefs that are known as the Baptist distinctives. Each individual belief is held by some other group, but no other group holds the whole bundle. Baptists are distinguished, not by the individual teachings, but by the combination of teachings that make up the Baptist distinctives.

While each of the Baptist distinctives is held by *some* other Christians, no Baptist distinctive is held by *all* other Christians. Therefore, each one of the distinctives sets Baptists apart from some other Christian group. When all of the distinctives are added together, the combination ends up setting Baptists apart from all other Christians.

The purpose of this book is both to articulate the Baptist distinctives and to discuss some of the practical issues that arise from applying them. Consequently, the book is in two parts. In the first part, each chapter takes up and discusses one Baptist distinctive, for a total of six in all. The second part deals with the application of these distinctives to practical problems that Baptists face. In the second part, each chapter deals with a particular problem.

Handling Scriptural Evidence

Before moving into the actual discussion of the Baptist distinctives, I should say something about how I will be handling the Scriptures. It can be perplexing to see how Christians of goodwill, all of whom acknowledge the authority of Scripture, can come to such different conclusions regarding denominational distinctives. Such realities force us to ask what is unique about the Baptists' way of handling Scripture that leads to their conclusions.

This question has several answers. One is that Baptists appeal specifically to the New Testament as their authority for the faith and order of the church. In fact, this appeal is really the first and most important Baptist distinctive. The first chapter of this book will discuss it in detail.

A second answer lies in the way that Baptists bring the Bible to bear on doctrinal questions. Different denominations draw contrasting conclusions partly because they employ distinct methods when handling the Scriptures. Baptists tend to read the Bible differently than other groups, though their starting place is the same as other gospel-believing denominations. With many other Christians, Baptists presuppose that Scripture interprets Scripture. This principle is crucial for churches that do not recognize an authoritative leader or church court to tell them what the Bible means. We allow the Bible to interpret itself by comparing Scripture with Scripture.

How does this principle work in practice? The answer to this question is the point at which the denominations begin to diverge. Unfortunately, many Bible teachers do not take time to make their method clear. Perhaps they simply assume an answer to the question.

Choices at this point will guide doctrinal and practical decisions later on. For this reason, I think that those who teach the Bible should describe their method up front. People ought to know how one reads the Bible and why one reads it that way.

Even Baptists differ to some degree in their method of understanding Scripture, though they are similar in most important respects. While I may not be able to speak for all Baptists at this point, I can at least state my own assumptions. In the main, these assumptions appear to be implicit in mainstream Baptist thought. These assumptions take the form of three rules for evaluating Biblical evidence when allowing Scripture to interpret Scripture.

The first rule is that teaching (didactic or doctrinal) passages should interpret historical passages. Historical passages tell us what happened, but by themselves they do not tell us what ought to happen. On the other hand, teaching passages are designed to instruct us in what to do.

The New Testament churches attempted a variety of practices. In at least one instance, the members of a church held all goods in common (Acts 2:44). All of the apostolic churches read the New Testament documents in Greek. These churches also met for prayer, preached the Word, and supported their widows (Acts 2:42; 6:1).

Which of these practices are churches obligated to adopt today? Unless we have clear teaching to tell us, we do not know. Holding all goods in common was practiced by some churches but not by others. Reading the New Testament in Greek was practiced by all churches, but may have been coincidental. Meeting for prayer, preaching the Word, and supporting widows were practiced by all apostolic churches—but were these practices coincidental or normative? Is a modern church sinning if it allows its widows to draw upon other sources of support? What if it has no widows at all?

The example of the early church may sometimes show us what is permissible. From the example of the Jerusalem church, we can probably infer that it is not *wrong* for a church to hold goods in common. By itself, however, the example does not show us what is required (e.g., that all churches *must* hold all goods in common). Teaching passages generally tell us what we ought to do, while historical passages illustrate how it was done.

Admittedly, distinguishing teaching passages from historical passages is not as easy as simply pointing out the difference between narratives and epistles. The epistles contain many personal references that are meant only for a particular time and place. For example, in 2 Timothy 4:16–21, the apostle Paul provides details about his trial, expresses his confidence that the Lord will bring him safely into the heavenly kingdom, extends greetings to several individuals, and tells Timothy to come before winter. Even though 2 Timothy is generally a teaching book, this passage is definitely historical in nature.

The opposite may also be true. Narrative may contain editorial comments or other indications that a passage is meant to be didactic. For example, Peter draws a doctrinal inference about Cornelius and his household in Acts 10:44–48, which he defends before the Jerusalem congregation in Acts 11:15–17. This inference is accepted by the church in Acts 11:18 and becomes the basis of advice in Acts 15:7–11 and 14–21.

While Acts is a narrative, its handling of the episode with Cornelius leads us to believe that an important doctrine is being communicated. Distinguishing historical passages from teaching passages sometimes requires skillful judgment, and occasionally a point of doctrine or practice will depend upon that judgment.

The second rule for Scripture interpreting Scripture is that clear passages should interpret obscure passages. One old Baptist confession puts it this way: "The infallible rule of interpretation of Scripture is the Scripture itself; and therefore when there is a question about the true and full sense of any Scripture which is not manifold, but one, it must be searched by other places that speak more clearly."[1] This principle is widely recognized, but its results are often disputed. The trick is determining which passages are clear and which passages are obscure. In view of this difficulty, I would like to restate the principle: a passage that can mean only one thing should be used to interpret a passage that could possibly mean several things.

For example, in 1 Corinthians 15:29, the apostle Paul refers to the custom of being "baptized for the dead." What is baptism for the dead? Guesses abound, meaning that this verse is capable of a variety of more-or-less plausible interpretations. Latter-day Saints believe that baptism is necessary to be admitted into the kingdom of God, and they understand this verse to teach that living Mormons can be baptized for their dead relatives. This understanding of baptism for the dead, however, contradicts clear passages that base salvation entirely upon personal faith in the cross work of Christ (e.g., Rom. 3:23–26) in the absence of any work or merit on the part of the one being saved (e.g., Eph. 2:8–9). We reject the Mormon interpretation because it is ruled out by the obvious teaching of other Scriptures.

When we are dealing with passages that could be interpreted in multiple ways, we are not free to choose whatever interpretation appeals to us. We are free only to choose those interpretations that do not contradict other Scriptures. When a text could mean either A or B, but a second text allows only B, we must not use the first text to justify a continuing belief in A.

The third rule is that deliberate passages should interpret incidental passages. The principle here is that the Bible speaks more clearly and directly when it is trying to answer a specific question than when it is talking about a different topic. Consequently, if we can find a passage that actually aims to answer the question that we are asking, that passage will be of greater value to us than a whole list of passages that touch on our question only incidentally.

For example, suppose we want to understand water baptism. We need to find passages that aim to teach us about water baptism. Granted, we will be

---

1. Baptist Confession of Faith (1689), 1.9.

interested in passages that mention baptism even when they are not aiming to teach us about it (e.g., Acts 22:16), but we will not base our doctrine on those passages. We will also hesitate to base any conclusions upon references that may not even be associated with baptism (e.g., the "washing of regeneration" in Titus 3:5 or being "born of water" in John 3:5). Instead, we will look for a passage that specifically aims to teach us about water baptism (such as 1 Pet. 3:20–21).

We cannot demonstrate the truth of our doctrine and practice simply by listing Scripture references. That is called proof-texting. Instead, we must demonstrate how the Scriptures answer the question that we are asking. Consequently, in the following chapters we will sometimes take the time to examine specific passages in greater depth rather than simply listing Biblical citations.

These three rules will guide the handling of Scripture throughout this book. When we weigh Biblical evidence, some evidence weighs more than other evidence. Teaching passages weigh more than historical passages. Passages that can mean only one thing weigh more than passages that could mean multiple things. Deliberate passages weigh more than incidental passages. I shall occasionally refer to these rules in order to explain the distinctive beliefs of Baptists and to show where and how these beliefs arise from the text of the Bible. Our next task then is to discover what those beliefs are. What is a Baptist? The following chapters will answer that question.

Part One:

The Baptist Distinctives

1 *The Authority of the New Testament*

MANY OF THE PAMPHLETS and books that have been written about the Baptist distinctives over the past half-century use the same approach. They take the word *Baptist* and turn it into an acrostic. Each letter of the word becomes the first letter of one distinctive. In this scheme, the initial *B* is always made to stand for *Biblical authority*.

This acrostic has helped many people gain a better idea of what a Baptist is, but it is a bit misleading. While Baptists certainly do recognize Biblical authority, it is not really a Baptist distinctive. Instead, the belief that sets Baptists apart from other Christians is their recognition of the absolute authority, not simply of Scripture in general, but specifically of the New Testament, in all matters of church faith and order. Let me explain what I mean.

Baptists and Biblical Authority

First, I certainly recognize that Baptists affirm the authority of the Bible. All genuine Christians acknowledge the authority of Scripture as the Word of God. This recognition of Biblical authority is one of the marks that distinguish Christians from non-Christians. It belongs to a class of ideas that is even more serious than the Baptist distinctives. Biblical authority is a fundamental of the Christian faith.

No one who denies the authority of the Bible is truly a Christian. Inasmuch as Baptists are true Christians, they do indeed acknowledge Biblical authority. If they did not, they would be neither Christian nor Baptist. Baptists, however, are not alone in affirming Biblical authority. True, historic Lutherans, Methodists,

Presbyterians, and others also recognize the authority of the Bible. Therefore, even though all real Baptists do acknowledge the authority of the Bible, Biblical authority is not properly a Baptist distinctive.

If Biblical authority is not specifically a Baptist distinctive, why do so many Baptists claim it as one of their distinguishing marks? The answer to this question has two parts, both of which are related to the fundamentalist-modernist controversy, which took place in the United States during the first half of the twentieth century. Modernists were theologians and churchmen who professed to be Christians but who denied the authority of the Bible. Some of these modernists (also called liberals) gained power in the major Baptist fellowships, especially in the North. Within these fellowships they were opposed by Baptists who still affirmed the fundamentals. These "fundamentalists" (as they were called) maintained that people who denied Christian distinctives (i.e., fundamental doctrines) should not be recognized as Christians at all. Obviously, if modernists were not Christians, they were not Baptists either. Thus Baptist fundamentalists insisted that anyone who denied the authority of the Bible was not a real Baptist.

As we have already seen, they were right. Modernists (liberals) who denied the authority of the Bible were neither Christian nor Baptist. Naturally, Baptist fundamentalists stood up to defend the fundamentals. The fight that ensued, however, was over a fundamental of the faith, not a Baptist distinctive. During this great battle, the Baptist distinctives tended to get lost in the scuffle. That is part of the reason that some current Baptists see Biblical authority as a Baptist distinctive.

The other reason that Biblical authority has come to be viewed as a Baptist distinctive is related. The modernists captured most of the Baptist seminaries during the fundamentalist-modernist controversy. Because they rejected the teachings of these denominationally controlled institutions, many Baptists were forced to attend inter- or nondenominational schools. Those schools, though strong on the fundamentals, did not emphasize the Baptist distinctives. Consequently, an important fundamental of the faith (Biblical authority) slowly began to edge out an important but more nuanced and baptistic understanding of the Bible's authority. Many of these Baptist leaders embraced a view of Biblical authority that was solidly fundamental but not distinctly Baptist.

As a result of these two historical forces, many contemporary Baptists believe that Biblical authority is a Baptist distinctive. To make their case, they may even go to great lengths to show how other denominations somehow infringe upon Biblical authority. The fact is, however, that all genuine Christians make the Bible their final court of appeal for doctrine and life.

Baptists and New Testament Authority

Baptists do affirm a distinctive that seems similar to Biblical authority, but the difference is significant once understood. Catching the distinction is fairly important, because this particular Baptist teaching is crucial for several of the others. The genuine distinctive that sets Baptists apart from many other groups of Christians is this: Baptists consistently affirm the absolute authority of the New Testament in all matters of church faith and order.

What does this mean? How is it different from the Christian fundamental of Biblical authority? Perhaps I should answer these questions first by saying what this first Baptist distinctive does *not* mean.

When Baptists affirm the authority of the New Testament for the faith and order of the church, they are *not* rejecting or ignoring the general authority of the Old Testament. Baptists agree with other Christians that *all* of the Scripture—Old and New Testaments alike—is both inspired (God breathed) and profitable for doctrine, reproof, correction, and instruction in righteousness (2 Tim. 3:16). Baptists hold the Old Testament in high esteem indeed.

The Bible is divided into two sections for a reason. In the outworking of God's plan, a new stage began when God the Son was born as a human being, died on the cross, rose from the dead, and ascended into Heaven. Something has changed in the way that God is dealing with the human race.

Baptists insist that the present form of the church is uniquely a New Testament institution. The church may or may not have been present in the Old Testament—Baptists disagree about that point. Dispensational Baptists, such as those of the General Association of Regular Baptist Churches, affirm that the church began on the Day of Pentecost. Even Baptists who believe that Israel was the Old Testament church, however, agree that the form and order of the church changed significantly with the death and resurrection of Jesus Christ. Even if the church existed in the Old Testament, its pattern of organization and mode of operation were dramatically altered by events that stemmed from the ministry of the Lord Jesus.

Where should we look to discover the church's nature, mission, and order? Baptists insist that the only divinely inspired textbook on the church is the New Testament. Only the New Testament tells us what the church is. Only the New

Testament tells us what the church is supposed to do. Only the New Testament tells us how the church is supposed to be organized. In fact, when Baptists speak about the church, they often specify that it is the "New Testament Church" that they have in mind.

Although the sole authority of the New Testament for church faith and order is the first principle of the Baptists, they are not the only ones who have acknowledged it. Ulrich Zwingli was led to begin the Reformation in Zurich after a careful study of the Greek New Testament. He also taught younger men like Conrad Grebel and George Blaurock to study the Greek New Testament, and it was this study that led them to perceive inconsistency in Zwingli's view of baptism. These young men became the fathers of the Anabaptist movement.[1] The authority of the New Testament has also been a guiding principle of the Stone-Campbell movement, which consists of the Churches of Christ, the Independent Christian Churches, and the Disciples of Christ (though because of their insistence upon baptismal regeneration, these groups should probably not be classified as Christian denominations). Baptists, however, have made the authority of the New Testament for church faith and order the key to their understanding of the church.

A few citations will help to evidence how widespread this belief is among different groups of Baptists. For example, J. M. Carroll, a leading voice of the Landmark Baptist movement, wrote in his famous booklet, *The Trail of Blood*, that the church has for "its laws and doctrines: the New Testament and that only."[2] While the Landmark movement has never included a majority of Baptists, Carroll's views on New Testament authority are very much in keeping with the mainstream.

Francis Wayland, one of the most famous Baptists in nineteenth century America, exerted exceptional influence among Baptists in the North. On the question of authority, Wayland wrote, "What is the creed, and what are the acknowledged standards of the Baptist churches in this country? To this, the general answer has ever been, 'Our rule of faith and practice is the New Testament.' We have no other authority to which we all profess submission."[3] As we shall see, Wayland was not disputing the value of confessions, but he was exalting the role of the New Testament as the authority for church faith and order.

---

1. This story is told briefly in William R. Estep, *The Anabaptist Story*, 3rd ed. (Grand Rapids: Eerdmans, 1996), 9–28.

2. J. M. Carroll, *The Trail of Blood* (Lexington, KY: Ashland Avenue Baptist Church, 1931), 55.

3. Francis Wayland, *Notes on the Principles and Practices of Baptist Churches* (New York: Sheldon, Blakeman, 1857), 13.

Another northern Baptist who articulated this principle was W. H. H. Marsh. Marsh was a generation or so removed from Wayland, but he, too, recognized the importance of New Testament authority.

> The constituency of the New Testament church should be determined by the New Testament itself. This accords with the facts of the case. True, the Old and New Testament together are the word of God. But the former was first given to the descendants of Abraham after the flesh. The New Testament was given to the constituencies of the churches established by the preaching of the gospel, and as an *ex post facto* [after the fact] interpretation of the Old. Therefore we must look into the latter, not the former, for the definition of the constituency of the New Testament church. Here is the real controversy between Baptists and evangelical Pedobaptists. The former as tenaciously hold the Old Testament to be part of the word of God as do the latter. The latter agree with the former, as we shall see, that the New is an *ex post facto* interpretation of the Old. We submit therefore, that while the Old Testament defines the constituency, government, and mission of the Hebrew Commonwealth, the New defines each and all of these for the visible Church of the New Testament.[4]

Southern Baptists have affirmed this principle with as much vigor as those in the North. One of the great Baptist theologians of the South was B. H. Carroll. Concerning the first Baptist distinctive, Carroll wrote:

> All the New Testament is the Law of Christianity. The New Testament is all the Law of Christianity. The New Testament will always be the Law of Christianity. This does not deny the inspiration or profit of the Old Testament, nor that the New is a development of the Old. It affirms, however, that the Old Testament, as a typical, educational and transitory system, was fulfilled by Christ, and as a standard of law and way of life was nailed to the cross of Christ and so taken out of the way. The principle teaches that we should not go to the Old Testament to find Christian law or Christian institutions. . . . This is not a question of what is the Bible. If it were, Baptists would not be distinguished from many Protestants in rejecting the apocryphal additions incorporated by Romanists in their Old Testament. Nor is it a stand with Chillingworth on the proposition, "The Bible, and the Bible alone, the religion of Protestants." If it were, Baptists would not be distinguished from

---

4. W. H. H. Marsh, *The New Testament Church* (Philadelphia: American Baptist Publication Society, 1898), 20.

many Protestants in rejecting the equal authority of tradition as held by the Romanists. But when Baptists say that the New Testament is the only law for Christian institutions they part company, if not theoretically at least practically, with most of the Protestant world, as well as from the Greeks and Romanists. . . .

The New Testament is the law of Christianity. All the New Testament is the law of Christianity. The New Testament is all the law of Christianity. The New Testament always will be the law of Christianity. Avaunt, ye types and shadows! Avaunt, Apocrypha! Avaunt, O Synagogue! Avaunt, Tradition, thou hoary-headed liar. Hush! Be still and listen! All through the Christian ages—from dark and noisome dungeons, from the lone wanderings of banishment and expatriation, from the roarings and sickening conflagrations of martyr fires—there comes a voice—shouted here, whispered there, sighed, sobbed, or gasped elsewhere—a Baptist voice, clearer than a silver trumpet and sweeter than the chime of bells, a voice that freights and glorifies the breeze or gale that bears it. O Earth, hearken to it: *The New Testament is the law of Christianity!*[5]

Probably no handbook on Baptist polity has been more widely used than Edward Hiscox's *New Directory for Baptist Churches.* It has served as a guide for millions of Baptists in the United States. Hiscox affirmed the absolute authority of the New Testament in the following words: "The New Testament is the constitution of Christianity, the charter of the Christian Church, the only authoritative code of ecclesiastical law, and the warrant and justification of all Christian institutions."[6]

Piling up so many quotations from old Baptist theologians may seem a bit pedantic, but it serves a purpose. These Baptists of yore represent very different branches of Baptist thought. They disagreed among themselves over several rather important issues. They all agreed, however, that the New Testament is the final and absolute authority in all matters related to church faith and order.

Their emphasis upon the New Testament does not mean that these Baptists ignored or depreciated the Old Testament in any way. Baptists continue to believe that *all* Scripture—Old and New Testaments alike—is both inspired and profitable. Many doctrines are revealed in the Old Testament with great clarity.

---

5. B. H. Carroll, *Baptists and Their Doctrines: Sermons on Distinctive Baptist Principles* (New York: Fleming H. Revell, 1913), 10–14.

6. Edward T. Hiscox, *New Directory of Baptist Churches* (Philadelphia: Judson Press, 1894), 11. This volume has been reprinted as *Principles and Practices for Baptist Churches* (Grand Rapids: Kregel Publications, 1980).

Baptists rely upon the Old Testament to help them understand the nature of God, the depth of human sinfulness, and the necessity of redemption. The New Testament church, however, is *not* revealed in the Old Testament. The doctrine and order of the church is revealed only in the New.

As we have seen, the inspiration and authority of the Bible is one of the fundamental doctrines of the Christian faith. Baptists hold this doctrine in common with all true Christians of whatever denomination. Christians from other denominations, however, frequently argue that some aspect of church polity or doctrine can be found in the Old Testament. Quite often they base this argument on the observation that Israel was the church of the Old Testament.

Some Baptists (I am among them) are dispensationalists who see a sharp distinction between Israel and the church. Others (perhaps the majority) believe that Israel was the church of the Old Testament. Even they agree, however, that something changed with the cross and resurrection of Jesus and with the descent of the Holy Spirit on the Day of Pentecost. That change deeply affected the constitution, purpose, membership, and order of the church. Therefore, one cannot simply appeal to God's people in the Old Testament to establish the pattern for the church in the New Testament.

Baptists insist that only the New Testament may be used to establish the doctrine and structure of the church. Thus Baptists are different from most other Christians because they restrict their doctrine of the church to the New Testament. They also differ from many other Christians in the way that they apply the teachings of the New Testament to church faith and order.

The Sufficiency of Scripture

To understand how Baptists bring the New Testament to bear upon church life, we need to revisit a dispute between Martin Luther and Ulrich Zwingli, leaders of distinct branches of the Reformation. The two men agreed that Roman Catholic beliefs and practices had corrupted the existing churches. To amend matters, both began a process of removing the most blatantly anti-Scriptural doctrines and forms. They disagreed, however, about what to do with Romanist doctrines, forms, and customs that, while not authorized by the Bible, did not obviously contradict Biblical teaching.

Luther argued that these teachings and customs could be retained as long as they did not directly violate Biblical doctrine. He recognized that ordinary church members had become used to these customs and rituals. The sudden removal of these teachings and practices might prove unnecessarily upsetting. Therefore, to avoid controversy and to deflect the charge of extremism, Luther allowed some Roman customs to persist even though he could find little direct Biblical support for them. If those practices did not contradict any Biblical teaching, he reasoned, then they would do no harm, and they might even do some good.

Zwingli gave just the opposite answer. He insisted that Christ is the Lord of the church and the Bible is the church's law. Zwingli believed that Christians have no liberty to introduce teachings or customs into the ministry of the church unless Christ authorized them. Therefore, if a ritual or observance (i.e., an element of worship) is not authorized in the Bible, the church must regard it as forbidden.

The principle that motivated Zwingli is called the sufficiency of Scripture. The idea is that Scripture reveals everything necessary to life and godliness. The New Testament reveals everything that is necessary to the right order of the church. Since Christ has addressed the question of how He wants His people to live and worship, and since He has (through His apostles) revealed how He wants His churches to be ordered, Christians do not have the liberty to invent these things.

The interesting thing about the dispute between Luther and Zwingli is that both of them wanted to reject ecclesiastical innovation. Both were prepared to insist that it is not up to Christians to redefine what the church is, what its mission might be, or how it ought to be ordered. Luther was willing to keep some of the older Roman teachings and practices in order to avoid the appearance of innovation. Zwingli insisted that, because these Roman customs and teachings were not grounded in Scripture, they were themselves innovations. Essentially, he took the position that even an old innovation is still an innovation.

In general, Baptists have taken Zwingli's side in this argument. One Baptist writer has expressed the principle in the following words.

> [I]t is assumed that the outward institutions of the Christian religion are of God, and that, therefore, their form and order as delineated in the New Testament, are of divine obligation. The Bible presents a definite and final constitution of the church, the ordinances, and the ministry, and is on these subjects the sufficient guide and the only authority; no man may set aside, alter, or supplement the divine model there given.[7]

7. Hezekiah Harvey, *The Church: Its Polity and Ordinances* (Philadelphia: American Baptist Publication Society, 1879), 13.

The above quotation is typical of the older Baptist theologians. In their attempt to formulate the doctrine and order of the church, they faced a double challenge. From Catholicism, Anglicanism, and Lutheranism they were confronted with the problem of ecclesiastical tradition as a source of authority for doctrine and practice. From sects like the Quakers, they were confronted with the problem of divine-light mysticism, in which religious teachers assumed the initiative to decide what teachings and practices ought to be acceptable to God. The Baptist response to both problems was identical.

> In the worship of God there cannot be either obedience or faith, unless we regard the divine appointments. Not *obedience*; for that supposes a precept, or what is equivalent to it. Not *faith*; for that requires a promise, or some divine declaration. If then, we act without a command, we have reason to apprehend that God will say to us, as he did to Israel of old, "Who hath required this at your hand?"[8]

The challenges that these early Baptists faced were not only theoretical, but also practical and numerous. Could churches be governed by monarchial bishops? Could the office of presbyter be divided between teaching and ruling elders? Could churches receive unimmersed members? Could ordinances other than baptism and the Lord's Table be recognized and practiced? Could church services include elements such as the burning of incense and the ringing of sanctus bells as part of their worship? Could deceased saints be asked to intercede on behalf of the living? Could the practice of auricular confession be maintained as part of the church's discipline? None of these doctrines or practices was specifically forbidden by the New Testament. The real question was whether churches were restricted to what the New Testament requires for their worship and practice, or whether they were permitted to adopt whatever ideas and practices seemed useful to them.

Baptists gave a uniform answer to this question. For example, one of the earliest Baptist confessions of faith was called the "Faith and Practice of Thirty Congregations." It was prepared in 1651 as an associational document of the General Baptists, one of two large groups of early Baptists. This confession states, "That whosoever shall preach, teach, or practise any doctrine in the worship of

---

8. Abraham Booth, "Vindication of Baptists from the Charge of Bigotry," in *The Baptist Manual: A Selection from the Series of Publications of the American Baptist Publication Society, Designed for the Use of Families; and As an Exposition of the Distinguishing Sentiments of the Denomination* (Philadelphia: American Baptist Publication Society, 1849), 17. The chapters in this book are separate works that had been published independently. Each chapter retains its own pagination in the collected volume.

God, pretending it in the name of Jesus Christ, which is not to be heard or read of in the record of God, which was given by inspiration of the holy Ghost; such teachers are lyable to the curse of God, howsoever, countenanced by men, Gal. i. 8, 9" (article 46). Clearly, the General Baptists restricted themselves to the sufficiency of Scripture in all matters of belief and practice.

The Particular Baptists were the other large group of early English Baptists. Like the General Baptists, they adopted a series of confessions, the most prominent of which was the Baptist Confession of Faith (1689), popularly known as the Second London Confession. This confession states that "the acceptable way of worshipping the true God, is instituted by himself, and so limited by his own revealed will, that he may not be worshipped according to the imagination and devices of men, nor the suggestions of Satan, under any visible representations, or any other way not prescribed in the Holy Scriptures" (22.1).

Over fifty years later, Baptists in America adopted the Philadelphia Confession of Faith (1742). This American confession was a close copy of the Second London Confession. It used exactly the same language in restricting the acceptable way of worshiping God to what has been instituted by His own revealed will, and in excluding human "imaginations and devices."

The Baptist position is really rather straightforward. Since Christ is the head and Lord of the church, He alone has the authority to define its nature, mission, constitution, order, membership, ordinances, offices, and worship. He has not left us to wonder about these matters, but has addressed them through His apostles in the New Testament. Since Christ has given us the authoritative word on these matters, we do not have the prerogative to introduce new doctrines, offices, ordinances, or forms of worship on our own initiative. If we do, then we are usurping a right that belongs to Christ alone. We believe that Scripture has given complete and sufficient guidance in all of these areas.

Hebrews 8:5 has often been a text from which Baptists and others have derived their understanding of the sufficiency of Scripture. The verse says, "Who [the Levitical priests] serve unto the example and shadow of heavenly things, as Moses was admonished of God when he was about to make the tabernacle: for, See, saith he, that thou make all things according to the pattern shewed to thee in the mount." Commenting upon this verse, Baptist theologian John Gill offered the following observations.

> It may be gathered from hence, that whatever is done in a way of religious worship, should be according to a divine rule; a church of Christ ought to be formed according to the primitive pattern, and should consist, not of all that are born in a nation, province,

or parish; nor should all that are born of believing parents be admitted into it; no unholy, unbelieving, and unconverted persons, only such as are true believers in Christ, and who are baptized according as the word of God directs; the officers of a church should be only of two sorts, bishops, elders, pastors or overseers, and deacons; the ordinances are baptism, which should only be administered to believers, and by immersion, and the Lord's supper, of which none should partake, but those who have tasted that the Lord is gracious; and this should be performed as Christ performed it, and as the Apostle Paul received it from him; the discipline of Christ's house should be regarded, and all the laws of it carefully and punctually put in execution; and a conversation becoming the Gospel should be attended to.[9]

The principle that Gill saw in Hebrews 8:5 is that God alone has the right to define what His people should believe and practice. Gill understood this principle to entail the sufficiency of Scripture. For Gill, whatever was not authorized in Scripture must never be introduced into the faith and order of the church.

The Sufficiency of Scripture and the Colossian Heresy

The principle of the sufficiency of Scripture draws upon a variety of Biblical evidences. One of the most direct arguments comes from Paul's response to the so-called Colossian heresy in Colossians 2. The heresy at Colosse was an odd mixture. It contained early elements of the religious philosophy that would eventually become known as gnosticism, but it also included Judaizing elements. It drew upon pagan philosophies while simultaneously attempting to introduce Old Testament rituals into New Testament worship.

Paul wrote to the Colossians to rebut this heresy. His refutation consisted largely in a focus upon the person and work of Christ. By explaining clearly who Christ was and what He had done on the cross, Paul was able to cut the ground out from under both the Judaistic and the proto-gnostic elements of the heresy.

While both sides of the heresy relied upon some form of tradition, the gnostic side was more creative in its doctrines and practices than the Judaistic side. The Judaizers restricted themselves to importing Old Testament patterns into the church. The gnostics, however, simply made up their doctrines and

9. John Gill, *An Exposition of the New Testament* (1853; repr. Atlanta: Turner Lassetter, 1960), 2:721.

practices as they went. The church father Hippolytus, writing in the third century, described gnostic rites in painful detail.[10] Hippolytus depicted more than thirty branches of gnosticism, some of which went to extremes of asceticism and others of which went to extremes of libertinism. To Hippolytus's portrait of the gnostics, the church fathers Irenaeus and Tertullian also offer confirming evidence.

The many versions of gnosticism all had one thing in common. Their doctrine and practice were sheer invention, employing sophisticated philosophies and often bizarre rites that were nowhere authorized in the New Testament. Given that the Colossian heresy represented an early prototype of gnosticism, it almost certainly incorporated at least some of the intellectual and liturgical inventions that characterized later gnostic worship.

For the Christians at Colosse, this heresy created a double problem. First, it introduced doctrines that were nowhere authorized in the Scriptures or the apostolic teaching (though gnostic teachings did not always explicitly contradict Biblical revelation). Second, it introduced rites of both Judaistic and gnostic origin that had no basis in the apostles' doctrine.

Paul's response to this religious amalgamation was a radical exaltation of the risen Christ. He opened Colossians 2 by asserting that all the treasures of wisdom (*sophia*) and knowledge (*gnosis*) are found in Christ. *Sophia* and *gnosis* both became code words within the gnostic heresy, and Paul was here co-opting those terms for Christ Himself. With respect to spiritual things, no true wisdom or knowledge can be found outside of Christ. Paul warned the Colossians against being deluded by pithy arguments (v. 4). Furthermore, he commanded them to walk "as ye have therefore received Christ Jesus," in other words, as Christ was announced and taught through the apostolic witness (v. 6).

Continuing his argument in verse 8, Paul warned against people who want to carry Christians into spiritual captivity (a clear reference to the heretics of Colosse). According to Paul, this captivation could take three forms. The first is through "philosophy and vain [empty] deceit," by which Paul meant philosophical and theological speculations carried beyond the warrants of revelation. The second is "the tradition of men," or rites, forms, and customs that people have made up for themselves. This is a reference to the gnostic side of the heresy and its invented liturgies. The third is the "rudiments [elements] of the world," a

---

10. The chief work in which Hippolytus discussed gnosticism is *The Refutation of All Heresies*, which can be found together with his other extant works in ed., Alexander Roberts and James Donaldson, *The Ante-Nicene Fathers* (1886; repr. Peabody, MA.: Hendrickson, 1994), 5:1–259.

controversial expression that is connected in Galatians with the transmission of Judaistic forms into Christian observance. In sum, Paul was warning that when doctrine and order go beyond what is revealed, this excess brings Christians into captivity—whether the imported teachings and customs arise from deceitful speculation, from human invention, or from Judaistic retention.

In verse 9 Paul stated his reason for restricting faith and order to what is revealed: the entire fullness (*pleroma*) of the Godhead dwells in Christ bodily. The term *pleroma* was also a gnostic code word. It stood for an entire series of divine beings called *eons*. Paul's use of the term *pleroma* constituted a direct assault upon gnostic doctrine. Against the gnostic view of many divine beings, Paul asserted that Christ Himself contains the entire Pleroma, that is, the entire fullness of the Godhead. What all the *eons* together were to gnostics, Christ alone is to Christians. This observations implies that Christians are complete (the word *complete* is *pleroma* turned into a verb) in Christ. In other words, Christians need nothing and can have nothing outside of Christ, Who is the head of all principality and power (two key gnostic terms that denote spiritual authorities).

The upshot of Paul's argument is that all spiritual authority resides in Christ. Christ's absolute authority provides a basis for critiquing both proto-gnostic and Judaistic doctrines and practices. Those forms do not have to be directly forbidden within special revelation. Since Christ is the center and sum of spiritual authority, He alone can authorize the doctrines that Christians must believe and the practices that Christians must employ in their churches. In matters of the church's faith and order, whatever Christ has not commanded is forbidden.

In fact, Christ has completely triumphed over every pretender to spiritual authority (v. 15). This triumph is most likely a reference to the resurrection, and is parallel to the assertion in Ephesians 4 that Christ "led captivity captive" (or "led captive a captive multitude"). He has completely vanquished and despoiled every alternative spiritual authority, and His resurrection proves His unconditional victory. No one and nothing can be set alongside Christ, Who is the absolute master of all things spiritual.

What this means for the individual Christian is that no one but Christ has the authority to bind the conscience (Col. 2:16–17). Only He has the power to forbid or to command. No mere human has authority to establish moral standards for any Christian. Only Christ can do that. Church authority consists only in the announcing of the standards that Christ has revealed.

By the same token, no human has the right to introduce new doctrines or practices (v. 18). Here Paul mentioned specifically the gnostics' habit of humbling themselves before the *eons* or angels, rendering veneration to them. Paul's intention, however, was not merely to forbid this one custom. On the contrary, he based his exclusion of this custom upon the supremacy of Christ, Who alone has the authority to impose patterns of worship. He argued that humans lack both the authority and the knowledge to specify how they ought to behave in the face of things they have not seen. He implied that people who think they can please God by making up new doctrine, practices, or forms of worship on their own initiative are "vainly puffed up" by their "fleshly mind." To make up new doctrines or modes of worship is to reject ("fail to hold firmly to") the Head, namely, Christ.

Concluding his argument in verses 20–23, Paul was evidently viewing both the Judaistic and gnostic sides of the heresy together. He presupposed that, in Christ, believers have died to the elements of the world (possibly a reference to the old Jewish rituals). Why, then, would Christians ever subject themselves to decrees that have been authorized by mere human beings?

In the context, these decrees work in two ways. Some decrees restrict the individual Christian where Christ does not. Other decrees introduce doctrine, order, or elements of worship that Christ does not. Paul saw these as two results of the same abysmal heresy. He denounced both as will-worship, that is, as the assertion of the depraved human self against the authority of Christ. Such ordinances, he declared, are utterly without spiritual value. There is no redemptive quality to them, wise though they may appear to be.

This passage contains two enduring lessons. The first is that Christians do not have freedom to make up moral rules for other Christians. If a requirement is not revealed in or cannot be soundly inferred from the Word of God, then it cannot be a matter of binding morality. The second is that Christians do not have freedom to make up their own doctrines, order, or worship. If a doctrine or practice is not revealed in or cannot be soundly inferred from the Word of God, it must not be introduced as an aspect of the Christian faith.

To reject either of these lessons is directly to assault the Lordship of Christ. Paul did not grant the Colossians permission to retain any element of Judaistic or gnostic ritual on their own initiative. Quite the opposite. He restricted the faith and order of the Colossian church to those doctrines, customs, requirements, forms, and elements authorized by Christ Himself through the apostolic testimony.

Today the apostolic testimony is mediated to God's people only through the written Scriptures. Consequently, the principle that Paul articulated in Colossians 2 entails the sufficiency of Scripture. Whatever we need for faith and life must be found in the Bible, and in the case of church doctrine and practice, it must be found in the New Testament. Any offices, ordinances, teachings, practices, or elements of worship that cannot be authorized from Scripture itself must not be adopted as part of Christian faith and order.

Parameters of the Sufficiency of Scripture

Baptists believe that the church's nature—its mission and ministry, its organization, officers, membership, ordinances, and worship—must be defined by the positive teachings of the New Testament. When it comes to operating their churches, Baptists do not ask, Does the New Testament forbid this practice? Instead, they ask, Does the New Testament authorize this practice? If it does not, they almost always regard it as forbidden.

I say "almost always" because there are one or two important exceptions to this rule. First, Baptists recognize that the New Testament does not always specify every means by which its own requirements are to be fulfilled. Second, Baptists acknowledge some administrative latitude in arranging the details of church life, even where Scripture is silent. Therefore, even though the New Testament does not specifically authorize church buildings (for example), it does require churches to meet, and the choice to construct a building is allowable as a means of expediting effective church meetings. Since the New Testament does not specify a time at which churches will meet, we assume that the congregation has a certain amount of liberty in determining the hour: after all, the church has to meet at *some* time. The distribution of gospel tracts is not specifically authorized, but Christians are commanded to evangelize, and handing out written messages is consistent with New Testament patterns of evangelization.

Like others who affirm the sufficiency of Scripture, Baptists occasionally disagree about whether a particular activity falls within the purview of New Testament church order. For example, we have sometimes debated whether instrumental music should be allowed in church services. We have also disagreed about whether we are permitted to sing nonbiblical hymns (as opposed to the psalms, hymns, and spiritual songs found in Scripture itself). Even where we have disagreed on the particular applications of the principle, however, Baptists have agreed about the principle itself.

Baptists are distinguished from some other groups of Christians by their authority for church faith and order. While some other groups of Christians find the church in both Testaments, Baptists find it only in the New. While some groups of Christians are willing to superimpose their church faith and order upon the silences of the Bible, Baptists insist that the doctrine and practice of the church must be derived from the positive teaching of the New Testament itself. Baptists believe strongly in the sufficiency of Scripture as their textbook for faith and practice.

Creeds and Confessions

The first Baptist distinctive is the absolute authority of the New Testament in all matters of church faith and order. Baptists appeal to the New Testament, and to the New Testament alone, as their authority for the doctrine and practice of the church. They also share with all other Christians a firm commitment to the Bible as their authority for all areas of belief and life. This leads to another important question. What is the appropriate role, if any, for creeds and confessions?

One might think that Baptists, with their emphasis upon the sufficiency of Scripture, would reject any authoritative role for creeds and confessions. A glance at Baptist history, however, reveals that wherever Baptists have existed, they have busied themselves with drafting confessions of faith. How can this incessant creed-making be reconciled with the Baptists' profession that they derive their faith and conduct from the Bible alone? The answer to this question lies in the nature of creedal authority, or in the way that Baptists use confessions.

For Baptists, creeds and confessions are simply summaries of what they believe the Bible teaches. Accepting the Bible's authority does little good if one misunderstands its teachings. Some cults even claim to accept the authority of the Bible while denying fundamental doctrines. For this reason, Christians have often developed short summaries of important Biblical teachings. That is what creeds and confessions are: summaries of what we believe the Bible teaches. All Christian confessions articulate teachings that distinguish Christians from non-Christians. Often, they also enumerate teachings that distinguish their adherents from other groups of Christians.

Some Baptists have tried to distinguish creeds from confessions. They have insisted that Baptists are confessional but not creedal. Confessions, they say, are merely descriptive, while creeds are prescriptive. In other words, a confession of faith is a summary of what the members of a church or denomination actually do believe. A creed, on the other hand, is a statement of what the members of the group must believe in order to be received into fellowship. Creeds are normative, while confessions are simply expressive.

Many Baptists have rejected this distinction between creeds and confessions, and for good reason. The distinction is neither useful nor convincing. What good does it do for an organization to describe its most important beliefs if it does not intend to maintain those beliefs? And how is an organization supposed to maintain its beliefs unless it intends to keep out (or put out) people who refuse to affirm those beliefs? Unless a church or denomination intends to enforce its confession (i.e., to make it prescriptive), the confession will likely cease to be descriptive in a very short time.

Some Baptists have argued that an authoritative confession violates the principle of Biblical authority. They ask how the Bible can be one's sole authority if one's confession is authoritative. The solution to this problem is to remember that the confession is simply a summary of what one (or one's group) believes that the Bible teaches. A confession has no authority of its own. Its only authority derives from Scripture, which is the true and only standard for doctrine and life. An organization may rightly enforce belief in a confession only insofar as the teachings of the confession come from Scripture itself.

Suppose that a member of your church is caught embezzling. When challenged with his sin, he replies that he believes the Bible permits some forms of stealing, and actually commands Christians to embezzle under some circumstances. He claims to acknowledge the authority of the Bible, but he understands the Bible to authorize him to embezzle. Furthermore, he insists that the church's stand against stealing is only descriptive and not prescriptive. He says that if the church actually tries to keep him from stealing, it is usurping the authority of Scripture. Therefore, he intends to keep right on embezzling, and there is nothing the church can do about it.

Of course you would be incredulous, and so would all the other members of the church. You would not see any difference between enforcing the Bible's commands and enforcing the church's standard. You would insist that they were one and the same: "Thou shalt not steal." You would argue that the whole reason the church stands against stealing is precisely because the Bible forbids it.

If a church can enforce practical standards without violating the absolute authority of the Bible, it can enforce doctrinal standards as well. We insist that church members must not steal just because the Bible forbids stealing. Similarly, we insist that they must not deny the deity of Christ just because the Bible teaches that Jesus is God. When we adopt a confessional affirmation of the deity of Christ, our confession does not take the place of Scripture. It simply states what we understand the Bible to teach. In no way does this diminish the Bible's own authority, and in no way does it make the confession a separate authority alongside the Scriptures.

Therefore, confessions may legitimately function to repel (or expel) those who do not share a group's view of what the Bible teaches. This is the negative function of confessions: they keep some people away. Confessions also have a positive function, however. While they keep out those who do not share an organization's beliefs, they also attract those who do share the beliefs.

A well-written confession serves as an advertisement of a group's doctrinal commitments. As such, it constitutes an invitation to others who share those commitments. Christians who hold substantially the same beliefs as the confession will often be drawn to the organization that adopted it.

In other words, the confession specifies the organization's basis of fellowship. We usually think of fellowship as an activity, perhaps centered on eating and drinking. However, the actual meaning of *fellowship* is that something is held in common. In Christian organizations, one of the things that must be held in common is a body of true and important beliefs that have been drawn from the Bible. Those who hold these beliefs are appropriate subjects of fellowship, while those who deny the beliefs are not. The function of a creed or confession is to enumerate the beliefs, thought to be Biblical, that are held in common by all the members of a given organization.

Baptists have adopted creeds and confessions from their very earliest days. Sometimes these confessions have been individual statements of belief. Sometimes churches have issued them. Often they have been adopted by associations, conventions, conferences, and other organizations. Moreover, Baptists have regularly used their confessions as a way of determining who could fellowship with the group and who could not.

The presence of these creeds and confessions in no way contradicts the first of the Baptist distinctives. Baptists affirm the absolute, final authority of the New Testament in all matters of church faith and order. They appeal to the New Testament alone to determine the nature, mission, polity, and ordinances of the church. Because they believe that Scripture is sufficient, they build their theory of the church from the positive statements of the New Testament rather than superimposing their own ideas upon its silences. They regard the New Testament as the constitution of the church, and that is the commitment from which all of their other distinctives flow.

2 *Believer Baptism*

IF YOU ASK most people how Baptists are different from other Christians, they will probably say something about baptism—usually about immersion. Baptists do indeed practice and understand baptism differently than many other Christian groups. It may not be the most central Baptist distinctive, but baptism is certainly the most visible.

How does the Baptist approach to water baptism differ from the perspectives of the other denominations? Baptists generally argue that their approach is defined by three emphases. They insist that valid, Scriptural baptism requires, first, proper subjects; second, a proper meaning; and, third, a proper mode. To these three, some Baptists add a fourth emphasis, maintaining that valid baptism must occur under proper authority or a proper administrator.

Perhaps I should offer a word of explanation about the expression *valid baptism*. When Baptists talk about a "valid" baptism, they mean real, or genuine, baptism. For Baptists, a valid baptism is simply a baptism. If a baptism is not valid, then it is not really a baptism at all. So when Baptists ask what constitutes a valid baptism, they mean to ask what constitutes an actual baptism as opposed to some other act that is not really a baptism at all, even though it may be called one. For Baptists, valid, or real, baptism requires at least a proper subject, a proper meaning, and a proper mode.

Proper Subjects

All Baptists agree that a baptism is not valid (it is not really a baptism) unless it is performed on the proper subjects. Who are the proper subjects of baptism?

According to Baptists, only those who have made a credible profession of faith in Christ as Savior ought to be baptized. This practice is often called believer's baptism, but it is properly denoted as believer baptism.[1]

Before stating the grounds for believer baptism, one minor objection should be answered. Occasionally someone will suggest that it is impossible to baptize only believers because we can never really know who the true believers are. Of course, Baptists admit the force of this argument. They do not claim that they can infallibly distinguish true professions of faith from false ones, but they insist that people should not be baptized until they have credibly professed faith in Jesus Christ as Savior. While not all who profess faith actually possess faith, Baptists maintain that those who do not even profess faith are certainly unfit subjects for baptism.

Why do Baptists limit baptism to professing believers? Specifically, why do Baptists deny that infants should be baptized? They offer several reasons.

First, the New Testament commands only believers to be baptized and shows baptism being performed only on professing believers. Matthew 28:19–20, for example, explicitly connect baptism with making disciples, and it is difficult to imagine a disciple who did not at least profess to believe on Jesus. In Mark 16:16, the order is belief and then baptism. This order is uniformly followed in the book of Acts. Those in Jerusalem who gladly received the word were baptized (Acts 2:41). The Samaritans were baptized only after they believed (Acts 8:12). When the Ethiopian eunuch requested baptism, Philip required him to profess faith first (Acts 8:36–38). Cornelius and his household were baptized only after they had received the Holy Spirit and—by implication—salvation (Acts 10:47). The Philippian jailer and his family were promised salvation if they believed on the Lord Jesus Christ; then they received baptism and rejoiced that they had believed on God (Acts 16:31–34).

Second, the New Testament does not contain a single command to baptize infants, and it never narrates a single indisputable incident in which an infant was baptized. Advocates of infant baptism point to Jesus' insistence that the little children be allowed to come to Him (Mark 10:14), as well as to the occurrence of household baptisms in such cases as Lydia (Acts 16:15) and the Philippian jailer (Acts 16:33). Nowhere, however, does the text intimate that these household baptisms included any infants. While Jesus certainly loves

---

1. Baptism is not possessed by the believer; it is administered to him—hence believer baptism, not believer's baptism. By the same token, we always speak of infant baptism and never of infant's baptism. Paul King Jewett, *Infant Baptism and the Covenant of Grace* (Grand Rapids: Eerdmans, 1978), 226.

children and wants them to be brought to Him, He never suggests that baptism is the way to do this. In fact, in the gospel accounts baptism was not practiced on little children. Therefore, the point stands: the New Testament contains no clear command to baptize any infants, and it offers no clear instance of an infant being baptized. Since Baptists affirm the sufficiency of Scripture for church faith and order, this silence is tantamount to forbidding infant baptism.

Third, Peter connects baptism with a clear conscience (1 Pet. 3:21). This connection is relevant to the problem of infant baptism because nothing that is done to us involuntarily can be a matter of conscience. For Peter to connect baptism with a clear conscience implies that those who are baptized must have a choice in the matter. Baptism must be a voluntary act. To perform it on someone (like an infant) who has not personally decided to be baptized runs contrary to its very nature. Consequently, infants should never be subjected to baptism.

Fourth, infant baptism does not appear in the records of the early church until the third century, and then it is mentioned as an objectionable practice. While there are references to baptizing *children* in the early church fathers, there is no indisputable reference to baptizing *infants* until Tertullian, who argued against it in a treatise on baptism written between AD 200 and 206. In other words, no mention is made of infant baptism and no example of infant baptism can be adduced for the first 150 years of Christian history.[2]

Fifth, Baptists reject infant baptism because the meaning of baptism implies that it should be limited to proper subjects. Of course, this observation raises the question of what baptism actually does mean. Therefore, we must discuss the meaning of baptism before we will be able to discuss the implications of that meaning for the subjects and mode of baptism.

Proper Meaning

Baptists maintain that for someone's baptism to be valid (i.e., real, or genuine), the baptism must be administered with the proper meaning. The person who is being baptized may not entirely understand the true meaning, but if either the administrator or the subject intends a false meaning, the baptism is not valid. Since professing Christians offer a variety of explanations about what baptism signifies, and since some of those explanations are false and damaging,

---

2. Jewett, *Infant Baptism*, 13–45, has an excellent summary of the practice of the early churches.

Baptists insist upon making sure that baptism communicates the correct meaning. When the meaning of baptism contradicts the gospel, the baptism is not Biblical baptism at all.

The Biblical Meaning of Baptism

One of the most important texts for understanding the meaning of baptism is 1 Peter 3:21. Some aspects of this verse are rather difficult to understand, but others are quite clear. One of the clear teachings of 1 Peter 3:21 is that the significance of baptism is tied to the resurrection of Christ. Since a resurrection is impossible unless a death has occurred first, to tie baptism to Jesus' resurrection is also to tie it to His death. This point is made forcefully in Romans 6:3–5, in which baptism is explicitly linked to the death and resurrection of Christ.[3]

The meaning of water baptism is connected to the death of Jesus for our sins and to His resurrection from the dead. Therefore, baptism is a picture of the gospel. It is a symbolic reenactment of Jesus' death and resurrection. In the New Testament, it is always performed upon those who have trusted Jesus as Savior. Indeed, it functions as their public profession of faith. In other words, people who submit to water baptism are symbolically stating that they have received Jesus Christ—Who died and rose again—as Savior. Water baptism becomes the badge or ensign of the believer's faith. It is a declaration to the world that the Christian is identifying with Jesus and acknowledging Him as Savior.

Baptism is a first step of Christian obedience. Jesus clearly intended water baptism to function as a major aspect of becoming His follower. In Matthew 28:19–20, He commanded baptism as a specific part of making disciples. For a believer to neglect baptism, therefore, is to disobey the Lord. Tellingly, the New Testament does not offer a single example of an unbaptized believer. Baptism is a Christian duty that stands at the head of the list of Jesus' commands for believers.

An unsaved person cannot offer any form of obedience to God except to receive Jesus as Savior. Persons who have not trusted Christ are already engaged in the worst form of disobedience. They are rejecting God's Son. The nature of baptism as a step of obedience implies that it ought to be restricted to those who profess faith in Jesus Christ.

Biblically, then, baptism possesses the following meanings. It is a picture of the gospel that symbolizes the death and resurrection of Christ. It is a public

---

3. Some Baptists and other Christians believe that Romans 6 is not about water baptism, but about baptism in or by the Holy Spirit. Almost everyone agrees, however, that 1 Peter 3 is about water baptism.

profession of faith in Christ, and consequently a badge of Christian identity. It is also the first step of obedience in the Christian life, where it serves as a commitment to ongoing obedience.

Baptism and Circumcision

Why do some Christians wish to baptize babies? One reason is because they think that baptism is a rite of entrance into the community of God's people. They suggest that it replaces circumcision as a mark of inclusion in the believing community. To understand this argument, we must understand how circumcision worked in the Old Testament.

In the covenant community of Old Testament Israel, circumcision was the enduring physical sign of God's covenant with the nation. As such, all male infants were circumcised at eight days of age. God's covenant was with the nation, and because those infants were members of the nation, they were given the mark. Of course, a circumcised baby would still have to make his own decisions about whether to follow the Lord. Circumcision did not save. What it did was to mark the child as a member of the community.

Some Christians believe that baptism functions the same way today. They reason that the church has taken the place of Israel as the people of God. They suggest that the children of church members should also be recognized as members of the community, just as infant Israelites were members of the community in the Old Testament. Community membership, they say, does not depend upon having personally trusted Christ as Savior. Since infants are members of the community, it is proper for them to receive the mark of inclusion in the community, and that mark is baptism.

Baptists reject this argument for two reasons. First, many Baptists object to drawing a parallel between baptism and circumcision. Colossians 2:11–12 mention the two together, but not everyone agrees that the connection is direct enough to establish an analogy between them. Second, even if baptism has replaced circumcision as the rite of entrance and mark of inclusion in the community, the nature of the community has changed between the Old and New Testaments.

The Old Testament community (national Israel) was defined by membership in a biological family. Those who were descended from Abraham, Isaac, and Israel were automatically included as members of that community, quite apart from any choice of their own. In other words, membership in the community of Israel was visible, external, and involuntary.

The community of the New Testament (the church) is defined differently.

Jesus made it clear that "one fold [flock]" (i.e., the church) is composed of those who follow Him (John 10:16).[4] "Following Christ" in this passage is another way of talking about saving faith. Therefore, a person gets into the New Testament community, not by being born into it, but by trusting Jesus. One is not a member of the community until one believes. The implication should be obvious: if people are not included in the community until they believe, they should not receive any marks of inclusion (specifically, baptism) until they believe. This is a powerful argument for baptizing only those who have professed faith in Christ as Savior.

Whether or not baptism replaces circumcision, it is a mark of identification with Christ. Identification with Christ implies some form of identification with His people. Baptists do not object to seeing baptism as a badge of membership in the Christian community. They contend, however, that the badge can be worn only by those who have entered the community voluntarily.

Baptism and the Washing of Sins

So far we have seen that baptism functions as a picture of the gospel, as a public profession of faith, as a first step of obedience, and as a badge of initiation and identification. We have rejected the suggestion that baptism replaces circumcision as the mark of inclusion for infants. Now we need to discuss the theory that baptism depicts the washing of sins.

Many professing Christians believe that baptism symbolizes the washing away of sins. Others believe that baptism actually constitutes the washing, that is, that baptism removes sins. To moderns, this seems quite reasonable: What could be more natural than to associate washing with an application of water? Nevertheless, Baptists have always insisted that baptism does not wash away sins. It does not even symbolize washing. Baptism (as we have seen above) is a picture of the death, burial, and resurrection of Jesus, a profession and badge of faith, and a first step of obedience in following Jesus.

Why do Baptists reject the notion that baptism either symbolizes or accomplishes the washing of sins? First, because the Bible teaches that sins are removed only when we turn to Jesus in saving faith, not when we are baptized. Second, because no text of Scripture clearly connects baptism with the washing of sins, but many texts connect it with something else. Third, because the New

---

4. The King James Version translates this as "one fold," but all Greek texts agree that the term is *flock*. Jesus is making the point that He has some sheep in the fold (national Israel), whom He will lead out. He has other sheep (Gentile believers) outside the fold. All these sheep together will comprise one flock with one Shepherd.

Testament shows people whose sins were washed away, even though they had not yet been baptized in water.

God's children have always been saved in exactly the same way: by grace, through faith. The way of salvation is seen with special clarity in the case of Abraham, who simply believed God, "and he counted it to him for righteousness" (Gen. 15:6). In Romans 4, the apostle Paul argued that Abraham was justified through faith without any works. Even Abraham's circumcision came after his justification: no external rites or rituals played any role in his salvation. Paul made Abraham the prototype for all saved people: whoever we are, and whenever we live, we are justified in the same way that Abraham was. We are justified through faith alone, without works (Rom. 4:23, 24).

In Ephesians 2:8–9, Paul wrote that we receive salvation as a gift by grace, through faith, without works. To the Philippian jailer, he announced, "Believe on the Lord Jesus Christ, and thou shalt be saved," with no mention of baptism as a condition of salvation (Acts 16:31). In Romans 10:13 he repeated the words of the Old Testament prophet Joel, "Whosoever shall call upon the name of the Lord shall be delivered" (see Joel 2:32). These and many other Scriptures indicate that God's plan has always been to save people upon the simple condition of faith.

Nowhere does the Bible ever make baptism a condition of justification. Nowhere does it ever depict baptism as a mechanism through which sins are removed. Nowhere does the Bible present baptism as a rite through which sins are washed away.[5]

No clear text of Scripture treats baptism as a washing, either literally or symbolically. Granted, regeneration either is or produces a washing (Titus 3:5), but the text does not associate this washing with baptism. Occasionally someone will point to being "born of water" as a reference to baptism (John 3:5), but the encounter between Jesus and Nicodemus occurred before the cross and antedated the establishment of Christian baptism.

One verse that does mention baptism together with the washing of sins is Acts 22:16. That verse, however, separates "getting baptized" from "getting your sins washed away" by placing the two verbs in separate clauses. Properly, getting sins washed away is not a function of baptism (either literally or symbolically), but of calling on the name of the Lord.

The apostle Peter clearly stated that the significance of baptism is *not* the

---

5. The principal proof texts for baptismal regeneration will be examined in chapter 10. None of these texts actually teaches that baptism washes away sins. In fact, baptism can never accomplish the forgiveness of sins, either in whole or in part.

washing of "filthiness from the flesh." While some translators understand this to mean that baptism does not merely wash dirt from the body, a better interpretation understands *filth* to mean "moral pollution" and *flesh* to mean something like "sin nature." If this interpretation is correct, Peter was actually denying that baptism can wash away sins or the sin nature.

To moderns in the West, any application of water seems to entail the notion of washing. That was not always the case, however. During the first century, baptism was typically used as a rite of identification. John's followers were baptized into identification with repentance (Matt. 3:11; Acts 13:24). Paul argued that the children of Israel were baptized into identification with Moses in the cloud and in the sea (1 Cor. 10:1–2). Paul was not willing to have anyone baptized into identification with him (1 Cor. 1:13–16). Clearly the significance of baptism is not as a symbol of washing, but as a symbol of identification.

Baptism does not wash away sins, either literally or symbolically. In case we have any doubt, the New Testament presents clear examples of people who were saved and whose sins were forgiven (washed away) before they were baptized in water. Among these examples are Cornelius and the members of his household. The story of Cornelius is found in Acts 10, then retold in Acts 11.

Cornelius was a Gentile who, drawn to some Jewish customs, had begun to worship the Lord in an uninformed and flawed way. An angel from God instructed Cornelius to send for the apostle Peter (Acts 10:22), promising that Peter would tell Cornelius and the members of his household how to be saved (Acts 11:14). Cornelius responded to the angel's instruction and sent for Peter, but according to the text, neither Cornelius nor the members of his household were yet saved people.

When Peter arrived, he announced Jesus as Lord and as God's anointed one (Acts 10:36–38). He declared the death and resurrection of Jesus (vv. 39–41). He preached that Jesus would someday judge the living and the dead (v. 42), and he stated that the way to receive the forgiveness of sins is to believe on the name of Jesus (v. 43).

Apparently, Peter had only completed the introduction to the sermon that he had planned to preach (Acts 11:15), when he was suddenly interrupted. The Holy Spirit fell on Cornelius and the members of his household, and they began to speak in tongues and to magnify God (Acts 10:46). Peter and his companions rightly interpreted this phenomenon as the gift of the Spirit (Acts 10:45) that Jesus had promised to His disciples (Acts 1:5). Peter further concluded that this was the very same baptizing work of the Spirit that had begun on the

Day of Pentecost (Acts 11:15–17), the exact same gift that had been given to the original followers of Jesus.

At this point, Cornelius and the members of his household were undoubtedly saved. They had heard the gospel. They had heard the invitation to believe. They had received the gift of the Holy Spirit, understood in terms of the Spirit's baptizing work. Elsewhere, the apostle Paul clearly specified that this baptizing work is what unites believers to the Body of Christ, making them the members of Christ Himself (1 Cor. 12:12–13).

Before Peter came, Cornelius was still an unsaved man. When he received the gift of the Spirit, that was a clear declaration that he had been accepted by God and forgiven. He was definitely saved and his sins were washed away. Significantly, however, he was not yet baptized.

Only after Cornelius received the gift of the Spirit did Peter mention water baptism. To his companions he asked, "Can any man forbid water, that these should not be baptized, which have received the Holy Ghost as well as we?" (Acts 10:47). Since all believers are to be baptized, and since Cornelius and the members of his household were clearly saved, it stood to reason that they should also be baptized. Only at this point, after Cornelius had clearly believed and been saved, did Peter command him and the others to be baptized (Acts 10:48).

The example of Cornelius illustrates the unvarying pattern of the New Testament. We believe on the Lord Jesus Christ and we are saved. Once we are saved, we are to be baptized. Baptism is the confession of forgiveness already received. It is never a means of gaining forgiveness.

Cornelius and his household are clear examples of people who were forgiven and saved before they were baptized. No passage in the New Testament ever places baptism before forgiveness or makes baptism a condition of forgiveness. Baptism comes after salvation, because salvation is always applied upon the condition of faith.

In sum, baptism neither symbolizes nor accomplishes the forgiveness of sins. Baptism is not a replacement for the circumcision of infants. Rather, baptism is a picture of the gospel. It shows Jesus' death and resurrection. It is a confession of faith, the badge by which we identify ourselves as believers in Jesus. Furthermore, baptism is a first step of obedience for the saved person.

Proper Mode

Baptists are characterized by many beliefs and practices, but none is more visible than their practice of immersing. Indeed, the only thing that some people know about Baptists is that they dunk. That is not necessarily a bad thing, because the insistence upon immersion is indeed an important Baptist distinctive.

The question is whether baptism must be performed by immersion, or whether it may be administered through different modes. Most professing Christians believe that baptism can be performed in a variety of ways: sprinkling (aspersion), pouring (affusion), or multiple ways of immersing. Thus they believe that baptism can be administered in different modes.

The leading Reformers were quite willing to allow for baptism by immersion, but they also wanted to allow other ways of baptizing. Martin Luther, in his Larger Catechism, spoke of baptism in terms of both pouring and immersion. Calvin also wrote, "Whether the person being baptized should be wholly immersed, and whether thrice or once, whether he should only be sprinkled with poured water—these details are of no importance."[6]

More recent writers have expressed the same opinion. Three examples can be listed here, all of whom were Presbyterians. Robert Lewis Dabney admitted "any application of water, by an ordained ministry, in the name of the Trinity, to be valid baptism." J. Oliver Buswell wrote, "We have no objection to the thought that baptism may properly be performed by immersion." Charles Hodge granted that baptism may be performed "by immersion, affusion, or sprinkling."[7]

The question is not whether baptism *can* be performed by immersion. Almost everyone admits that it can.[8] The question is whether baptism *must* be administered by immersion. Baptists insist that genuine, or valid, baptism must be administered by immersion in water. According to Baptists, people who have been subjected to sprinkling or pouring have not been baptized at all. Before

---

6. Martin Luther, "Larger Catechism," in *The Book of Concord*, trans. and ed. Theodore G. Tappert (Philadelphia: Muhlenberg Press, 1959), 442, 444; John Calvin, *Institutes of the Christian Religion*, ed. John T. McNeill, trans. Ford Lewis Battles (Louisville, KY: Westminster John Knox, 1960), 2:1320.

7. Robert Lewis Dabney, *Lectures in Systematic Theology* (1878; repr., Grand Rapids: Zondervan, 1972), 764; James Oliver Buswell, *A Systematic Theology of the Christian Religion*, (Grand Rapids: Zondervan, 1962), 2:243; Charles Hodge, *Systematic Theology* (New York: Charles Scribner's Sons, 1885) 3:526.

8. A few Christians have reacted against the Baptist insistence on immersion by discouraging immersion or even refusing to immerse at all, but this is not typical. Instances include Presbyterian Lewis Sperry Chafer, *Systematic Theology* (Dallas: Dallas Seminary Press, 1947), 7:35; and Lutheran Edward W. A. Koehler, *A Summary of Christian Doctrine*, rev. ed. (1952; repr., St. Louis: Concordia Publishing House, 1971), 204.

they are received as members of Baptist churches, such persons must be immersed. As Baptist theologian A. H. Strong noted, baptism "is immersion, and immersion only."[9]

Why do Baptists insist so strongly upon immersion as the only mode that can properly be called baptism? They appeal to three lines of evidence. The first is the meaning and use of the Greek verb *baptizein,* which is translated *to baptize* in most English versions of the Bible. The second is the meaning of the ordinance of baptism. The third is the practice of the early churches.

The Meaning and Use of Baptizein

Almost everyone recognizes that the verb *baptizein* has the strict and proper meaning "to immerse." Widely used in secular Greek before and during the New Testament era, the verb always carries the idea of complete submergence. Even when used figuratively, *baptizein* relies upon the literal notion of immersion. For example, a drunken person could be said to be "immersed in wine," a vivid picture of the effects of alcohol.[10]

Some arguable uses do occur in the Apocrypha and in the New Testament itself. Non-Baptists often point to these passages as proof that *baptizein* could be used to denote some version of sprinkling or pouring. Space does not permit a detailed examination of these passages. At best, however, they are ambiguous: in no instance is immersion impossible or even unlikely.[11]

Obscure or ambiguous passages are of less theological value than clear passages. Texts that can rightly bear only one meaning must be used to understand texts that could bear more than one interpretation. Ambiguous passages, therefore, are of little value in deciding whether baptism must be done by immersion. To date, no one has suggested a passage in which *baptizein* clearly means something other than immersion. In a number of instances, however, one finds baptism clearly depicted as immersion.

---

9. Augustus Hopkins Strong, *Systematic Theology* (Valley Forge, PA: Judson Press, 1907), 933.

10. The classic treatment of *Baptizein* is Thomas Jefferson Conant, *The Meaning and Use of* Baptizein (1864; repr. Grand Rapids: Kregel, 1977). Conant pursued *baptizein* and its cognates comprehensively through Greek literature. His conclusion is that the term always bears the meaning *to immerse.*

11. In the Apocrypha, Ecclesiasticus 34:25 refers to the Jewish practice of baptism after touching a dead body, while Judith 12:7 has the protagonist baptizing herself (bathing) at a spring. In the New Testament, Mark 7:4–8 has cups, pots, bronze vessels, and "tables" (probably sleeping mats) being baptized. Hebrews 6:2 and 9:10 refer to baptisms that were part of the Jewish levitical system. First Corinthians 10:2 speaks of Israel being "baptized unto Moses in the cloud and in the sea."

One such instance occurs in the description of John's baptism in Mark 1:4 and 5. While John's baptism was not Christian baptism, it was still baptism, and it illustrates how baptism was performed. Mark 1:5 states that those who came to John were baptized by him "in" the Jordan River. Some non-Baptists suggest that John waded out into the river with his converts so that he could sprinkle or pour a bit of water on them. This suggestion might be believable if the people who make it ever took their converts out into a river to sprinkle water on them. That they never do is an indication of how preposterous their suggestion actually is. John certainly immersed his converts in the Jordan River.

Similarly, Philip certainly immersed the Ethiopian eunuch (Acts 8:36–38). The text is quite clear that Philip and the eunuch went down into the water and came up again. If all that Philip needed to do was to sprinkle or pour, he could easily have used some of the drinking water in the eunuch's chariot. Any uncontrived reading of this text will understand that an immersion was taking place.

Thus in its usage outside the New Testament, the verb *baptizein* simply means *to immerse*. The New Testament contains no text in which this meaning is impossible and some in which it is so evident as to be undeniable. Consequently, Jesus' command to baptize is a command to immerse. That is why Baptists insist that until one has been immersed, one has not been baptized.

Meaning Determines Mode

Whatever points they may dispute, all Christians agree that baptism is, at some level, symbolic. Most Christians instinctively seek for a mode of baptism that adequately pictures whatever meaning baptism is supposed to symbolize. For example, if baptism symbolizes the washing away of sins, then sprinkling or pouring might be adequate and admissible pictures.

This is the point at which Baptists turn to the Biblical texts that explain the meaning of baptism. Most Baptists believe that Romans 6:3–4 explicitly make water baptism a symbol of the death, burial, and resurrection of Christ. Those who disagree still recognize that 1 Peter 3:20–21 connect the significance of baptism with the resurrection of Jesus, and a resurrection implies a death and burial. Consequently, baptism serves as a symbolic picture of the gospel itself, specifically a picture of Jesus' death for sin and His victorious resurrection from the dead.

Immersion in water is an adequate and even obvious symbol of death, burial, and resurrection. By submitting to immersion, we confess our faith that Jesus died and arose for us. We are symbolically buried in the likeness of His death and raised to walk in newness of life. Many Baptist ministers even utter these words when performing a baptism—"buried in the likeness of His death, raised to walk in newness of life." Whether they do or not, however, the subject's confession of faith is tied directly to the meaning of the symbol itself.

On the other hand, neither sprinkling nor pouring provides an adequate depiction of death, burial, and resurrection. Nothing in these acts would lead an observer to believe that the subject is confessing the death or resurrection of Christ. Sprinkling and pouring are completely inadequate as vehicles for the symbolic meaning of the ordinance. Since they cannot depict what baptism is supposed to symbolize, they should never be viewed as baptism.

To repeat, water baptism is a symbol of the death, burial, and resurrection of Jesus. Only immersion can adequately picture death, burial, and resurrection. Therefore, only immersion should be practiced as baptism. Sprinkling and pouring are not modes of baptism. They are not baptism at all. This understanding of baptism is virtually universal among Baptists.

The symbolic meaning of baptism is also important for determining the correct way of immersing. Baptists typically practice single immersion, but some Anabaptist groups practice what is called trine immersion—the practice of immersing three times, once in the name of the Father, once in the name of the Son, and once in the name of the Holy Spirit. Baptists normally reject trine immersion as valid baptism.

Their reasoning draws upon the significance of the ordinance. If baptism is meant to picture the death, burial, and resurrection of Jesus, then trine immersion cannot be correct. Jesus did not die three times. He was not buried three times. He did not rise three times. Neither the Father nor the Holy Spirit died for the sins of the world. For water baptism to symbolize the death, burial, and resurrection of Christ, it must be single immersion.

Thus, in regard to the mode of baptism, Baptists do not recognize either sprinkling or pouring as baptism at all. Although trine immersion does involve immersion, it destroys the symbolic value of baptism, so most Baptists do not recognize it as valid New Testament baptism. People who have been sprinkled, poured, or trine immersed are required to be singly immersed before they are received as members of Baptist churches. Properly speaking, they are not rebaptized. Rather, they are Biblically baptized for the very first time.

Practice of the Early Churches

The earliest churches—the churches of the New Testament—gave no evidence of baptizing by sprinkling or pouring. They established a pattern of immersing that was maintained after the apostolic era. The earliest Christian documents after the New Testament indicate that the churches were still immersing converts.

The label *church fathers* is used for the generations of Christian pastors and thinkers who wrote from the close of the apostolic period to the beginning of the Middle Ages. These ancient authors vary in their value for present-day discussions of doctrine and practice. Since Baptists look to the New Testament for final authority in church faith and order, the church fathers are never determinative. They are often useful, however, because they help us to understand how the early Christians read and implemented the Bible.

One of the very earliest Christian documents outside of Scripture is the *Didache*, or *The Teaching of the Twelve Apostles*. It represents an attempt by one early Christian writer to summarize what the apostles taught in a variety of areas. One of the topics that the *Didache* addresses is baptism.

> Now concerning baptism, baptize as follows: after you have reviewed all these things, baptize in the name of the Father and of the Son and of the Holy Spirit in running water. But if you have no running water, then baptize in some other water; and if you are not able to baptize in cold water, then do so in warm. But if you have neither, then pour water on the head three times in the name of Father and Son and Holy Spirit.[12]

Some writers believe that the *Didache* "says that baptism may be performed by pouring."[13] That is not correct. What the *Didache* does is to permit the practice of pouring as an emergency substitute for baptism. It does not suggest that pouring is baptism, but that pouring may sometimes be performed instead of baptism. Baptism itself is not understood to include pouring.

The author of the *Didache* clearly understood baptism to be equivalent to immersion. Pouring—if it was done at all—was for extreme circumstances. Even then, the author seems uncomfortable with pouring, for while he requires only a single immersion, he insists upon triple pouring. Perhaps he thought that the repetition would somehow compensate for the deficiency in mode.

The pattern of baptism by immersion held true until the fourth century. Baptism was simply immersion in water. Only with the introduction of so-called clinic baptism (the baptism of the sick and dying) did pouring become

---

12. Michael Holmes, trans. and ed. *The Apostolic Fathers in English*, 3rd ed. (Grand Rapids: Baker, 2006), 166.

13. William G. T. Shedd, *Dogmatic Theology* (1889; repr., Grand Rapids: Zondervan, 1953), 2:582.

widespread. Even then it was practiced almost exclusively in the West. The descendents of Eastern (Greek-speaking) Christianity have continued to practice immersion down to the present day. Granted, these churches practice infant baptism, but the mode is immersion. In both the East and the West, the baptisteries of the most ancient churches were designed to be used for immersion, not for sprinkling or pouring. No one seriously questions that professing Christians practiced immersion almost exclusively during the early centuries of the church.

To conclude, the earliest churches recognized only immersion as baptism. Pouring originally arose as an emergency measure to be substituted for baptism when immersion could not be performed. Even then, it remained a rare exception during the first several centuries of Christian history. In fact, major segments of professing Christianity (i.e., the churches of the East) have practiced immersion exclusively. While this historical evidence is not determinative for church faith and order, it does illustrate that the earliest church fathers understood the New Testament to require immersion. Thus history corroborates the Baptist perspective that only immersion qualifies as baptism.

Proper Authority

One of the most important and disputed issues among Baptists concerns the proper authority for baptism. The question of authority has two parts. The first is, Who has proper authority to baptize? The second is, What becomes of those who are baptized under improper authority?

Baptism as a Church Ordinance

Who has authority to baptize? This authority was granted by Jesus Himself in Matthew 28:19–20. In that passage, baptism is a required aspect of making disciples. Inasmuch as the apostles were authorized to make disciples, they were also authorized to baptize.

Was this authority unique and specific to the original apostles, or does it extend beyond them? Jesus answered this question; for when He authorized the apostles to make disciples, He added, "I am with you alway, even unto the end of the world [age]." Jesus promised His presence would accompany those who make disciples. This promise specifically extended throughout the age. Consequently, it must reach beyond the original apostles, all of whom died either before or very shortly after the end of the first century.

If baptism is an ongoing aspect of discipleship, is every individual Christian authorized to go around baptizing converts? Most Baptists have answered this question in the negative. The nature of baptism requires more than simple, individual initiative on the part of an administrator.

As we have already seen, baptism is a confession of faith in the death, burial, and resurrection of Jesus for one's sins. This confession is not merely a private activity, as if one could be baptized by simply taking a bath at home. Instead, it is a public profession of faith that needs to be witnessed, at minimum, by the church.

Baptism also stands at the head of the list for obedience in the Christian life. It is connected with a clear conscience (1 Pet. 3:21). It is the prerequisite to being taught to obey all that Christ commanded (Matt. 28:19–20). As such, it surely falls under the purview, or responsibility, of "the house of God, which is the church of the living God, the pillar and ground of the truth" (1 Tim. 3:15), a clear reference to the local congregation.

Baptists have been nearly unanimous that baptism is an ordinance reserved for the local church. One way they have expressed this opinion is in their confessions of faith. For example, Article 33 of the London Confession (1644, The First London Confession) specified that a church is a "company of visible Saints, called & separated from the world, by the word and Spirit of God, to the visible profession of the faith of the Gospel, being baptized into that faith, and joyned to the Lord, and each other, by mutuall agreement, in the practical injoyment of the Ordinances, commanded by their head and King." Later, in Article 39, the same confession stipulated that baptism is such an ordinance.

The Baptist Confession of Faith (1689), popularly known as the Second London Confession, echoed this theme. It stated that a fully ordered church consists of "Officers, and Members; And the Officers appointed by *Christ* to be chosen and set apart by the Church . . . for the peculiar Administration of Ordinances" (26.8). The confession later defined baptism as an "Ordinance of the New Testament, ordained by Jesus Christ" (29.1). The wording of the Second London Confession is closely followed by the Philadelphia Confession, one of the early statements adopted by Baptists in America.

The General Baptists of England in 1678 produced a confession they called The Orthodox Creed. According to this confession, a rightly organized church consists of officers and members, and the officers have the responsibility of administering the ordinances (article 31). While the Particular Baptists and the General Baptists experienced some differences of opinion, they were united in believing that baptism ought to be administered under the authority of a local church.

Baptists in America fully agreed with the English Baptists on this point. As we have seen, the Philadelphia Baptist Association simply adopted the wording of the Second London Confession in its own statement of faith. One of the most famous Baptist confessions was the New Hampshire Confession (1833), which simply states that a visible church of Christ is a "congregation of baptized believers, associated by covenant in the faith and fellowship of the Gospel; observing the ordinances of Christ" (article 13). This wording implies that the church was tasked with "observing the ordinances." Later on, fundamental Baptists tended to copy this language very closely.

While there have been instances of dissent, the vast majority of Baptists have understood the New Testament to imply that authority for baptism rightly belongs to local congregations.[14] Baptisms ought not to be performed in non-church settings such as camps or tours of the Holy Land. They should not be administered by individuals who lack authority from a local congregation.

Usually a pastor of the church will administer baptism. In the absence of a pastor, a deacon may be assigned the responsibility. The church may, however, appoint any member of its choosing (or even a member of another church, such as a visiting minister) to act in its behalf in baptizing new believers. No matter what the circumstance, however, Baptists maintain that the proper authority for baptism rests with the local church.

The Problem of Alien Immersion

By holding that baptism is a church ordinance, Baptists often find themselves confronting a second problem. How should they evaluate the baptisms of people who were immersed, but not under the authority of a local church? For that matter, what are the qualifications for an organization to be recognized as a church with the right to administer baptism?

This is a very real problem. Some people get baptized by tour guides in the Jordan River. Others get baptized at summer camps when they trust Jesus as Savior. Still others may choose to be immersed in churches that also baptize infants or that practice pouring or sprinkling. Some have even been immersed in churches that teach baptismal regeneration (the belief that one must be baptized before one can be saved). Which baptisms should Baptists accept and which should they not?

---

14. One dissenting voice is that of early Baptist theologian John Gill. See *Body of Divinity*, 3rd ed. (1839; repr., Atlanta: Turner Lassetter, 1965), 896.

The answer to this question has several parts. The first part is that, if baptism is a church ordinance (as most Baptists believe), then baptism without a church's authority is always irregular (to Baptists, this is a technical term for a baptism that is out of order). Practices that result in irregular baptism should not be encouraged, for to practice irregular baptism is to fail to do things "decently and in order" (1 Cor. 14:40). That is why Baptists discourage baptisms at camps, on tours, or under other circumstances that lack authorization from a local congregation.

Irregular baptisms, however, are not necessarily invalid. To say that they are irregular is to say that they should have been performed under different circumstances. To say that they are invalid is to suggest that they are not Christian baptisms at all. Baptists are unanimous that baptism is invalid when it has the wrong subject, meaning, or mode. They have not come to the same unanimity regarding baptisms that lack proper church authority.

The distinction between irregular and invalid baptism hinges on the meaning of the ordinance. The primary meaning of baptism is symbolically to confess one's trust in the death, burial, and resurrection of Jesus. An infant is in no position to make such a confession, so infant baptism is invalid. Modes other than single immersion destroy the symbolism, so they are invalid. When baptism is performed irregularly, however, it still retains its full significance as a confession of faith in the death, burial, and resurrection of Christ. Therefore, even though proper meaning, mode, and subjects are essential to valid baptism, proper authority may not be. Under most circumstances, baptisms performed without church authority are valid Christian baptisms and should be recognized by Baptist churches (though they should not be encouraged). These baptisms are rather like a couple who elopes: the parents might have wished for a more orderly wedding, but the marriage is still a marriage.

Baptisms that destroy the symbolism of the ordinance, however, are not valid. Baptism is a confession of faith in the death, burial, and resurrection of Jesus. When baptism is being performed as a saving act (as in Roman Catholicism or the Churches of Christ), it constitutes a denial of the gospel. Its meaning is profoundly subverted and even negated. For that reason, baptisms performed as part of baptismal regeneration are not valid. People who have been baptized in gospel-denying churches have never been Scripturally immersed.

The same is true of non-Trinitarian baptism. Mormons baptize, as do Jehovah's Witnesses, but their baptisms cannot be recognized as Christian. The doctrine of the Trinity is essential to the gospel: it is a fundamental of the faith. Baptisms performed by cults, as well as baptisms performed by anti-Trinitarians such as the Jesus-Only Movement (e.g., the United Pentecostal Church), entail a denial of the gospel. They are not valid Christian baptisms, and people who have gone through them must still receive baptism.

What about baptisms performed in gospel-preaching churches that are not baptistic? Perhaps such churches also sprinkle or pour. Perhaps they believe that they can baptize babies. Are people who receive immersion in these churches really baptized?

Baptism that is performed in non-Baptist churches is sometimes called alien immersion. Over the past 150 years, Baptists have disagreed sharply over whether to recognize alien immersion as valid baptism. The followers of James R. Graves (called Landmarkers) have insisted that alien immersion should never be recognized. Most Baptist churches, however, have been willing to receive members who have been immersed in other gospel-preaching churches. As long as the meaning and symbolism of baptism is preserved—as long as it functions as a public profession of faith in the death, burial, and resurrection of Jesus Christ—then most Baptists recognize its validity.

Landmark churches typically require those who have received alien immersion to be rebaptized (according to their view, baptized the first time). If baptism from other churches is valid, however, then submitting to rebaptism is a sin. For believers to repeat baptism that they have already received is to destroy its symbolism. Jesus died only once, was buried only once, and was raised from the dead only once. A person who has once received baptism as a profession of faith should never submit to a second baptism.

The most visible distinguishing mark of Baptists is their view of Christian baptism. Baptists believe that valid, or genuine, baptism requires a proper subject, a proper meaning, and a proper mode. Baptists generally emphasize the proper authority of the local church in administering baptism. They see baptisms performed in non-church settings as irregular, but not necessarily as invalid. Most Baptist churches are happy to receive members who have been immersed in other evangelical congregations.

3 Pure Church Membership

WE HAVE SEEN two ways in which Baptist churches differ from other gospel-preaching churches. First, Baptists appeal to the absolute authority of the New Testament in all matters of church faith and order. Second, Baptists insist that only believers ought to be baptized and that only immersion qualifies as baptism. Now it is time to examine the third Baptist distinctive.

Baptist churches differ from many other gospel-preaching churches in their understanding of church membership. Many churches knowingly admit unregenerate individuals into membership. Others admit unbaptized believers. Still others are willing to receive or retain members whose lives are a scandal to the gospel. On the other hand, some groups deny that local church membership is even possible. They stress that no one can be a member of any church other than the universal Body of Christ.

Baptists differ with all of the above by emphasizing pure church membership. This chapter will examine the idea of pure church membership by investigating its three central themes: regenerate membership, baptized membership, and church discipline. In connection with church membership and discipline, this chapter will also explore the Baptist understanding of the Lord's Table, or Communion. Before beginning any of those investigations, however, we must first ask whether we ought to practice church membership at all.

Church Membership and Church Covenant

If church membership is important, then where is it explicitly taught in the New Testament? Neither Acts nor the Epistles contain any particular formula for the

55

admission and recognition of church members. Nowhere does the New Testament mention membership rosters. Can membership really matter as much as Baptists believe it does?

In answer to this question, we first notice that the New Testament describes several different kinds of relationships between Christians. "Church membership" is the name that Baptists and some others apply to one of these relationships. What does this relationship look like?

In the New Testament, Christians have the responsibility to hold one another accountable and even to exercise discipline over one another. This relationship is detailed in 1 Corinthians 5:1–13, where a professing brother was engaged in scandalous conduct (v. 1). Consequently, the apostle Paul instructed the church to take specific action toward this man. In fact, he insisted that they should already have taken this man out of the church (v. 2). Paul stated that he had heard enough to judge the situation for himself, and he instructed the church, when it "gathered together" (v. 4), to "deliver such an one unto Satan for the destruction of the flesh" (v. 5). Paul reminded the Corinthians that God would judge those who were outside the church, but they themselves were responsible to judge those who were inside (vv. 12–13). Consequently, they were to put away this wicked person from among themselves (v. 13).

Clearly Paul believed that some people were inside the church at Corinth while others were outside it. Those inside were accountable to the whole congregation for their conduct. The congregation possessed the authority to expel anyone whose error was sufficiently grievous. This authority was mediated through the assembled church, not through private individuals or subgroups of the congregation.

In other words, some mechanism existed to determine who was in the church and who was not. Some mechanism existed to decide who should participate in a congregational decision and who should not. This mechanism had to involve more than physical presence in the assembly, for unbelievers frequented the assemblies (1 Cor. 14:23). It had to involve more than simply being a Christian, for Paul himself did not participate in making the decision (though he told the church what it was obligated to do). Some way had to exist to distinguish those who were bound by this relationship of accountability from those who were not. In other words, whether written or unwritten, formally or informally, some kind of list must have existed.

The church at Corinth displayed a relationship of mutual accountability and discipline between individual believers and the entire congregation. This relationship is exactly what Baptists call church membership. To become a member of a church, an individual deliberately submits to this relationship. Christians who take this step become accountable to the congregation as a whole. Since they are part of the congregation, they also participate in holding others accountable.

This relationship is deliberate and voluntary on the part of the church member. It never happens accidentally. The only way in which Christians become members of a New Testament church is by agreeing to submit to that congregation's accountability and spiritual oversight. In other words, each member accepts certain responsibilities toward the congregation, while the congregation accepts responsibilities toward the members. Becoming a church member involves a solemn agreement, a promise that church members make to one another.

This agreement is embodied in the church's covenant. Next to the Bible, the covenant is the most important document that the church possesses. There are two reasons for its importance. First, the covenant represents the agreement of the members actually to be a church. Not every gathering of believers is a church for the simple reason that not every gathering of believers intends to be one. Youth camps, seminaries, Bible conferences, and mission agencies are gatherings of Christians, but they are not churches. The covenant is what distinguishes a particular assembly or congregation by stating its intention to be a church according to the pattern of the New Testament.

Second, the covenant states an agreement about what it means to be a church. Different churches understand their nature and function differently. These differences are a major part of what distinguishes the various Christian denominations from each other. They have different understandings of what a church is, what a church ought to do, and how a church ought to operate in order to do it. In a Baptist church, the covenant and its attendant documents (usually a confession and a constitution) represent the church's commitment to a particular vision of being a church. Whether it is written, spoken, or merely assumed, whether formal or informal, the covenant is what turns a gathering of believers into a church.

Of course, church membership involves more than just mutual accountability and discipline, and most church covenants recognize this fact. The duties and privileges of membership correspond to the various "one another" requirements found in the letters to the New Testament churches. Church members are obligated to show brotherly love and affection for one another, to prefer one another, to honor one another, and to take care of each other's material needs (Rom. 12:10, 13). They are to avoid judging one another, taking care not to trip one another up (Rom. 14:13). They must receive one another just as Christ has received them, and they have a duty to warn one another (Rom. 15:7, 14; Col. 3:16). They are responsible to bear one another's burdens (Gal. 6:2), to put up with each other in love (Eph. 4:2), to forgive one another (Eph. 4:32; Col. 3:13), to teach one another (Col. 3:16), to comfort one another (1 Thess. 4:18), and to edify one another (1 Thess. 5:11).

In some sense, these are also general duties that all believers owe toward all other believers. We recognize, however, that none of us can fulfill these duties toward all Christians all the time. In some cases, Christians do not even agree as to what their duties entail. For example, baptism is an ordinance that is given to the local church, but one church may sprinkle while another immerses. To organize as a church, a body of believers must agree about the nature of their mutual obligations and promise to fulfill these obligations toward each other. Christians may or may not fulfill these obligations for other believers in the next county or (for that matter) halfway around the world, but they solemnly promise to fulfill them for those who enter together into their church covenant.

Regenerate Membership

Church membership is a covenant relationship. One becomes a member of a church only when one freely assumes the duties and privileges of the covenant. In other words, church membership is always a voluntary decision for both the member and the church. Inasmuch as an infant is incapable of voluntarily assuming the responsibilities of the covenant, infants must not be received as church members.

The covenant of a New Testament church is spiritual in nature. When they enter into the church covenant, members receive spiritual blessings and they undertake to perform spiritual responsibilities. Consequently, only those who have been given spiritual life are suitable subjects for church membership. An individual who is still dead in trespasses and sins and who is by nature a child of wrath (Eph. 2:1–3) is in no position to assume spiritual responsibilities toward the children of God.

In the New Testament, a saint is a person who has been set part, or sanctified, by God through salvation. Everywhere we look in the Epistles, church members are addressed as saints. Paul used this label for the members of the churches at Rome (Rom. 1:7), Jerusalem (Rom. 15:26), Corinth (1 Cor. 1:2), Ephesus (Eph. 1:1), Philippi (Phil. 1:1), Colosse (Col. 1:2), and even "in all churches"

(1 Cor. 14:33). If the members of these churches were saints, then they were clearly regenerate people.

He also used the term *brother* for church members. For Paul, members of the church at Rome were brothers (Rom. 1:13), as were members of the churches at Corinth (1 Cor. 1:26), Galatia (Gal. 1:11), Ephesus (Eph. 6:23), Philippi (Phil. 1:12), Colosse (Col. 1:2), and Thessalonica (1 Thess. 1:4). Writing to Timothy, Paul made it clear that the word *brother* denotes a relationship between fellow believers (1 Tim. 6:2). Inasmuch as the members of New Testament churches were brothers, they must have been believers.

The New Testament also addresses church members as children of God (Rom. 8:16), sons of God through faith (Gal. 3:26), servants of righteousness (Rom. 6:18), temples of the Holy Spirit (1 Cor. 6:19), fellow citizens of the saints and members of the household of God (Eph. 2:19), and those who are washed, sanctified, and justified (1 Cor. 6:11). Some of these words are spoken to church members who are in serious doctrinal error or whose lives are badly disordered. Nevertheless, the universal assumption of the New Testament is that church members are saved people.

True, professions of faith may sometimes be false, and for that reason unbelievers may sometimes get into a church's membership. Baptists do not claim to be able to examine people's hearts. They can, however, evaluate two external things: the credibility of applicants' testimonies (i.e., whether they profess to believe the true gospel or whether their profession is tied to some false gospel), and the veracity of applicants' lives (whether their conduct is in keeping with a profession of salvation or whether it somehow contradicts their profession).

Unbelievers might sometimes become members of Baptist churches. Some unbelievers have learned to repeat the right words, and they live outwardly moral lives. They may present themselves for church membership, and they may be received into churches. Some heretical teachers may pretend to be Christians to get the opportunity to propagate their aberrant doctrines. Such devious individuals are false brothers who sneak in (Gal. 2:4). Nevertheless, the goal of New Testament churches is not to include such individuals, but to exclude them.

Some churches include baptized infants in their membership. Other churches define their membership geographically so that everyone who lives within a "parish" is considered a member. Baptists, however, affirm that one becomes a church member only by entering a covenant. The nature of this covenant is such that it can be fulfilled only by believers. In the Epistles, churches always comprise believers only. In Acts, the ones who were "added to the church daily" were the ones being "saved" (Acts 2:47). For these reasons, Baptists insist that the members of a rightly ordered church must be professing believers. This practice is generally called regenerate church membership, and because of it, Baptist churches are sometimes called believers' churches.

Procedurally, no one can become a member of a Baptist church except by application. At one time, most people understood what was expected of them as Baptist church members, and the application procedure was simple (often as straightforward as going forward at the end of a service). Typically, the pastor(s), and often the deacons, of the church would meet with applicants and listen to their testimonies before recommending them to the congregation for church membership. In all cases, the congregation would act to receive new members, because no one is a member until accepted by the church itself.

These days, many Baptist churches have discovered the need to make their membership process more deliberate. Potential members are expected to apply in writing, often on a form that the church provides. They are schooled in the church's covenant, confession of faith, and constitution. On their application they indicate their willingness to accept the provisions of these documents. Very often they are asked to share their testimony, not simply with the church's leadership, but with the entire congregation.

At one time, it was possible for church members to transfer their membership from one Baptist church to another by letter of dismission. This practice assumed that both churches understood membership in the same way and had comparable standards for their members. In recent generations, many churches have relaxed their doctrinal and moral standards—without bothering to drop the name *Baptist*. Consequently, no judgment can be made about the suitability of a particular member based on the fact that she or he comes from a church that calls itself Baptist. For the most part, the practice of accepting members on the basis of their letter has been dropped. It is still practiced, however, among some churches that are closely associated and well known to each other.

Baptized Membership

In addition to their practice of regenerate church membership, Baptists are also known for the requirement of baptized church membership. This insistence upon baptized church membership stems directly from their understanding of what baptism means. Baptists believe that baptism is not an optional accessory of the Christian life, but rather a direct command from Jesus Christ. To be baptized is the first step of obedience as a Christian, implying a commitment to live a life of faithfulness to the Lord Jesus. By submitting to baptism, one symbolically declares one's trust in Jesus' death, burial, and resurrection for the forgiveness of sins.

The apostolic churches included no unbaptized members for the simple reason that there were no unbaptized Christians. During the apostolic era, Christians could not have imagined that anyone would profess faith in Christ but refuse to be baptized. For them, baptism was a solemn obligation without which one could not be called a Christian. Though water baptism could in principle be separated from saving faith (as it was with Cornelius in Acts 10:44–48), it invariably followed faith as soon as possible. The New Testament pattern is exactly the one that occurs in Acts 2:41, namely, that those who gladly received the word (regeneration) were baptized, then added to the church.

Water baptism was commanded by the Lord Jesus Christ. It was universally practiced by the apostolic churches. Its significance was explained by the apostles in their writings. Peter explicitly connects its meaning with a clear conscience before God (1 Pet. 3:21). Professing believers who refuse to be baptized are walking in disobedience to the Lord and to His revealed Word. If such people wish to become members of New Testament churches, the first thing they must do is to get themselves baptized. When such people apply for membership in Baptist churches, they should be kindly instructed in their Biblical obligations and baptized as soon as possible. By action of the congregation they can become members once they are baptized.

Church membership is not automatically conferred by baptism. If a pastor or missionary baptizes an individual without a church's knowledge, that individual does not thereby become a member of the church. Instead, the congregation must agree to receive the new member. Usually this decision is made in advance of baptism. The church will hear the candidate's testimony of salvation and vote to receive him or her upon baptism. In this case, the candidate becomes a member of the church when baptized, but not because of baptism. Baptism is a prerequisite for membership, but only the deliberate choice of the congregation can bring a candidate into the church's covenant.

Given their strong emphasis upon baptized church membership, Baptists sometimes confront two related questions. The first is what to do about people who want to be baptized, but do not want to become church members. The second is how to regard churches of other denominations that do not insist upon baptism for church membership. For the moment, we will deal only with the first question, but we will return to the second one later.

People sometimes wish to submit to baptism while holding aloof from church membership. Baptists disagree in their responses to this situation. Two opinions are generally expressed. On the one hand, some Baptists view water baptism as a door to church membership. They reason that baptism is a promise of obedience to Christ, and that church membership is the next logical step of obedience. They infer that it makes no sense for someone to promise obedience while already planning to disobey. They conclude that someone who already plans not to be a church member cannot rightly make the commitment of baptism; therefore, baptism should be withheld until the candidate is prepared to enter the covenant relationship of church membership.

On the other hand, some Baptists argue that it makes no sense to talk about subsequent steps of obedience until the first one has been taken. An individual who has become convinced that Christ commands baptism is responsible to obey that command first. Understanding and agreement to other commands will follow once obedience has been initiated.

This second group also notes that some New Testament examples seem to separate baptism from church membership. The classic illustration is the baptism of the Ethiopian eunuch (Acts 8:35–39). Nothing in Philip's teaching or the eunuch's understanding seems to imply the covenant relationship of church membership. Some suggest that the eunuch was tacitly received into membership in the Jerusalem congregation, which is possible. For that reason, some missionaries in unevangelized fields will baptize their converts into the membership of their sending church. When there is no church on the field and when the missionary's sending church is halfway around the world, does it mean anything to speak of new converts being baptized into church membership?

Lawyers have a saying that "hard cases make bad law." What they mean is that trying to define a rule to cover all of the apparent exceptions often ends up in a morass of stipulations and qualifications. Perhaps the lawyers' dictum should be applied here. What is clear in the New Testament is that the usual order of events is for believers to be baptized and then to bring themselves under the covenant of church membership.

Church Discipline

When people are regenerated, they receive new life. They are changed. Their thinking, sensibilities, and priorities are transformed. While they do not attain sinless perfection until they stand in the presence of their Lord, they do begin the process of sanctification. That process continues as they are progressively transformed by the renewing of their minds (Rom. 12:2). They put off the old man whose corruption and deceitful lusts characterized their former lives; and, as they are renewed in the spirit of their minds, they put on the new man, who according to God is created in righteousness and true holiness (Eph. 4:22–24).

Those who are truly born again will increasingly forsake their former patterns of life. The gospel itself dictates that their lives will change. A relapse into the old life is, in effect, a denial of the gospel. Returning to the old ways is inconsistent with a profession that one has believed on Jesus Christ and been saved from one's sins (1 Cor. 6:9–11). Consequently, the practices of the old life should never be named among Christians (Eph. 5:3–11). To live according to the sinful patterns and habits of the unsaved is a scandal and an affront to the gospel.

Baptists believe in regenerated church membership. To join a Baptist church, prospective members must first be able to articulate a credible profession of faith in the gospel. If they are living according to the patterns of the unsaved life, however, the credibility of their profession is severely undermined. Therefore, a corollary of regenerated church membership is pure church membership.

By "pure church membership" Baptists do not mean that church members must be living sinless lives. What they do mean is that a church must not permit its members to return to the sinful ways of living that characterize the unsaved. Sins will be committed, but they must be dealt with properly. Scandalous conduct will be challenged and, if persisted in, will result in the disfellowshipping of the erring member. This process is known as church discipline.

Church discipline is any activity by which church members hold one another accountable for growing as disciples of Jesus Christ. Church discipline may include informal instruction, encouragement, or rebuke. It may also include more formal steps when a church member persists in conduct incompatible with the gospel. Two passages of Scripture are especially important for their instruction in handling different kinds of church discipline.

Personal Offenses and Matthew 18:15–20

Private grievances between church members may eventually lead to public church discipline. The key text for dealing with private grievances is Matthew 18:15–20. Jesus was speaking. His words assume that a brother has committed a private sin, that is, a sin that is known only to another brother. Most likely it involves a transgression that was committed personally against that brother. The passage outlines four steps that the aggrieved party should take to reclaim the offending brother for the Lord.

The first step is simply to confront the erring brother privately about his sin. In some instances, a private exhortation will be adequate, and the brother will repent. If so, the episode never needs to be made known to a larger circle.

If the erring brother does not repent, the offended brother is to confront him again. This time the confrontation is to take place before one or two witnesses. In part, the witnesses are for the purpose of observing and verifying what is said by both parties, "that in the mouth of two or three witnesses every word may be established." Yet the witnesses are not merely neutral observers. Once convinced of the legitimacy of the complaint, they, too, bear a responsibility to exhort the erring brother. Even though he would not listen to a private appeal, he might listen to the witnesses and repent.

If, however, the sinning brother does not hear the witnesses, the third step is to take the matter to the entire church. At this point the problem becomes a public affair. In the nature of the case, going before the church entails a more formal procedure than the previous confrontations, and Jesus' words in Matthew 18 assume that both brothers appear before the assembly. Presumably each is permitted to describe the situation as he sees it. The witnesses are also asked to verify the results of their appeal. After hearing the entire matter, the assembly must make a decision. It must determine whether the brother has indeed sinned, and if so, it must decide what genuine repentance should look like.

In bringing the matter to the church, both brothers are in principle submitting themselves to the authority of the congregation. They are recognizing the right of the church as a whole to offer a judgment that will bind their future conduct. What the church decides will carry important implications; indeed, in the immediate context Jesus made it clear that whatever the church binds or looses on earth will have been bound or loosed in Heaven. What is more, Jesus promised that during the decision-making process, He Himself will be with those who are gathered. To reject the decision of one's church, made under the authority of Jesus Christ, is a grave matter indeed.

Yet Jesus envisioned just such a possibility. He anticipated a situation in which the sinning brother would not hear the church. Under those circumstances, Jesus said, "Let him be unto thee as an heathen man and a publican" (Matt. 18:17). Within the community of Israel, Gentiles (heathens) were reckoned as outsiders, and tax collectors (publicans) were accounted as renegades. Jesus' words imply that a complete break must take place in the covenant relationship between the sinning brother and the congregation. He is no longer to be recognized as a part of the assembly. He is no longer counted as a member of the church.

To summarize, the four steps of church discipline prescribed in Matthew 18 are (1) confronting the erring brother personally and privately, (2) confronting the erring brother in the presence of witnesses, (3) appealing to the entire church for a judgment, and (4) disfellowshipping the erring brother if he will not hear the church. This is the only procedure that the New Testament prescribes for mediating personal offenses between church members. Taking such offenses into the civil courts is expressly forbidden (1 Cor. 6:1–8). In all instances of private transgression, Matthew 18 provides the pattern that Christians ought to follow.

Public Offenses and 1 Corinthians 5

Matthew 18:15–20 is the key text for dealing with private offenses among church members. When dealing with public offenses, however, and especially offenses of a scandalous nature, 1 Corinthians 5 is the crucial text. This chapter, written by the apostle Paul to deal with an episode of public scandal in the church at Corinth, not only articulates the procedures that the church should employ in discipline, but also establishes the rationale behind those procedures.

The immediate situation in Corinth was that a church member had entered into a sexual liaison with his father's wife, possibly his stepmother (1 Cor. 5:1). Paul was deeply indignant that the church would allow this conduct to remain unchallenged (1 Cor. 5:2–3). As he articulated principles for dealing with sexual immorality, he also extended them to include other situations. He specifically named greed, fraud, idolatry, verbal abuse, and inebriation as offenses that require the same kind of response (1 Cor. 5:10–11). He probably meant these as a list of typical or sample offenses rather than an exhaustive table of sins that require church discipline. What they have in common is that, first, they are incompatible with a profession of the gospel and, second, that they constitute public scandals.

How should a church respond when a member becomes embroiled in such abhorrent conduct? Paul offered some rather pointed instructions. Church members who do such things should be "taken away from among you" (1 Cor. 5:2). They should be delivered "unto Satan for the destruction of the flesh" (v. 5). They are like leaven that the church needs to "purge out" (v. 7). The church is "not to keep company" with them nor even to eat with them (vv. 9, 11).

When a man that is "called a brother" commits this kind of offense, the church must "put away from among yourselves that wicked person" (vv. 11–13).

Some Christians have understood these strictures to imply a practice called "shunning." Shunning entails a complete cessation of all normal social relationships with the errant church member. Some who practice shunning teach that a wife should not even live with her husband if he has been put out of the church.

Most likely, however, the text does not require a complete shunning of the offending party. What it clearly does require is the cessation both of the privileges of church membership and of any form of interaction that could be construed as Christian fellowship. This is precisely the treatment that Jesus had in mind in Matthew 18:17, when He commanded, "Let him be unto thee as an heathen man and a publican," that is, an outsider and a renegade. While the two passages begin at different points, they end up in the same place.

The authority of a local church extends exactly as far as the privileges of membership. A congregation has no authority over people who are not members (1 Cor. 5:12). The ultimate disciplinary step that any church can take is to remove the privileges of membership from an offending party, thereby placing that individual outside the fellowship of the church. When a member's conduct becomes an affront to the gospel, the church is obligated to take this step.

Why is this final step of church discipline so important? In 1 Corinthians 5, Paul touched on at least four goals of the discipline process. The first has to do with the church's testimony in the broader community. The offending member in Corinth was engaged in conduct that was "not so much as named among the Gentiles" (1 Cor. 5:1). Evidently, even the unsaved community was scandalized by this man's behavior. The church's reputation was being damaged and its testimony harmed. By putting the offending party out of its fellowship, the church would make a public statement that would distance it from the sin.

The second goal of church discipline is ultimately to restore the offending member. Paul said that the church was to turn him over to Satan "for the destruction of the flesh" (1 Cor. 5:5). Evidently Paul anticipated that severe physical affliction would follow the final step of church discipline. To anticipate these calamities was not unloving, however, because the purpose of the affliction was "that the spirit may be saved in the day of the Lord Jesus." The idea is that the chastening would help to lead the erring brother to repentance and, subsequently, to restoration.

A third goal of church discipline is to halt the spread of sin. In 1 Corinthians

Paul compared the immoral man's behavior to yeast or leaven, expressing the concern that a little leaven would permeate the entire lump of dough (1 Cor. 5:6). Sin, if it is tolerated and remains unchallenged, can spread. The church can become corrupted. Church discipline acts as a decontaminant and deterrent against the further encroachments of sin within the body.

The fourth goal of church discipline is to maintain the clarity of the gospel and the purity of fellowship with Christ. This goal is implied by Paul's discussion of Christ as our Passover (1 Cor. 5:7–8). The first Passover was the occasion upon which God redeemed Israel from slavery and made it a nation. During the Passover, God killed the firstborn in every Egyptian household, but He spared the firstborn in Israel through the blood of the sacrificial Passover lamb. In 1 Corinthians 5, Paul stated that Christ has been sacrificed as the Passover lamb for believers. Because of His death on the cross, we have been liberated from sin. If that is true, then to place ourselves back under sin would be a serious betrayal of the gospel. It would introduce an element of pollution, or leaven, into our relationship with Christ Himself. This pollution is eliminated when the offending party is removed from the membership of the congregation.

Does church discipline still work? Sometimes a member may be disciplined by one church, only to drive down the street and secure membership in another congregation. If that is going to happen, why even bother to disfellowship offending members? The answer is simple: church discipline is designed to accomplish multiple goals. Even when one or two of those goals are subverted, the other goals remain worthwhile. Whenever an errant brother or sister is led to repentance, church discipline works. Whenever the spread of sin is halted, church discipline works. Whenever a congregation's reputation before the community is guarded from scandal, church discipline works. Whenever an encumbrance or pollution is removed from a church's fellowship with Christ, church discipline works.

How should the church behave toward a disfellowshipped member? Since such persons are viewed as "heathen" and "publican," should they be barred from attending the church meetings? Can church members continue any personal relationships with those who have been disfellowshipped? Baptists have never answered these questions in exactly the same way. What seems clear is that the disfellowshipped member has no right to claim any of the privileges of church membership. Furthermore, all church members must be careful never to engage in any interaction with such an individual that could be understood as Christian fellowship.

Excommunication and the Lord's Table

Some refer to church discipline as excommunication, meaning that the disciplined member is barred from the Lord's Table (also called Communion). This procedure is thought to be especially grave in churches that view the Lord's Supper as a means of grace or perhaps even of salvation. In those churches, being barred from Communion is to run the risk of eternal condemnation.

To understand how Baptists view excommunication, one must first understand how Baptists view Communion, or the Lord's Table. The Baptist view differs sharply with the views of Roman Catholics, Lutherans, and some of the Reformed. The difference focuses on the significance or meaning of the Lord's Table.

According to Roman Catholicism, the elements of bread and wine are actually transformed into the body and blood of Jesus when the priest speaks the words of institution ("This is my body . . . this is my blood"). The change is called *transubstantiation*. While the elements still look, smell, and taste like bread and wine, they are believed to be the real body and blood of Christ. According to Catholics, the Lord's Table (which they call the *Eucharist*) is a re-presentation of the sacrifice of Christ. It is offered for the sins of the living and the dead. Receiving the Eucharist forgives venial sins and preserves the recipient from grave sins.[1]

Lutherans reject transubstantiation, believing instead that they receive the true body and blood of Jesus "in and under" the bread and wine. They believe that the "sacrament of the altar" is food for the soul, nourishing and strengthening the new man. It functions as a symbol of the gospel, and those who receive it while believing what it symbolizes obtain the forgiveness of sins through it.[2]

Presbyterian and Reformed theologians follow two influences in their thinking about the Lord's Table. None of them believe that the material body and blood of the Lord Jesus are present in the elements. They differ, however, in the exact significance of the ordinance.

Those who are closer to Calvin believe that when Christians partake the Supper worthily, they do "really and indeed" receive and feed upon Christ crucified, and that Christ's body and blood are spiritually present in the ordinance to

---

1. *Catechism of the Catholic Church: Modifications from the* Editio Typica (New York: Doubleday, 1995), 368–96.

2. See Martin Luther, "Larger Catechism," in *The Book of Concord*, trans. and ed. Theodore G. Tappert (Philadelphia: Muhlenberg Press, 1959), 447.

the faith of believers.[3] It is sometimes difficult to know what this means, since different emphases can be found among different Reformed theologians. In some cases, the thought seems to be that by consuming the Communion elements, the participant spiritually consumes the body and blood of Jesus and receives some objective grace that increases faith or advances sanctification.[4]

Other Presbyterian and Reformed theologians follow Ulrich Zwingli, the Reformer of Zurich. Zwingli taught that the Lord's Table functions primarily as a memorial of the sufferings of Christ. For those who follow Zwingli, participation at the Lord's Table does not objectively increase faith or advance sanctification. The benefit of the Table consists rather in the subjective or psychological change that might occur while a devout individual reflects upon the meaning and benefits of Jesus' death.

Baptists have accepted the Zwinglian understanding of the Lord's Supper. They see it primarily as a memorial service or a commemoration of Jesus' death on the cross. They emphasize the activities of remembering and reflecting upon the nature of Jesus' love and suffering for sinners. This remembrance and reflection is not merely individual, but a corporate activity of the assembled church. Because it is a shared reflection, it constitutes genuine fellowship or communion among brothers and sisters. Since the church's remembrance and reflection is directed toward the once-crucified, now-risen-and-ascended Jesus, it also constitutes fellowship or communion with Him. While the body and blood of Jesus are not present in the elements, Christ is personally present among His people for the observance of the ordinance.

In Catholicism and most Protestant churches, to be "excommunicated" is to be deprived of some definite, objective transfer of divine grace. If this were really what happened, it would be calamitous. Since Baptists see the Lord's Table as a memorial service, the effects of "excommunication" extend only as far as the corporate fellowship of the church. For this reason, Baptists prefer to speak of "disfellowshipping" errant members rather than of "excommunicating" them.

Baptists and the Lord's Table

The foregoing has shown that Baptists are distinguished from some other Christians by their understanding of the Lord's Table. In fact, most Baptists prefer

---

3. Westminster Confession of Faith, 29.7.
4. Belgic Confession, Article 35.

not to use the word *sacrament* when referring to either baptism or the Lord's Supper. The term has too often been appropriated by those who see some objective transfer of grace taking place in the observance of these practices. Baptists would rather speak about the ordinances of the New Testament. Baptists also rarely use the term *Eucharist*, which has often become associated with a highly sacramental or even sacerdotal understanding of the Supper. They generally talk about the Lord's Table, the Lord's Supper, or the Communion service. Their objection, however, is to the connotations that these terms have acquired and not to the terms themselves. Baptists do occasionally use language like *sacrament* and *Eucharist*.

The Meaning of the Lord's Table

In seeking to understand the Lord's Supper, Baptists rely primarily upon 1 Corinthians 11:17–34. They supplement this key passage with certain references in the preceding and following chapters, as well as with the Gospel accounts of the Last Supper. Baptists give priority to 1 Corinthians 11 because it is a teaching passage in which the apostle Paul is deliberately aiming to define the Lord's Table and to instruct the Corinthian church in its proper administration.

As in many other places, in 1 Corinthians 11:17–34 the apostle Paul was writing to correct a problem. The church at Corinth was subverting the meaning of the Lord's Table so badly that it could no longer be recognized as a Biblical ordinance (v. 20). They were using the Table as an occasion for both personal indulgence and self-aggrandizement, despising their Christian brothers in the process (vv. 17–20). Paul responded to this problem by refocusing attention upon the significance of the ordinance.

He began by relating the story of Jesus' Last Supper, namely, how Jesus distributed both bread and cup to His disciples with the instruction to do this "in remembrance of me." These words clearly mark out the Supper as a memorial in which the bread and cup symbolize the body and blood of Jesus. The Lord's Table is first of all a look backward to the sufferings of Jesus, particularly to the body that He gave and the blood that He shed. The Supper is a sobering reminder of the appalling price that Jesus had to pay to secure salvation. Therefore, the observance of the ordinance should never be an occasion for lightness or frivolity.

The Lord's Table requires not only a look backward, but also a look upward. It is His Table, and His people gather there by His commandment in order to commune with Him. He died for them, but He also rose gain and ascended to His Father. Baptists do not believe that the body and blood of Jesus are uniquely present in the Communion elements, but they do believe that their risen Lord is present at His Table. Their observance of the Table is an act of obedience to Him, carried out in His presence, motivated by a desire for the fellowship that has been secured by His sacrifice. They commune with Him in His body and blood (1 Cor. 10:16). By doing so, they consecrate themselves solely to Him, symbolically turning away from any fellowship with idols (1 Cor. 10:21). As Charles Spurgeon wrote,

> *Amidst us our Belovèd stands,*
> *And bids us view His piercèd hands;*
> *Points to the wounded feet and side,*
> *Blest emblems of the Crucified.*
> *If now, with eyes defiled and dim,*
> *We see the signs, but see not Him;*
> *O may His love the scales displace*
> *And bid us see Him face to face!*

This remembrance is not merely individual, but corporate. It is to be observed when the church comes together (1 Cor. 11:33). The bread symbolizes not only the material body of Christ that was crucified, but also the union of individual believers with one another (1 Cor. 10:17). Their union in Christ's spiritual body joins Christians to each other (1 Cor. 12:12–26). In view of this spiritual union, church members have a fundamental obligation to care for one another. Any factiousness in the church destroys the imagery of the Lord's Table, rendering it invalid as a memorial of Jesus' death (1 Cor. 11:17–20). Consequently, the Lord's Table involves not only a look backward and a look upward, but also a look around at fellow church members.

Furthermore, the Lord's Table necessitates a look within. To appear at the Table with unrepented, unconfessed sin is to eat the bread and to drink the cup unworthily. The consequence of this act is to become guilty of the body and blood of the Lord (1 Cor. 11:27). People who eat and drink this way bring judgment upon themselves because they do not discern the Lord's body (v. 29). To escape the calamitous consequences of judgment (v. 30), they must examine themselves (v. 28), and by judging themselves avoid divine chastening (v. 31). Looking within is a necessary antecedent to rightly observing the Lord's Table.

Finally, the Lord's Table implies a look forward. Those who observe the ordinance do so with anticipation of the coming of their Lord (v. 26). Every

Lord's Supper includes the anticipation of that day when Jesus Himself will lift His cup with us in His Father's kingdom (Matt. 26:29).

In sum, the Lord's Table is both a memorial and a fellowship service. In both these respects, it is all about communion. It should be a high point in every believer's communion relationship with Jesus. We should be moved by the recollection of the terrible price that Jesus had to pay for the forgiveness of our sins. We should be moved by the recognition of His presence with us at His table. We should be moved with compassion and care for our brethren to whom we have been united in His body. We should be moved to examine ourselves, confessing any unrepented sin that impedes our communion with Jesus. We should be moved with anticipation, knowing that Jesus will bring us into His bodily presence when He returns, perhaps very soon.

Some Christians describe the Baptist understanding as a "mere" memorial or a "low" view of the Lord's Supper. On the contrary, the recognition of our communion with the Lord ought to move us deeply as we look backward, look upward, look around, look inward, and look forward. Rightly administered and thoughtfully attended, the Communion service ought to be a time of increased desire for and commitment to our Lord Jesus.

As one of only two ordinances that Jesus left to His church, the Lord's Table is a crucial element of Christian worship. It should never be observed thoughtlessly or flippantly. It should never simply be tacked onto the end of another service as an afterthought. Because it is a corporate ordinance for the assembled church, it should never be administered to private individuals. Every observance of the Lord's Supper should be solemn, dignified, and thoughtful. While the elements themselves impart no objective grace, the Lord does graciously work in the hearts of His people as they ponder the matters to which the Supper rightly directs their attention. Properly observed, the Lord's Table is an important aspect of pure church membership.

The Participants at the Lord's Table

Baptists and other Christians have long debated who should be permitted to participate at the Lord's Table. Three major positions have been staked out in the debate. These are labeled Open Communion, Closed Communion, and Close Communion.

Those who advocate Open Communion believe that the qualifications for the Lord's Table should be minimal. Some churches invite all who profess faith in Christ to participate in the ordinance. Other churches will accept any mode of baptism as a proper qualification. In some instances, churches have even opened the Lord's Table to members of the community, irrespective of whether they have even believed on Christ. While some Baptists have favored Open Communion, the practice is inconsistent with the meaning of the Lord's Table. How can a church conscientiously invite people to participate in an event that will bring them under God's chastening? A warning (at minimum) is more appropriate than an invitation.

Those who affirm Closed Communion wish to restrict the participants at the Lord's Supper to members of the local church that is administering the ordinance. Some churches believe that this restrictiveness is the only way of protecting the Communion service from the "leaven of malice and wickedness" (1 Cor. 5:8). Closed Communion has been widespread in some Baptist circles, particularly among Primitive and Landmark Baptists. Churches that practice Closed Communion sometimes regulate physical access to the elements of the Supper, offering them only to members or requiring a card or certificate in order to participate at the Table. This practice is sometimes called a "fenced Table."

The third option, Close Communion, is also common among Baptist churches. In Close Communion, the Table is open to believers who are not members of the administering church, but only if they are walking in visible obedience to the requirements of Scripture. Most Baptist churches understand these requirements to include believer immersion, membership in a New Testament church, and confession to God of any known sin. In this arrangement, the officiant will state the requirements, but leave the participants to judge for themselves whether they ought to participate.

Most Baptist churches ought to favor Close Communion over Closed Communion for several reasons. First, the ordinance is the Lord's Table and not the church's table, implying that the Communion being observed is with Christ and His people, not merely with the members of the individual congregation. Second, 1 Corinthians 11 places a strong emphasis upon self-examination, while it places none upon examination of communicants by the church's leadership (such as a fenced Table requires). Third, no Scripture actually restricts the ordinance to members of the local congregation, meaning that the practice of Closed Communion is a human invention. The New Testament does state qualifications for the Lord's Table, and these qualifications should certainly be announced. Making this announcement, however, is not the same as closing the Table to nonmembers. Generally, the Table should be open to obedient believers, in other words, to members of churches of like faith and order.

Baptists place a high premium upon participation in the Lord's Supper, not because it magically conveys some objective spiritual benefit, but because it symbolizes Christ's death for their sins and serves as an emblem of their fellowship with Him and with each other. While they have disagreed about who should participate in communion, there are good reasons for insisting that only those who belong to Jesus and are seeking to obey Him should be invited to the Table. After salvation, the first step of obedience is baptism. Visible obedience also entails a life that is free of scandalous conduct. While no believer lives a sinlessly perfect life, all are responsible to walk according to the position that they have been given in Christ Jesus. Any return to the ways of the old life (unless repented of) should not merely bar an individual from the Lord's Table, but also attract the warning and discipline of the congregation. The gospel must be reflected in the changed lives of church members. This is what Baptists mean when they talk about pure church membership.

4 *Individual Christian Responsibility*

BAPTISTS BELIEVE that every Christian has received tremendous privileges and consequently bears tremendous responsibilities. We also believe that the Lord Jesus Christ, through the work of the Holy Spirit, has made each believer competent to fulfill these responsibilities in company with other believers. Baptists typically discuss these privileges, responsibilities, and competencies under two rubrics: the priesthood of the believer and the soul liberty of the believer.

The Priesthood of the Believer

Most Protestants affirm the priesthood of the believer, but Baptists tend to stress this teaching more distinctively than others. Baptists understand the priesthood of the believer to mean that Christians require no separate priesthood (separate from the community of believers) other than that of the Lord Jesus Christ. Because Christ is the only mediator between humans and God, each believer has the privilege and duty of direct access to God. This direct access places the believer in a position to make intercession for other believers.

The Function of Priests

The basic duty of a priest is to represent humans before God. A priest is a go-between or mediator who speaks to God on behalf of people who are unworthy to appear before Him. Consequently, the first responsibility of a priest is to secure forgiveness on behalf of those whom he represents (Heb. 5:1–3). To gain forgiveness, the priest offers a sacrifice that propitiates (satisfies) God's justice and expiates (wipes away) the guilt of the sinner. Once the guilt of sin has been dealt with, the priest may also offer other kinds of sacrifices representing devotion, thankfulness, or praise.

In the Old Testament, God ordained a separate priesthood to perform this function on behalf of the children of Israel. The sons of Aaron were called to act as priests for the entire nation. Even though individual believers could and did enjoy personal fellowship with God, the offering of sacrifices for sins and trespasses was the exclusive business of the priests.

The Old Testament priesthood, however, could neither satisfy God's justice nor remove the guilt of sin. Since priests and the sacrifices alike were flawed and finite, neither could accomplish the work of salvation. Rather, these Old Testament institutions were teaching tools designed to lead people to place their faith in God for forgiveness.

Looking back from our perspective, it is difficult to tell how much Old Testament believers may have understood about God's ultimate provision. Probably their knowledge increased over time as God progressively revealed His plan. God's full revelation—and the perfect Sacrifice and Priest—came in Jesus Christ. The book of Hebrews describes Christ's priestly work in rich detail. This description can be found in Hebrews 10:1–18.

The Priesthood of Christ

According to Hebrews 10, the sacrificial system of the Old Testament law was a shadow or picture of the sacrifice that God would provide some day. Because it was not the reality, however, it could not make the participants perfect by forgiving their sins (v. 1). Even Old Testament believers should have realized this, for if the sacrifices could have made people perfect, they would not need to be offered continually. Forgiven people would no longer bear the consciousness of their sins (v. 2). The fact that the sacrifices were offered year after year should have reminded people that their sins could not be forgiven through the sacrificial system (v. 3).

Why did the levitical sacrifices not remove sin? Part of the problem lay in the sacrifices themselves. The sacrificial animals—bulls and goats, for instance—were merely brute creatures. It was not possible for their blood to remove sins (v. 4). God took no pleasure in such sacrifices and burnt offerings (v. 6). In contrast to animal sacrifices, however, the perfect sacrifice was provided through the Incarnation, when Jesus Christ as God's Messiah was born as a human being. His body would become the sacrifice that could genuinely propitiate God's justice and expiate human sins (v. 5). Messiah took a genuinely human body specifically so that He could accomplish God's will in salvation (v. 7). In other words, Jesus came as Messiah to fulfill the office of a priest. He is both the priest who offers the sacrifice and the sacrifice that is offered.

The animal sacrifices of the Old Testament stand in sharp contrast to the work of Christ. Ultimately, God neither desired nor took pleasure in animal sacrifices that were offered according to the law (v. 8). Such sacrifices were only shadows, pointing to a greater reality. That reality—God's ultimate will—was the very thing that Jesus Christ came to achieve (v. 9). In accomplishing God's will (i.e., the forgiveness of sins), Christ did away with the sacrificial system. The result is that believers are fully forgiven (sanctified) once-for-all by the offering of the body of Jesus (v. 10).

The implication is clear. Animal sacrifices were offered repeatedly because they could not sanctify sinners or bring them to perfection. Christ, by sacrificing His own body, has brought sinners to perfection once-for-all. Consequently, His sacrifice must be a one-time, unrepeatable event.

The following verses draw out this implication explicitly, again employing a sharp contrast between the Old Testament priesthood and the priesthood of Christ. It is important to remember that when these verses were written, every Jewish child was taught about the tabernacle and its sacrifices. Every Israelite knew in detail how the tabernacle was furnished and what the priests did as they worked. They all knew that every priest had to show up for work each day, repeatedly offering the same sacrifices because those sacrifices could not take away sins. The tabernacle had no chairs because the priests were not allowed to sit down. As long as they were on the job, they were busy, repeating the same offerings (v. 11).

The Messiah, however, offered a single sacrifice for all sins for all time (v. 12). When His sacrifice was complete, He sat down (v. 13). In contrast to the ceaseless activity of the Aaronic priests, the Lord Jesus Christ is at rest, His work done. Now He is simply waiting until His Father subjects His enemies to Him by placing them under His feet. In contrast to the Old Testament priests, whose repeated sacrifices could never make sinners perfect (v. 1), the single sacrifice offered by Jesus Christ perfects believing sinners for all time (v. 14).

To be saved, sinful humans need a priest. This priest must represent them before God, presenting a sacrifice that will propitiate God's justice and expiate their sins. The Aaronic priests could not fulfill this responsibility, because neither they nor their sacrifices were adequate. However, by offering His own body as a sacrifice for our sins, Jesus Christ has perfectly satisfied all priestly requirements. His work is complete. It need not be repeated. In fact, it cannot be repeated. No one else can offer anything that will supplement or improve upon the finished work of Jesus. Those who believe on Jesus for salvation are fully forgiven, and God no longer remembers their sins and transgressions (v. 17). No other priesthood or sacrifice will ever be needed for their salvation (v. 18). None is even possible.

If Hebrews 10:1–18 is rightly understood, it absolutely forbids a separate priesthood that offers sacrifices for the salvation of sinners. It is a great error to create such a priesthood or to transform the Lord's Supper into a sacrifice that supposedly secures grace for sinners seeking salvation. Any system in which a priest other than Jesus stands between humans and God constitutes a usurpation of the priestly office of Christ and a denial of His finished work. Baptists emphatically deny the possibility of any separate priesthood today.

Access to God

Christ as high priest has offered a once-for-all sacrifice for all sins. The provision of salvation stands forever complete. As Hebrews 10:19–25 shows, this truth affects not only the Christian's vertical relationship with God, but also the Christian's horizontal relationship with other Christians, by providing each believer with access to God.

Toward God, believers ought to experience great confidence. Drawing upon imagery from the Old Testament temple, the writer of Hebrews states that Christ, acting as priest, has through His flesh opened a way through the veil (vv. 20–21). Believers can now enter boldly into the very holy of holies (v. 19). This was a privilege that was reserved only for the high priest in the Old Testament, who could enter the holy of holies only on the Day of Atonement. The implication is that each believer now exercises the highest privileges of priesthood, having been granted access to the very presence of God.

Since believers have the right of entry into the presence of God, they are expected to use it. They are to draw near to God with true hearts in full assurance of faith, grounding their confidence upon the cleansing that they have received in Jesus Christ (v. 22). Because Christ is our mediator, we need go through no other agent to gain admission to the presence of the Almighty. We have the privilege of worshiping Him directly, of thanking Him directly, of petitioning Him directly. No one has greater access to God, and no one has a higher standing in God's presence, than the most ordinary Christian.

This right of access to God also carries implications for relationships between believers. Since each has full access into the presence of God, each is to stir up other believers to love and good works (v. 24). In other words, the privilege of priesthood entails the duty of exhortation. This mutual encouragement is not supposed to be merely an individual and occasional activity, but a regular function of the assembled church (v. 25). The implication seems to be that the gathered church is a convocation of priests, each exercising his or her priestly functions on behalf of the others.

Concerning priesthood, Hebrews 10 presents a careful balance. On the one hand, with reference to offerings for sins and trespasses, Jesus Christ is the only possible priest. His completed sacrifice has provided the satisfaction of God's justice and the removal of sins for all believers for all time. In this sense, no other person can ever act as a priest, and those who claim that they can are denying the gospel itself.

On the other hand, because every believer has the right of direct access to God, mediated only through Christ, each believer is qualified as a priest. Every Christian has the privilege of standing face-to-face with God for worship, thanksgiving, and petition. The greatest imaginable intimacy with God is given as a gift to the most ordinary believer.

Sometimes the priesthood of the believer is taken to mean that all Christians simply act as their own priests, but that is a distortion of the teaching. No Christian can act as his own priest in the removal of sins. Only the offering of Christ can wash away guilt. Nevertheless, in some sense every Christian is able to act as a priest for any other Christian. With the right of direct access to God through Christ, each Christian can encourage and exhort other Christians. If Christians are to live as God wishes, then each needs to be a priest for others and each needs the priesthood of others.

This priestly function is seen especially in the ministry of intercessory prayer. Because each believer can approach God directly in prayer, each believer can pray effectively for other believers—and, indeed, even for unbelievers (1 Tim. 2:1–2). Whenever Christians intercede for someone else, they are representing that person before God. They are acting as priests. Intercession is a vital aspect of each believer's priesthood.

Sacrifices of Believer Priests

The function of a priest is to offer sacrifices. It stands to reason that, if believers are truly priests, then they ought to bring offerings to God. Granted, Christ's sacrifice has satisfied God's justice and wiped away sins. Other kinds of sacrifices are possible, however, and believer-priests bear a responsibility to offer these.

Believers have a responsibility to offer their bodies as living sacrifices to God (Rom. 12:1). This offering is reasonable in view of the great salvation that God has provided and His inexorable purpose to bless His people. The offering of their bodies is a form of worship (the word translated *service* is *latreia*, a term that is used for worship). This is perhaps the most fundamental form of sacrifice that believers are able to present.

Another sacrifice is for believers to spend themselves on behalf of those to whom they minister (Phil. 2:17). Paul was prepared to be martyred if his death would help to increase the faith of the Philippian believers. He compared the prospect of his death to a drink offering that would be poured out as a libation in divine worship. To spend one's self for the good of one's fellow-believers is a rich sacrifice indeed.

The apostle Paul also speaks of sharing the gospel as a priestly service (Rom. 15:16). When he preached the gospel among the Gentiles, his goal was to present them as an acceptable offering to God. When Christians share the gospel with lost people, those who receive it become an offering in which God delights. This is another sacrifice that believer-priests are privileged to offer.

Often Christians will give material gifts to alleviate the needs and aid the ministries of God's servants. When the apostle Paul was imprisoned in Rome, the church at Philippi sent him a generous gift. Out of their poverty they gave Paul what was actually necessary for their own livelihood (Phil. 4:15–19). When Paul spoke of their gift, he used Old Testament language for the sweet-savor offering, stating that their sacrifice was acceptable and well pleasing to God. When believer-priests give sacrificially to God's servants and God's work, their offerings are a delight to God.

The same is true when believer-priests engage in good deeds and share their possessions (Heb. 13:16). True, the good works and gifts of Christians are directed toward other people, but they are also directed toward God Himself. God is pleased with such sacrifices.

One very important offering that believers can present to God is the sacrifice of praise (Heb. 13:15). In the Old Testament, the prophet Hosea compared praising God to offering calves (Hos. 14:2). Perhaps that is the image that the writer to the Hebrews has in mind when he speaks of the "fruit of our lips" that confess the name of God. The conscious adoration of the Lord God is a priestly act, and it is the precious privilege of all Christians.

Clearly, believer-priests in the New Testament church possess many sacrifices that they can present. They have been granted the privilege of appearing before God, and they need not appear empty-handed. Jesus Christ has given them the ability and opportunity to offer sacrifices that bring delight to God. These sacrifices represent the very activities in which believer-priests should be encouraging one another when they assemble.

Priesthood and Ordination

As Baptists understand the Bible, every believer is a priest. The priesthood of the believer entails the right of direct access to God, mediated only through the high-priesthood of Jesus Christ. It also entails the obligation to act as a priest, interceding for the brethren and offering sacrifices that are well pleasing to God. Every believer is equally equipped for these responsibilities.

Consequently, Baptists completely reject any distinction between clergy and laity. While they do ordain ministers, Baptists do not believe that ordination confers any special grace, anointing, unction, chrism, authority, or standing with God. Pastors are priests only in the same sense that all Christians are priests, no more and no less. The only distinction between pastors and other church members is functional (although, as we shall see, the functional difference matters a great deal).

The Baptist rejection of the distinction between clergy and laity is seen most vividly at the Lord's Table. In many non-Baptist churches, the Lord's Supper is served from an altar that stands behind the minister. The minister acts as a mediator between the congregation and the altar, which represents the presence of God. In Baptist churches, however, the entire congregation gathers around a Communion table. Usually a pastor will administer the elements, but in principle the church could appoint any brother to perform this task. In fact, if none of the church's men are comfortable administering the elements, then the congregation may even invite a member from another church to lead the service. The administrator exercises no particular spiritual authority, but merely distributes the elements so that the ordinance is conducted decently and in order.

The same is true of baptism. One need not be ordained in order to baptize. The church can ask any brother to perform the ordinance, and the baptism will be just as valid as if it had been administered by an apostle. In fact, the validity of the baptism does not depend in any sense upon the personal qualifications of the administrator. If the subject, mode, and meaning of baptism are preserved, then it is a genuine and valid ordinance.

Nor must one be ordained in order to preach in a Baptist church. Baptists have a long tradition of preachers and pastors who have been farmers, tradesmen, physicians, or lawyers. These men may seek ordination, but they may not. A church is at liberty to call an unordained man to its pulpit, and he has liberty to accept.

One activity that most church members are not allowed to perform is to solemnize marriages. Most governments require a minister to be ordained or at least licensed in order to perform this task. Though many people assume that marriage is a church function, the New Testament never actually assigns it to churches. A minister is not essential to a valid marriage. A union that is solemnized before a civil authority such as a justice of the peace has all the weight and binding force of one that is solemnized before a minister. If a minister does officiate at a wedding, then he is acting as an agent of the state rather than in his proper capacity as a minister of the gospel. He may (and should) add a Christian emphasis to the event, but his authority to marry does not come from his ordination.

If ordination confers no special gifts, then why ordain at all? In the New Testament, ordination was indistinguishable from holding the pastoral office. When a church called a man to be its elder, it was ordaining him. Usually that man came up through the congregation; and once he became an elder, he would pastor the church until he died. The New Testament contains very little evidence of pastors moving from one church to another.

Today, pastors often move between churches. While this mobility does not necessarily violate New Testament requirements, it does pose special problems. How can churches know that a particular pastor possesses the calling and gifts for the responsibilities of ministry? How can they know that he has been found faithful? Ordination as it is practiced by Baptist churches today is one solution to that problem.

When a Baptist church ordains a man, it is putting its stamp of approval upon him. It is saying that he has been examined and has given evidence of doctrine, calling, and gifts that are suitable for Baptist ministry. It is saying that the man is not a novice, but that he has been tested in ministry and found faithful. Normally a congregation will call a council of messengers from other churches of like faith and order to assist in examining a candidate for ordination. The council does not ordain, but it does offer its recommendation to the church. When the church ordains the candidate, it issues a certificate that is signed by the church's leadership and by the members of the examining council.

Ministers who are not yet prepared for ordination can be licensed. A Baptist church issues a license to an individual who shows promise of a calling and the gifts for ministry, but who still needs to improve his gifts and to gain experience. Before a church licenses a minister it will hear him preach. It will conduct a brief examination of his doctrine and Christian experience, but it will not call a council of messengers from other churches. Typically, a license will expire after a year or two, at which time the minister can be re-licensed or examined for ordination. Since the license is issued by a single church, unassisted by advice from other congregations, the license becomes void if the minister removes himself from the membership of that church.

Unlike licensing, ordination does not expire. If the minister becomes a member of another church of like faith and order, he retains his ordination. He does, however, become accountable for his ordination to the church of which he is currently a member. If he simply removes himself from any church membership, or if he becomes a member of a church not of like faith and order, then the last Baptist church of which he was a member should revoke his ordination when it dismisses him from membership.

Among Baptists, ordination serves a purpose. It identifies a minister as an individual who has been examined as to his doctrine, experience, call to ministry, and giftedness. It places upon him a stamp of approval, not only from the ordaining church, but also from the advising council. It does not, however, confer any special spiritual grace or ecclesiastical authority. Among Baptists, an ordained minister does not belong to a separate caste of Christians. He is simply one of the brethren who has been formally designated to perform the functions of vocational ministry.

Soul Liberty

Closely related to the priesthood of the believer is an idea that is called *soul liberty*. Broadly defined, soul liberty is the responsibility that all believers share to understand and obey God's requirements for themselves. This duty cannot be delegated or assigned to another believer. Each individual believer is personally responsible for understanding and obeying God.

Personal Responsibility

Christians are priests who stand directly in the presence of God. On the one hand, this means that they have the right of addressing God without having to go through any separate priesthood. On the other hand, it also means that when God addresses them in Scripture, they bear the personal responsibility of grasping God's message and obeying it.

Obviously, obedience includes doing what God says to do. Conduct or practice is an aspect of obedience. Doctrine is also part of obedience. God reveals truths in His Word, and Christians are responsible to believe accurately what God has revealed. To believe a doctrine that is contrary to Scripture is to disobey God.

Consequently, each individual believer is responsible to read and to understand the Scriptures correctly. Soul liberty is not liberty to believe whatever one wishes to believe. It is liberty to believe what Scripture teaches. It is liberty to obey God.

Every Christian has a duty to study the Bible. Every Christian has a duty to know the Bible. This duty involves more than reading through the Bible every year or so, and it involves more than being able to recite isolated verses. To understand the Bible, one must know how it is put together and how to interpret it rightly. Gaining these skills is a fundamental duty of every believer. Consequently, fostering these skills is a fundamental duty of every church, for unless Christians know how to understand the Bible, they will falter in their duty to obey God.

Of course, this entire discussion assumes that the Bible was written to be understood. While some parts of the Bible are harder to understand than others, and while the more difficult parts may require more advanced interpretive skills, the Bible was not written in a secret code and it does not communicate its message using secret symbols. Some parts of the text are more technical in nature, and reading them is akin to reading other rigorous and thoughtful literature. Nevertheless, an ordinary person who can read a thoughtful journal of opinion can also understand Isaiah or Paul. Indeed, much of the Bible requires no more skill to understand than a daily newspaper does.

No one can understand the Bible for a believer. No one can obey God for a believer. All believers must understand and obey the Bible for themselves.

Spiritual Competence

Does understanding the Bible require some special spiritual competence, perhaps some special anointing or chrism of the Holy Spirit? At first glance, the Bible seems to teach this. For example, the apostle Paul spoke about a natural person who does not receive the things of God and to whom those things seem like foolishness (1 Cor. 2:14). According to Paul, this person cannot understand spiritual things because they are spiritually discerned. Paul seems to have been quite certain that something more than natural knowledge is necessary to comprehend Scripture.

Yet in the immediate context, Paul also declared that to those who are saved, Christ has become wisdom, righteousness, sanctification, and redemption (1 Cor. 1:30). The idea is that believers receive all these things when they trust Christ as Savior. In other words, those who have believed have already received spiritual wisdom.

Paul followed up this thought in 1 Corinthians 2. There he argued that the gospel message does not rest upon the kind of wisdom that unsaved people naturally employ. Rather, it carries its own power (vv. 1–5). While the gospel does not rely upon human wisdom, it does include a spiritual wisdom that is hidden from unsaved intellectuals (vv. 6–8). If the unsaved elite had understood the wisdom of the gospel, they would never have crucified Christ. The gospel is a thing that not even the cleverest unsaved mind could have invented, but God has now revealed it through the Holy Spirit (vv. 9–10). The Spirit knows the mind of God in intimate detail (vv. 10–11). The same Spirit who has revealed the deep things of God—the same Spirit who comprehends all spiritual wisdom— has been given to believers so they might understand spiritual truth (v. 12). The Holy Spirit provides believers with an inner mechanism for grasping the truth of God's Word (v. 13).

Paul's point was that every believer has access to the mind of God through the Word and through the Spirit. Whatever special wisdom or anointing is necessary is supplied by the Holy Spirit. Paul was making approximately the same point that John made when he stated that, because believers have an unction or anointing from the Holy One, they know "all things" (1 John 2:20). In context, the "all things" to which John refers do not include such matters as astrophysics or infinitesimal calculus, but the essential truths of the gospel and gospel living. The Holy Spirit has already convinced all saved people of these truths so they will recognize error when they see it.

Paul's remarks in 1 Corinthians 2 certainly include the anointing to which John refers, but Paul goes further. He appears to say that believers experience an ongoing ministry of the Holy Spirit that helps them apply Scripture. While there is some debate about the identity of the spiritual man in 1 Corinthians 2:15 (the spiritual man may be one who has the Spirit, one who is controlled by the Spirit, or one who has been brought to maturity by the Spirit), Paul clearly intended to articulate God's ideal for all believers, and that ideal is that they should discern the entire realm of spiritual truth. Such discernment is possible because, through the mediation of the Spirit, all believers have the mind of Christ (v. 16).

How does the Spirit help believers to understand the Scriptures? Not by reading the text for them, certainly. Nor by doing the hard work of interpretation—the Holy Spirit does not identify parts of speech, parse verbs, diagram sentences, or ascertain literary genres. These are things that all readers—even believers—must do for themselves, and Christians are responsible to develop the necessary skills.

We can tell what the Spirit does for believers by contrasting it with what unsaved people cannot do for themselves. Unbelievers are capable of interpreting the Biblical text, sometimes with great skill. They can learn the meanings of terms, identify the grammatical and rhetorical connections in the text, and gain a fairly precise understanding of what the text is saying. The problem is, however, that they do not receive or welcome the message of the text (1 Cor. 2:14). It is one thing to understand what a text says; it is another to become so convinced of its truth that it completely rearranges one's perspective. Because natural people do not welcome the message of Scripture, it seems to contradict everything they think they know about the world. The Bible gives them a set of perspectives and priorities that makes absolutely no sense within the world as they perceive it. Since the Biblical perspective radically contradicts their own, they reject it as foolishness. This rejection completely disables them from understanding the significance or spiritual applicability of the Word of God.

The Holy Spirit does not perform a miracle of interpretation for believers. What He does is so to change their hearts that they welcome what they once rejected. As they submit themselves to the authority of God's Word, it transforms their perspective. They begin to see all things—God, sin, the world, themselves, and other people—as they never have before. As they come back to Scripture again and again, they find in it a wealth of help for confronting reality as they now perceive it—reality as it really exists. When they were unbelievers, they might have understood what the text was saying, but as believers they begin to understand what difference it makes. They grasp not only meaning but also significance. They are capable not only of interpretation but also of application.

This work of the Holy Spirit is what theologians call *illumination*. In His illuminating work, the Holy Spirit takes the meaning or interpretation of Scripture and helps God's people grasp its relevance. He makes sense, not of terms and grammatical structures, but of the importance of the text in facing the variegated challenges of life. Through this illuminating ministry, the Holy Spirit grants to every believer the spiritual equipment to know and obey the Word of God.

In short, all believers already possess the spiritual qualifications for understanding and obeying God. They do not need to wait to receive some additional anointing. They do not need to rely upon some separate class of interpreters who have been granted a special spiritual ability to understand the Bible. Each Christian has the duty to comprehend and to obey God as He has revealed Himself in His Word.

Teachers and Learners

Since each believer is spiritually qualified to understand the Bible, all believers are responsible to understand and obey it for themselves. This is what Baptists mean when they talk about *soul liberty*. Nevertheless, all Christians do not understand the Bible equally well.

Sometimes one meets Christians who are convinced that they should never use humanly written tools, such as commentaries, in understanding the Bible. They seem to think that the responsibility of the Holy Spirit is to ensure that they will grasp everything necessary in the Bible without the advice of human teachers. In its extreme forms, this attitude can lead some Christians to set themselves up as judges over pastors and other teachers of the Word of God. Probably every pastor has had the experience of laboring for weeks to understand and preach a text, only to be informed by some listener that the Holy Spirit had given him or her a superior interpretation.

While Baptists certainly recognize the illuminating work of the Holy Spirit, they also note that the Bible has much to say about teaching and learning. Believers are commanded to teach and admonish (warn) each other (Col. 3:16). This is necessary because some believers are not skillful in the "word of righteousness" (Heb. 5:13). Consequently, Christians must recognize the spiritual authority of certain individuals who have labored among and admonished the congregation (1 Thess. 5:12). Individual believers are to follow the example of those who hold this spiritual authority, paying attention to their teaching of the Word of God (Heb. 13:7). Christians are responsible to obey and to submit to these spiritual leaders, for the leaders will someday have to answer for the souls committed to their care (Heb. 13:17).

These passages neither present a picture of unqualified egalitarianism in the church nor allow an unrestrained individualism. While all believers experience the illuminating ministry of the Holy Spirit, three factors account for their different levels of Biblical understanding. First, some are more skilled interpreters than others. Second, some are able to invest much more time and effort in studying the Scriptures. Third, some are more spiritually mature than others, and with maturity comes an increased ability to apply the Scriptures rightly (Heb. 5:14).

Some people are more skillful interpreters because they have mastered the art of reading and understanding. The Bible is rightly interpreted grammatically and historically; but all believers are not equally adept at grammar and not everyone knows history uniformly well. All other things being equal, those who have mastered disciplines like grammar (particularly of the Biblical languages) and history will be far better interpreters of texts in general, and of Scripture in particular, than those who have not.

Some people are in a position to give themselves to Bible study, while others must take such time as they can make. Pastors are among those who are supposed to immerse themselves in Scripture, spending significant time and energy in mastering the text. All other things being equal, those who spend more time with the Bible, and those who are more focused during the time that they spend, will be better interpreters of the Word.

All Christians begin the life of faith at a level of immaturity. Immature believers must be fed the elementary teachings of Scripture, which the New Testament compares to milk rather than solid food (1 Cor. 3:1–2; Heb. 5:12–14). As Christians grow to spiritual maturity, they become more skilled in handling Scripture. Beyond a certain point, they are expected to be able to teach the Scriptures to others. All other things being equal, mature believers will understand the Scriptures better than immature believers.

Pastors ought to be superior teachers of Scripture for all three of these reasons. They ought to be trained in the disciplines of skilled interpretation. They ought to be granted time to pore over the text of Scripture, pondering it in detail (this is one reason that Baptist churches normally pay their pastors). They ought to be spiritually mature individuals, not novices. If they do not meet these qualifications, they should not be pastors. If they do meet these qualifications, church members should listen to them carefully and heed what they say, not because they have some special mystical qualification, but because they have become wise in the Scriptures.

Church Standards

Soul liberty means that Christians are responsible to obey God as they understand His requirements revealed in Scripture. They must bring both their opinions and their conduct into conformity with divine revelation. Yet churches are covenanted communities, and in their covenants they specify which teachings and practices are obligatory for members of the church. New Testament churches hold their members accountable for their beliefs and their practices, and they may even disfellowship erring members. Does this create a conflict between the soul liberty of the believer and the authority of the church?

The answer to this question lies in the nature of the local church as a voluntary association. A voluntary association is one that people may join or leave without coercion. An involuntary association is one that people are forced to be part of, whether they want to or not. The best example of an involuntary association is the state. Under normal circumstances, people have no choice about whether they will be citizens of the country into which they are born. They are assumed to be citizens of the nation, and they are extended both the privileges and duties of its citizenship. The obligations are not voluntary—generally the citizen must obey certain laws, pay certain taxes, and perhaps participate in military service. If a citizen attempts to evade these duties, the state responds with force. It may fine, imprison, or even execute recalcitrant citizens.

Baptist church membership, on the other hand, is entirely voluntary. True, God requires church membership, but no one is coerced into joining any Baptist church. Members enter of their own free will, and they can depart of their own free will. They may be disciplined by the church, but the church's right to discipline extends no further than the privileges of membership. No Baptist church can rightfully expropriate property from recalcitrant members. It certainly cannot incarcerate or execute them.

When an involuntary association such as a state attempts to control the ideas of its members, the result is tyranny. An involuntary association may rightfully impose only those strictures that are essential for the common welfare. To go beyond that is an abuse of its power, and such abuses may well call for correction by opposing force to force.

Voluntary associations, however, are distinguished precisely by their ideas and activities. A stamp club exists to promote stamp collecting. A genealogical society exists to study ancestors. A political party exists to advance a platform. To the extent that these or other voluntary associations deviate from their purpose, they dilute their influence and lose their identity. Their nature as voluntary societies is defined by the boundaries that they erect. These boundaries constitute the very identity of the association.

To be forced to join a voluntary society is tyranny. For the society to be forced to accept a member who does not share its interests is also tyranny. This is the fundamental difference between voluntary and involuntary societies. In order to be just, involuntary societies must exercise tolerance toward variations in their membership. Voluntary societies, however, must necessarily be intolerant in matters of membership, or they lose their identities.

The same is true of Baptist churches. Because they are voluntary societies, Baptist churches are defined by their commitment to a certain set of ideas and practices. They specify those commitments in their covenanting documents. Anyone who wishes to become a member of a Baptist church should be fully aware of these commitments and should embrace them wholeheartedly. If people disagree with the covenanting documents, then they should not become members of the church. They are perfectly free to go elsewhere.

Of course, a church may change its commitments. It may either add or detract from the doctrines and practices that constitute its identity. Members who disagree with these changes may leave for a different church, or they may start a new church that conforms to their ideals. They exercise their soul liberty by either retaining or relinquishing their membership.

An individual Baptist church possesses the sovereignty to specify whatever beliefs and practices it believes are necessary in order to obey Scripture. It may also specify procedures for housekeeping, that is, rules that are not necessarily Biblical but that are designed to facilitate decent and orderly conduct. Whether its rules are Biblical, extra-Biblical, or even anti-Biblical, the rules themselves do not constitute a violation of the soul liberty of any member. Members who agree are free to stay. Members who disagree are free to leave. That freedom— the freedom of voluntary association—is what preserves the soul liberty of the church's members.

While other denominations do speak of the priesthood and soul liberty of the believer, Baptists have made these teachings a distinguishing mark. They believe that, under Christ, every Christian is a priest who possesses the right of direct access to God. They believe that each Christian is personally responsible to understand and obey the Bible. They affirm the competence of each believer for these tasks, but they also recognize the importance of spiritual leaders who guide and assist church members in performing spiritual duties at the highest level. They also understand that, as believer-priests, church members have a responsibility to hold one another accountable for obedience to God in both belief and practice. Accountability, however, is not coercion, and Baptists affirm the freedom of each Christian both to unite with and to depart from local church membership.

5 *Congregational Government*

THE WORD *polity* designates any form of organization or government. Differ-ent denominations practice different polities—in other words, they are orga-nized and governed differently. Catholicism is governed by the bishop of Rome and the other bishops who are in communion with him. The various branches of Anglicanism, Eastern Orthodoxy, and Methodism are governed by bishops (sometimes called district superintendents) acting collegially. Presbyterian and Reformed churches are governed by representative bodies that operate at various levels of authority. Plymouth Brethren assemblies are governed by self-perpetuating boards of elders, a system that has become popular among many independent evangelical churches.

Baptists differ from all these churches in the form of polity that they adopt. Baptists believe that churches ought to be governed congregationally. They be-lieve that the final authority under Christ for making the church's decisions is invested in the congregation as a whole.

For Baptists, congregational polity is not merely a matter of practicality, as if they were trying to fit themselves to Western democratic sensibilities. Rather, Baptists believe that congregational government does the most justice to the pattern and teaching of the New Testament. Some other denominations believe that the Bible is largely silent on matters of polity so that churches are free to adopt whatever form of organization seems to work best. Baptists disagree: they believe that the New Testament does teach a form of church government, and they aim to implement that government in their congregations.

One misconception concerning congregational polity should be corrected at the outset. Congregational church government is not the same thing as de-mocracy—especially not as it is practiced in secular politics. Democracy is the brute rule of majorities. In a democracy, all voices are equal, and a bare 51 percent majority has the power to enforce its will upon the minority. For a Baptist church to behave in such a way, however, would dishonor Scripture and bring reproach upon the name of the Lord.

Granted, in congregational polity a vote still needs to be taken. At the end of the day, some proportion of the membership must be sufficient to make a decision that binds the entire congregation. A unanimous decision is not always necessary for a church to move forward. The factor that distinguishes this procedure from pure democracy is that before a church begins to count votes, it must weigh counsel. Some counsel weighs more than other counsel. The church's weightiest counselors can rightly be called its leaders. Most churches have both unofficial and official leaders. Legitimately, unofficial leaders are those who have won a hearing by virtue of their Biblical understanding, spiritual maturity, and service for the Lord. The New Testament also assigns official leadership to specific individuals within the congregation. When these officers speak authoritatively, the church ignores their counsel at the peril of God's displeasure.

Congregational polity includes several elements. The first is the competence and authority of the congregation to make its own decisions under Christ. The next element involves the church's official leadership, the office of pastor-bishop-elder. The next element requires a discussion of the office of deacon. This discussion will indicate that New Testament deacons are not officially leaders so much as helpers, though they must exercise a kind of leadership to fulfill the responsibilities of their office. Finally, the explanation of Baptist congregational polity will close with a reaffirmation of the importance of church unity.

Congregations Decide

To discuss congregational decision-making, we need to address two related questions. The first is whether congregations, which typically comprise Christians at all stages of spiritual development, are really competent to make spiritual decisions. The second is whether the New Testament actually thrusts upon congregations the duty of making their own decisions, and if so, which decisions fall within the congregation's purview.

Congregational Competence

Some people have argued vigorously against congregational polity. Not uncommonly, they suggest that ordinary church members are too immature, obtuse, or recalcitrant to be entrusted with the responsibility of making decisions for the church. For example, one writer who argues for elder rule describes sheep that he has observed, then states, "Sheep are really dumb animals! . . . Since the Lord calls us sheep, the above description gives us a rude awakening as how we must really be spiritually. Helpless, hopeless, and untrainable by nature! Thus, we need shepherds."[1]

This description contrasts sharply with the Baptist understanding of soul liberty, including the competence of the believer, as it was explored in the previous chapter. Furthermore, it fails to explain how elders, who are also among the Lord's sheep (John 10:16), manage to escape the shortcomings that the writer attributes to sheep in general. Some anti-congregationalists seem to believe that only church leaders have been granted spiritual wisdom. Baptists, however, understand the New Testament to teach that all church members possess the competence to make spiritual decisions.

The New Testament teaches that Christ has become wisdom from God to all believers, not just to elders (1 Cor. 1:24). The Holy Spirit has been given to all believers for understanding, not just to bishops (1 Cor. 2:12). All believers, not just pastors, have the mind of Christ (1 Cor. 2:16). Even those who are least esteemed in the church have sufficient qualification to render judgment in disputes among brothers (1 Cor. 6:4). Every genuine believer, no matter how humble, has been given access to spiritual wisdom as a gift from God.

The competence of congregations to make decisions is illustrated by the fact that the churches of the New Testament actually did make decisions. They were even required to make decisions, sometimes very important ones. For example, the apostles faced a situation in which the Greek-speaking widows of the Jerusalem church were being neglected in the church's daily distribution of food (Acts 6:1–6). The apostles' solution was to have the congregation select seven men to manage this distribution. Some have argued that the apostles could rightfully have made this decision themselves. Whether or not that is true, by telling the congregation to make the choice, the apostles expressed their confidence in the ability of ordinary church members to make an important decision about the direction of the church. The apostles would hardly have committed this choice to the congregation if its members had been spiritually inept.

Similar examples could be multiplied. These examples, however, raise another question. What kinds of decisions do we actually see congregations making in the New Testament?

---

1. Mal Couch, ed., *A Biblical Theology of the Church* (Grand Rapids: Kregel, 1999), 166.

Congregational Authority in the New Testament

The first main area in which New Testament congregations made their own decisions was in the selection of their servants. To be sure, the text of the New Testament never specifically assigns the selection of servants to congregations, elders, deacons, or any other particular group or individual. Nevertheless, if we look at the cases in which servants were actually chosen, we discover a number of instances in which congregations did the selecting. We find no clear instances, however, in which the church leadership did the selecting without congregational approval.

The first instance involved a conflict within the church (Acts 6:1–6). This episode supports two observations. The first is that the apostles provided leadership, advancing a solution to the problem. Congregational polity does not obviate the necessity of church leadership. Second, when the actual decision was made, the congregation was responsible to choose the seven servants. The congregational choice was then ratified by the apostles, who confirmed the choice by laying their hands on the servants. This passage provides a beautiful illustration of apostolic leadership and congregational selection working together. The congregation chose and the apostles appointed, or ordained, the seven servants.

The next instance occurred when, after Stephen was martyred, the church at Jerusalem heard reports of conversions in Antioch (Acts 11:19–24). The church (i.e., the congregation) sent Barnabas to Antioch to encourage the brothers. Comparable episodes occurred frequently. During a theological dispute, the church (congregation) at Antioch sent Paul and Barnabas to the church at Jerusalem to investigate the doctrinal deviation of some of Jerusalem's members (Acts 15:1–3). In its response, the church (congregation) at Jerusalem selected Silas and Judas Barsabas to accompany its reply (Acts 15:22). Later still, when Paul was traveling with a financial offering for the Jerusalem church, the churches (congregations) of Macedonia selected a brother to travel with him for the sake of accountability (2 Cor. 8:18–21). In each of these episodes, the text specifies that the assembly or congregation made the choice.

The situation in Acts 13 is a bit less clear. Five prophets and teachers from the church at Antioch are named. The text then states that they ministered to the Lord and fasted, and that when the Holy Spirit told them to set apart Barnabas and Saul, they laid hands on them and sent them away. The problem consists in deciding who sent Barnabas and Saul away. Does the pronoun *they* in Acts 13:2 refer to the five prophets and teachers, or does it refer to the whole congregation? Grammatically, *they* could refer to the prophets and teachers.[2] Most commentaries, however, understand *they* to include the entire church.[3] The passage is ambiguous: it could be taken either way. Given the ambiguity, it should probably not be taken as evidence either for or against congregational selection.

What about evidence against congregational government? Do any passages mention decisions that were made for or imposed upon the church? Opponents of congregational polity appeal to two passages that, at first glance, seem to indicate that church leaders were sometimes selected for and imposed upon local churches. In Acts 14:23, Paul and Barnabas are said to ordain elders in every church. Similarly, Paul commanded Titus to ordain elders in every city (Titus 1:5). Do these texts constitute clear evidence that congregations should not choose their own elders?

This question has a two-part answer. The first part is that both of these cases involved apostolic authority. Even Baptists and others who favor congregational polity believe that apostles had authority to command churches and to compel obedience. The only apostolic authority today, however, is mediated through the written Scriptures. With no apostles on the scene, the question of whether an apostle could override a congregational action is no longer relevant.

The other part of the answer is that the evidence in these two passages is not as clear as some people suppose. For example, Paul used a form of the Greek verb *kathistemi* when he told Titus to "ordain" elders (Titus 1:5). This is the very same verb that Acts 6:3 uses for the apostles "appointing" the seven servants. As we have already seen in Acts 6, the congregation did the choosing, and the apostles confirmed or ratified the congregational choice by appointing the seven. Apostolic appointing (*kathistemi*) did not rule out congregational selection. Neither does it rule out congregational selection in Titus 1:5. Paul was simply telling Titus that he wanted him to make sure that elders were in place. Paul did not specify the method of selection that Titus ought to use.

What about Acts 14:23? This verse employs a different verb when it says that Paul and Barnabas ordained (a form of *cheirotonein*, a term often used for

---

2. Ben Witherington III. *The Acts of the Apostles: A Socio-Rhetorical Commentary* (Grand Rapids: Eerdmans, 1998), 393.

3. Examples include John B. Polhill, *Acts*, The New American Commentary 26 (Nashville: Broadman, 1998), 290; Richard N. Longenecker, *The Acts of the Apostles*, The Expositor's Bible Commentary 9 (Grand Rapids: Zondervan, 1981), 417; Simon J. Kistemaker, *Exposition of the Acts of the Apostles*, New Testament Commentary (Grand Rapids: Baker, 1991), 455; Kenneth O. Gangel, *Acts*, Holman New Testament Commentary 5 (Nashville: Broadman & Holman, 1998), 209–10.

voting) elders. The same principle applies, however. Even if Paul and Barnabas presided over the selection and ordination of elders, congregational choice may well have been involved. Indeed, this fact has been recognized by many who do not necessarily affirm congregational polity. Lechler (a Lutheran) suggested that "the apostles may have appointed and superintended a congregational election."[4] Barnes (a Presbyterian) stated that "probably all that is meant by it is, that they [Paul and Barnabas] presided in the assembly when the choice was made."[5] Alford (an Anglican) added, "The apostles may have admitted by ordination those *presbyters whom the churches elected.*"[6] These citations show that the text is certainly capable of being taken in a sense that is compatible with congregational selection.

In other words, both Titus 1:5 and Acts 14:23 are ambiguous passages. When we make theological decisions, we ought to make them on the basis of passages that are clear rather than passages that can be taken in more than one way. Several passages in the New Testament unambiguously show congregations choosing their own servants. No passages unambiguously show these choices being made apart from congregational selection. The reasonable conclusion is that New Testament churches possess the authority to select their own servants.

A further evidence of congregational responsibility is seen as the New Testament shows churches holding their servants accountable. Even the apostles seem to have welcomed congregational accountability. For example, after the conversion of Cornelius and his household, Peter was called into account by members of the Jerusalem church (Acts 11:2). Rather than simply pulling rank, Peter explained carefully why he had done what he had. His explanation proved satisfactory, silencing Peter's critics and leading the church to glorify God (Acts 11:18).

Similarly, when Paul and Barnabas returned from their first missionary journey, they did not simply report to the prophets and teachers at Antioch. Rather, they gathered the church together to tell all that God had done with them (Acts 14:27). This accountability to the whole congregation seems to have become Paul's regular policy. Much later in his ministry, while administering

---

4. Gotthard Victor Lechler, *The Acts of the Apostles: An Exegetical and Doctrinal Commentary*, trans. Charles F. Schaeffer, in John Peter Lange, *Commentary on the Holy Scriptures: Critical, Doctrinal, and Homiletical* (1868; repr. Grand Rapids: Zondervan Publishing House, 1960), 9:272.

5. Albert Barnes, *Barnes' Notes on the New Testament Complete and Unabridged in One Volume*, ed. Ingram Cobbin (Grand Rapids: Kregel Publications, 1962), 467.

6. Henry Alford, *The Greek Testament*, 5th ed. (London: Rivingtons, 1865), 2:161.

a financial gift to Jerusalem, he welcomed a messenger from the donating churches, affirming that the extra accountability would prevent any appearance of impropriety in handling the funds (2 Cor. 8:18–21).

New Testament churches held both members and servants accountable. Nowhere is this more clearly seen than in the gathering of Acts 15. Sometimes called the Jerusalem Council, this assembly was not really a church council at all. It was a business meeting of the local church at Jerusalem. The need for the meeting developed when teachers from Jerusalem came to Antioch with the message that circumcision was essential to salvation (v. 1). This teaching obviously contradicted the message and practice of Barnabas and Paul, who sharply opposed these Jerusalem teachers (v. 2). As the result of this confrontation, the Antioch church decided to send Paul, Barnabas, and others to alert the church at Jerusalem to the situation (v. 3). Nothing in the text indicates that anyone in the Antioch church needed help from Jerusalem in deciding the theological point.

Then why send messengers to Jerusalem? Two reasons are likely. First, the false teachers were from the Jerusalem church, and it was up to the Jerusalem church to call them into account. Second, the church at Antioch may have wished for a formal statement or clarification of the actual position of the church at Jerusalem. This was a new issue, one that no church had yet addressed publicly.

Arriving at Jerusalem, Paul and Barnabas were welcomed by the church and its leaders (v. 4). Their report of missionary activity instantly provoked controversy (v. 5), however, and it quickly became evident that the Jerusalem church was divided in its understanding of the role of circumcision. The debate took place primarily among the apostles and elders, but apparently it was conducted in the presence of the congregation (v. 6). Peter's address (vv. 7–11) proved to be a turning point after which Paul and Barnabas again rehearsed God's dealings through them (v. 12). Finally, James articulated a Biblical rationale for a solution to the problem (vv. 13–19). The congregation quickly agreed to James's recommendation. A letter was prepared and messengers were selected to travel with Paul and Barnabas to Antioch (vv. 22–23).

The letter accomplished three things. First, it repudiated those members of the Jerusalem church who had been teaching aberrant doctrine (v. 24). Second, it successfully clarified the doctrinal position of the church at Jerusalem, distancing that church from the teachings that Paul and Barnabas had opposed. Third, it offered words of counsel to Antioch and other Gentile congregations. This counsel was judged necessary in view of the fact that these Gentile congregations often occupied cities that featured significant Jewish populations

(v. 21). The thrust of the counsel seems to have been that Christian Gentiles should avoid practices that might identify them with idolatry and unnecessarily alienate Jews (vv. 28–29).

Notably, the church at Jerusalem was home to the apostles. During the meeting, the apostle Peter spoke to the issues, but at no point did the apostles exert their official authority to deliver a verdict in the debate. The congregation, led by James, arrived at the correct decision, subsequently offering both an explanation and words of counsel to the Antioch church.

In no sense was the church at Jerusalem imposing its authority upon the congregation at Antioch. The point of the conference was for the church at Jerusalem to clarify its own position and to call its own members into account. This happened rather decisively. The Jerusalem congregation also offered words of counsel to the Gentile churches—counsel that eventually turned out to be anything but open-and-shut regulation (for example, see 1 Corinthians 8—10 on meat offered to idols). The authority that Jerusalem exercised was authority to define its own doctrine and to call into account certain individuals who were teaching in its name. The clearest lesson from Acts 15 is that a congregation does have the authority to hold its servants accountable.

Thus the evidence indicates that New Testament congregations had authority to choose their own servants. It also indicates that congregations had authority to hold their servants accountable. Furthermore, the evidence of the New Testament clearly shows that congregations held authority in matters of church membership, especially in the discipline and dismission of members.

The key text on church discipline is 1 Corinthians 5. That text has already been examined in the chapter on pure church membership, but one aspect of that discussion needs to be reinforced here. The erring brother was not put out of the church by the apostle Paul or even by the Corinthian church's leadership. He was put out by the congregation as a whole. He was to be delivered to Satan for the destruction of the flesh by the assembled church (vv. 4–5). The church had no authority to judge those who were outside its own membership, but it was obligated to judge those who were within (v. 12). Consequently, the congregation as a whole was responsible to put away from among themselves the sinning brother.

The counterpart of this situation can be found in 2 Corinthians 2:4–11. There the church was dealing with a member who had already been disfellowshipped and who had subsequently repented of sin (it is unclear whether this was the same person referred to in 1 Corinthians 5). Paul clearly stated that this punishment was inflicted "by the majority" (2 Cor. 2:6), a clear indication of congregational action. Now, however, the congregation was behaving too severely and refusing to restore the repentant brother. Paul begged the congregation to forgive and comfort this brother and to confirm him in their love (vv. 7–8). Clearly, the responsibility for the restoration of erring members was laid upon the congregation as a whole.

The New Testament contains no explicit references to the procedure for accepting new members into a church. Since erring members are disfellowshipped by the whole congregation, and since repentant members are restored by the whole congregation, the most reasonable procedure would be for new members to be received by the whole congregation. This is all the more likely in view of the many "one another" commands that are given to the members of New Testament congregations: to receive one another (Rom. 15:7), to forbear one another in love (Eph. 4:2), to warn one another (Rom. 15:14; Col. 3:16), to forgive one another (Eph. 4:32; Col. 3:13), to comfort one another (1 Thess. 4:18), to bear one another's burdens (Gal. 6:2), to care for one another (Rom. 12:10, 13), to teach one another (Col. 3:16), to speak to one another in psalms, hymns, and spiritual songs (Eph. 5:19), and to edify one another (1 Thess. 5:11). In view of the nature of these duties, it is unthinkable that new members could be imposed upon a church without the congregation's recognition and consent.

For churches, as for all organizations, two of the most important concerns that must be addressed are boundaries (who is out and who is in) and leadership (who is in charge). Within the local church of the New Testament, both of these areas are subject to the decision of the congregation as a whole. These are the most important decisions that a church must make. While other kinds of decisions are left unaddressed in the New Testament, we can certainly reason from the greater to the lesser. If the most important decisions are placed in the hands of the whole congregation, then the less important decisions must not be withheld from them. Consequently, Baptists believe that under Christ, local churches must be governed by the congregation and not by bishops, councils, colleges, committees, boards, elders, synods, district superintendents, general assemblies, conferences, associations, presbyteries, or popes. In the decisions of the local church, the congregation is answerable only to Christ.

Pastors Lead

Baptists place a strong emphasis upon congregational church order. One might think that this emphasis would produce a corresponding devaluation of spiritual leadership, but that is not the case. Baptists highly value the office of pastor. They recognize it as an office that Christ has invested with the duty to lead. Consequently, a full discussion of church polity must include an examination of the office of pastor.

The Identity of the Pastor as Bishop and Elder

The word *pastor* simply means "shepherd." A pastor is responsible, under Christ, to shepherd a flock of believers—a church. The office of pastor is clearly established in the New Testament, but it is not usually given that label. The office can also be designated by two other terms. These terms are actually used interchangeably in two separate texts, and two of the terms are used together in another.

The first text is Acts 20, in which, from the seaport town of Miletus, the apostle Paul sent for the elders (presbyters) of the church at Ephesus (v. 17). He told them that the Holy Spirit has made them overseers, or bishops, over the flock, and he instructed them to pastor, or feed, the church of God (v. 28). In this text, every elder is identified as a bishop and is given the responsibility to pastor.

The same kind of interchange occurs in 1 Peter 5. Peter announced that he was exhorting elders (v. 1). He commanded them to pastor, or feed, the flock of God (v. 2). He also commanded them to oversee the flock, and the word *oversee* is a verbal form of the noun for *bishop*. Here the elder is given the responsibility of both pastor and bishop.

Passages like these lead Baptists to believe that the terms *pastor* (shepherd), *bishop* (overseer), and *elder* all refer to the same office. They find further evidence in Titus 1:5–7, in which elders are named as bishops (though the title *pastor* is not used). In the absence of contrary evidence, Baptists conclude that every pastor is also an elder and a bishop. Every elder is also a pastor and a bishop. Every bishop is also a pastor and an elder. Baptists do not believe in elders who are not also pastors or bishops.

Of course, some other churches see this matter differently. Some believe that the New Testament teaches two offices of elder: the teaching elder (who is also a pastor, sometimes called *minister of the Word*) and the ruling elder (who is not a pastor). Typically, these churches believe that all pastors are also elders who rule, but not all ruling elders are pastors.

The most important proof text for this position is 1 Timothy 5:17, "Let the elders that rule well be counted worthy of double honour, especially they who labour in the word and doctrine." Those who wish to distinguish two offices of elder believe that this verse sets up a contrast between elders who rule and elders who teach. All ruling elders (which includes teaching elders) are together responsible for making decisions within the church, but some of these elders receive double honor because they labor in preaching and teaching ("the word and doctrine"). Some non-Baptists take this verse as sufficient warrant to insist that eldership be divided between two offices.

Their interpretation of 1 Timothy 5:17 is possible, but another is more likely. Granted, the verse does set up a contrast. The contrast, however, is not between ruling elders and teaching elders. It is between elders who rule adequately and elders who rule well. The characteristic of elders who rule well is that they labor (as opposed to merely functioning) at preaching and teaching. In other words, some elders simply fulfill their duty by preaching and teaching adequately. They are to receive honor. Other elders do more than their duty. They actually labor at their calling, which is primarily preaching and teaching. These elders are to receive double honor.

Because the second interpretation is the less complicated, it is to be preferred. Nevertheless, 1 Timothy 5:17 ought to be recognized as an ambiguous text. Either interpretation is possible. For just that reason, it cannot be used as a proof text by either side of the debate. In other words, if this is the strongest evidence for dividing the office of elder into teaching and ruling elders (and it is), then the evidence is not strong enough.

Obviously, Baptists tend to favor the second interpretation. They believe that all elders rule, but that some elders give themselves to ruling by laboring at preaching and teaching. If they are right, then this verse also implies something about the nature of pastoral leadership. It implies that preaching and teaching are ways in which elders rule. In other words, pastoral leadership does not necessarily look like making decisions for the church. It may look like equipping the church to make decisions for itself.

Sometimes theologians appeal to evidence outside the New Testament to determine the nature of eldership. They ask how elders functioned within Jewish or pagan societies, and then attempt to understand the New Testament office of elder against this extra-Biblical background. The idea is that the office of elder developed out of some preexisting social station, so its nature, qualifications, and functions can be determined by examining the position out of which it developed.

The church office of elder may well represent a new development, created by the Holy Spirit during the New Testament era. Whether or not the office of elder was developed out of some preexisting station is not really important. Baptists affirm the absolute authority of the New Testament in all matters of church faith and order. Consequently, Baptists do not look to the patterns of Jewish synagogues or Greek cities to determine how elders ought to function within the church. They look to the New Testament as their sole and sufficient authority in this important area of church order.

The Number of Elders per Church

Baptists have debated the question of how many elders a church can or should have. Some have strongly favored a plurality of elders, while others have insisted upon the sufficiency of a single pastor. The debate has sometimes been aggravated by the failure to realize what is and is not being asked. Consequently, certain stipulations must be stated before this conversation can proceed.

First, plural eldership is not the same thing as elder government. Plural elders may function as spiritual leaders and advisors while not functioning together as a decision-making board. Simply because a church has multiple elders does not mean that those elders exercise decision-making authority over the congregation.

Second, plural eldership need not divide the office of elder. Some churches have both ruling elders and teaching elders. Many churches with plural elders, however, recognize that each of their elders is also a pastor and a bishop.

Third, plural eldership does not obligate a church to utilize unpaid volunteer elders. Some churches do expect some of their elders to support themselves through some other vocation. However, many churches with plural eldership believe that they are Biblically obligated to support all of their elders.

Fourth, plural eldership does not necessarily destroy any administrative order or structure among the pastors of a church. Some churches believe that all elders should be absolutely equal in every respect. Other churches recognize that elders may be functionally unequal (they may have an authority structure among them) even if they remain equal in terms of their eldership. In other words, plurality does not require complete parity in every respect.

Fifth, the question of how many elders a church *may* have is not the same as the question of how many elders a church *must* have. Permission does not constitute a mandate. If the New Testament does give churches permission to have more than one elder, this permission does not entail a requirement for multiple elders.

Is a church permitted to have more than one elder? Even a cursory reading of the New Testament leads to the conclusion that plural eldership was quite common during the apostolic era. During their first missionary journey (Acts 14:23), Paul and Barnabas ordained elders (plural) in every church (singular). The church at Jerusalem was led by apostles and elders (Acts 15:6, 22; 21:18). Paul sent for the elders (plural) of the church (singular) at Ephesus (Acts 20:17). In Crete, Titus was to ordain elders (plural) in every city (Titus 1:5), and it is not likely that every city had multiple churches. When Paul wrote to the church at Philippi, he greeted the church's bishops (Phil. 1:1). In the absence of any contrasting examples, this evidence indicates that plural eldership was fairly consistent among the New Testament churches.

While the apostles never announced that this practice was mandatory, it did not proceed without their sanction. If plural eldership were impermissible, surely the apostles would have corrected the churches that implemented it. They did not. Rather, the apostles themselves appear to have been responsible for it. In view of the widespread practice of the New Testament churches, it hardly seems possible to argue that every church must be limited to a single pastor.

Still, this pattern of plurality may be occasional rather than normative, and though it shows that plural eldership is permissible, it does not necessarily enjoin the practice as mandatory. To conclude that plural eldership is obligatory, we would have to find a Biblical passage that states it as a requirement. Examples alone are not sufficient authority. Even the most widespread habits of the early church are not necessarily requirements for all churches at all times. Practices do not become normative simply because they are typical or average, even when they are typical or average among apostolic churches. Therefore, to determine whether plural eldership is the New Testament norm, we need to discover whether any passage of the New Testament actually states that individual churches must always have more than one pastor-bishop-elder.

The logical place to look is 1 Timothy 3, the importance of which lies in two considerations. First, it is a normative (didactic) passage rather than a merely descriptive passage. Second, it actually aims to deal with questions of church order. Most of the chapter is devoted to a discussion of the offices and qualifications of bishops and deacons. Paul's stated reason for focusing on this topic was so that, if his arrival was delayed, Timothy would know how to conduct himself in the house of God. Paul identified the house of God as the church (1 Tim. 3:15). Consequently, the conduct that Paul expected from Timothy was not simply his individual deportment, but the right ordering of the church. Timothy had to know how to set the church in order because he was Paul's delegate, responsible for the assembly while Paul could not be present.

The passage is both didactic and deliberate. This makes 1 Timothy 3 the single most important text on church offices in the New Testament. If any passage were to require a plurality of elders, this chapter should be it. Of course, the New Testament could state the requirement elsewhere, but if plural eldership is a requirement for New Testament churches, we would expect to find it stated here.

In 1 Timothy 3, the apostle Paul first discussed the office of bishop (vv. 1–7), then turned his attention to the deacons (vv. 8–13). His references to deacons are all in the plural, implying that the normal pattern of a fully organized church is to have multiple deacons. His references to the bishop, however, are all in the singular. This is the case whether he is referring to the office (v. 1) or to the individual who fills the office (vv. 1–7).

What is the significance of these references to a single bishop? Certainly not that a church is limited to only one bishop, for in many other texts, New Testament churches are shown with multiple elders. Rather, the significance is simply that plural eldership is never stated as a requirement. Even in 1 Timothy 3 (the most important passage on church order), Paul did not require a church to have multiple bishops or elders. In the key text dealing with church offices, a single bishop is sufficient to fulfill the requirement.

Sometimes the objection is raised that the shift between singular and plural in 1 Timothy 3 (*bishop* versus *deacons*) is merely stylistic. That may be the case—the apostle Paul was certainly allowed to vary his wording for the sake of style. It is, however, not relevant. The question is whether the text requires a church to have multiple bishops or elders. The answer is that it does not. A single bishop is adequate to fulfill the requirements of 1 Timothy 3. If the text does not require plural elders, we have no right to require plural elders.

Might the requirement be stated in some other text? The only other passage that might be taken to require a plurality of elders is Titus 1:5. In this verse, Paul stated that he had left Titus in Crete to set the churches in order and to ordain elders in every city. What follows is a description of the qualifications for an elder or bishop (vv. 6–9).

Though it is narrower in scope than 1 Timothy 3, this passage also aims to discuss church order. Clearly, Paul wanted multiple elders to be distributed throughout the cities of Crete. Some have suggested that these cities may have contained more than one church, but while possible, this suggestion seems unlikely. Whether this passage requires plural eldership for all churches, however, is subject to two considerations.

First, the expression "in every city" is not a literal translation of the Greek text. What Paul actually wrote is that he wanted Titus to ordain elders "according to city," or, as we might say, "city by city." The idea may not be that Paul wanted plural elders in every city, but that Paul wanted elders to be distributed throughout the cities of Crete, irrespective of the number of elders in each individual city.

Second, in this verse Paul stated in a factual way how he had instructed Titus when he sent Titus to Crete. In other words, Titus 1:5 is autobiographical and, consequently, historical in nature. It indicates what Paul's wishes and directives were upon a particular occasion. This particularity contrasts with the clearly general principles that he articulated in the subsequent verses (e.g., "if any," v. 6).

Even supposing that Paul wanted Titus to ordain elders in every city, we still must answer an important question. Is his instruction meant simply as a local reference to the work that Titus was doing in this particular situation, or is it meant as a general principle for all churches in all cities? The reference is sufficiently ambiguous that it should not be used as a proof text in either direction. It does not clearly establish plural eldership as normative for church order.

That is why most Baptist churches have believed that a single pastor is sufficient to meet the Biblical requirement for a fully ordered church. They believe that a Biblical requirement actually ought to be articulated in the Bible somewhere. Neither 1 Timothy 3 nor Titus 1:5 articulates a requirement for plural eldership that clearly applies to all churches everywhere. For that matter, neither does any other New Testament passage. To state the obvious, since the New Testament nowhere requires plural eldership, then plural eldership must not be treated as a New Testament requirement.

Plural eldership is clearly permissible and was even typical during the New Testament era. Consequently, churches may have more than one elder if they find a plurality useful. Nevertheless, Baptists usually stop short of concluding that plural eldership is a Biblical requirement. If a single pastor is sufficient to meet the needs of a church—for example, a small congregation in a rural community—then the church is not violating a New Testament standard if it does not add other pastors.

Pastoral Authority

The New Testament assumes that the local church has rulers or leaders. Paul spoke of elders who rule well (1 Tim. 5:17) and of those who are "over you in the Lord" (1 Thess. 5:12). The writer to the Hebrews exhorted submission and obedience to those who rule (Heb. 13:17). These passages presuppose an authority structure within the congregation. In that structure, some members are held particularly accountable to other members. Interpreters are nearly unanimous that elders are the ones who occupy this leadership position.

Since Baptists equate the office of elder with that of pastor and bishop, Baptists infer that pastors are to rule or lead. The recognition of this leadership function raises important questions that Baptists are obligated to answer. How do pastors lead? What does pastoral authority look like, and what are its limits? How do congregations follow? How can pastoral leadership be balanced with the decision-making authority of the congregation?

Several considerations indicate that a pastor's authority (his leadership or his rule) consists primarily in his teaching and example rather than his ability to make decisions that bind the congregation. The first consideration is that the New Testament shows churches, and not simply pastors, making the most important decisions. New Testament churches regularly chose their own servants and called them into account. New Testament churches possessed the authority to disfellowship erring members and to readmit repentant ones. Paul stated that the church, and not simply the pastor, is the pillar and ground of the truth (1 Tim. 3:15), which indicates that the church as a whole is responsible to maintain pure doctrine. There is no clear instance in Scripture of a pastor making the most important decisions on behalf of a church.

The second consideration is that fiat, decision-making authority is explicitly forbidden to the pastor. Writing to elders, the apostle Peter said that they must not act as lords over God's heritage (1 Pet. 5:3). The verb for "as being lords" means "to be master" or "to rule" in the sense of making and enforcing decisions by fiat. The word does not refer to the elders' attitudes as they make decisions but to the kind of authority that they must not exercise.

The third consideration is that the pastor's authority is regularly associated with his preaching and teaching ministry. According to Paul, preaching and teaching are characteristics of elders who rule well (1 Tim. 5:17). This should come as no surprise, because one of the few functional qualifications that Paul listed for the bishop is that he be a skilled teacher (1 Tim. 3:2). So important is teaching to the pastoral office that Paul even designated those who hold this office as "pastors and teachers" (Eph. 4:11). Along with teaching in general, Paul cited warning, or admonishing, as an aspect of spiritual leadership (1 Thess. 5:12), meaning that a pastor's teaching must not remain abstract, but must be applied to real situations. The writer to the Hebrews described church leaders as those who have "spoken unto you" the Word of God (Heb. 13:7). Such teachers, he said, are the individuals to whom church members are required to submit.

The fourth consideration is that the pastor's example is also connected to his authority. While Peter forbade pastors to exercise fiat, decision-making authority over the church, he required them to be examples to the flock (1 Pet. 5:3).

According to Hebrews 13, part of submitting to church leaders involves imitating their faith (Heb. 13:7). These teachings accord well with the ministry of the apostle Paul. He led the churches by pointing to his own example (1 Cor. 4:16; 11:1; Phil. 3:17; 2 Thess. 3:9). He also instructed Timothy and Titus to act as examples (1 Tim. 4:12; Titus 2:7). Clearly, the pastoral example is a significant aspect of New Testament spiritual leadership.

These two elements—teaching and example—come together in the comparison between a bishop's authority in the church and a father's authority in the home (1 Tim. 3:4, 5). Paul taught that a man who cannot manage his household will not be able to care for God's church. This comparison becomes especially relevant if one remembers how a household was likely to be structured during the first century. It was more than the "nuclear family" of the modern era. To be sure, it would include a husband, a wife, and possibly small children, yet it might also include adult children, elderly parents, in-laws, household servants or slaves, and often guests. Such a Christian household could hardly be managed well by a man who contented himself with simply barking orders. His leadership would have to involve instruction, persuasion, coordination, and illustration through example, all bathed in an attitude of sacrificial interest. Paul implied that the leadership of a church would be even more difficult, probably because a father can make certain decisions unilaterally, while a pastor cannot.

The New Testament epistles draw a fairly clear picture of pastoral leadership. Pastors are expected to lead, but their authority is moral rather than fiat in nature. They do not make decisions for the church, but they teach the Scriptures in such a way as to prepare the church to make wise decisions for itself. They live out their faith so transparently that their congregations can see by their example how Biblical principles come to bear upon life. They do this all in a spirit of gentleness, patience, and meekness that resists becoming embroiled in quarrels (2 Tim. 2:23–24).

In other words, a pastor has no authority of his own. He operates strictly with the authority of Jesus Christ—an authority mediated only through the Word of God. A pastor's private opinions are no more authoritative than the opinions of any other person. His authority consists in the proclamation of the Scriptures as he rightly explains their meaning, brings them to bear upon life, and illustrates their truth through personal example. When he has done these things, God's people are morally obligated to submit to him and obey him. Their submission is not personally directed to him as a man, nor is it even directed toward the pastoral office per se. Their submission is directed to the Word of God that he has proclaimed, explained, applied, and lived. If they fail to obey him under these circumstances, they will find themselves in a less-than-advantageous position when their pastor gives account for their souls (Heb. 13:17). Jesus Christ will hold them responsible for their disobedience.

A good illustration of pastoral authority at work can be found in the meeting of the Jerusalem church in Acts 15. This meeting had been called because some members of the church had been teaching deviant doctrine to another congregation (v. 1). As it turned out, some of the members at the Jerusalem meeting agreed with those teachers (v. 5). Considerable debate arose, not simply among the church's membership, but even among its leadership (vv. 6–7). Peter's testimony of the conversion of Cornelius opened the door for a serious consideration of the issue (vv. 7–12). Finally James spoke, bringing the Old Testament Scriptures to bear upon the problem and proposing a solution (vv. 13–21). His teaching and application were so compelling that the entire church adopted his recommendation (vv. 22–29). This situation clearly involved pastoral leadership on the part of James. Nevertheless, it also involved a congregational decision before James's proposal was implemented.

Pastoral authority, then, consists primarily in preaching, teaching, and example. Pastors do not exercise decision-making power over the congregation. Yet pastors do hold the authority to make decisions in one important area. If pastoral authority is a matter of teaching, then pastors must be able to decide what will be taught. If theirs is a teaching office, and if their duty is to teach the congregation, they must oversee the teaching ministry of the church.

As a covenanted body, the congregation itself specifies the acceptable doctrinal parameters for the church. Since he is a member, a pastor knowingly submits to those parameters and cannot ethically transgress them. When the church calls him to be a pastor, however, it lays upon him the duty of instructing the congregation. To fulfill that responsibility, it must also grant him the right to decide what and how the church is to be taught. Pastors should not have to gain congregational permission to preach an unpopular message, and they should not be saddled with programs and practices that work against a right grasp and application of Biblical principles.

The pastor or pastors must have the final word, not only over what takes place in the pulpit, but over any area of the church's ministry that communicates truth and shapes pious responses to God. Of course, non-pastors may also teach in various areas of a church's ministry, but whoever else leads the church's teaching ministries (such as Sunday School superintendents or youth leaders) must be accountable to the pastors. The teaching authority of the pastors includes such areas of the church's ministry as music, men's and women's groups, children's and youth ministries, and home Bible studies involving members. Indeed, it includes any area that communicates Biblical or doctrinal content or shapes Christian sensibility. It may even include aspects of architectural design and interior ornamentation. The pastor's authority in these areas should not merely be recognized, but welcomed.

The principle here is simple. If the pastor's authority consists in teaching, he must be able to teach the congregation. He must be able to teach without constantly having his teaching subverted or contradicted within the church's ministry. (Of course, he may encounter personal opposition, but how he handles that is a different matter.) The pastor's ministry will be most powerful and his leadership most effective when the whole teaching ministry of the church is, under his oversight, coordinated to accomplish the same goals. Whether the church should emphasize one area or de-emphasize another at a given time is really a pastoral decision. By calling a pastor, a congregation, in principle, recognizes this delegation of authority.

In other words, a local church that is ordered according to the New Testament will have two centers of authority. On the one hand, the congregation will possess the authority and bear the responsibility of making decisions about the church's leadership, membership, policies, direction, and programs. As a member of the church, the pastor is obligated to submit to the authority of the congregation. On the other hand, the pastor will possess the authority to preach, teach, apply, and illustrate the Word of God. Whenever he faithfully and accurately brings the Scriptures to bear upon life, the congregation is obligated to obey him. Furthermore, when the congregation makes decisions, it must do more than count votes. It must weigh counsel, and the pastor's counsel (informed by the Scriptures and reinforced by his example) ought to weigh very heavily. The church submits by listening carefully, evaluating the pastor's teachings in the light of God's Word and, where they are accurate, obeying.

Sometimes one hears of situations in which churches and their pastors have fallen out and are fighting one another. Though these situations arise from a variety of causes, they are always grievous. Most often such strife occurs when either the congregation or the pastor has failed to recognize the legitimate authority that belongs to the other. There is a real sense in which pastors need to submit to their churches, but there is also a real sense in which churches need to submit to their pastors. If either side fails in this mutual relationship of submission, trouble is almost certain to follow.

In sum, Baptist churches are congregationally governed. Baptist churches are also pastorally led. Congregational polity and pastoral leadership are not contradictory, but complementary. A church requires both if it is going to function well.

Relationships between Pastors

As most Baptists understand the New Testament, a church is not required to have more than a single elder or pastor. Nevertheless, the churches of the apostolic period generally did have multiple elders. A church today may choose to call multiple pastors for various reasons. If it does, it has to answer another question. How should pastors in the same church relate to one another? Should they function collegially as equals, or should they recognize an order of authority among them? An argument can be made in each direction.

In favor of collegiality is the fact that the New Testament does not distinguish different classes or offices of pastor. As Baptists understand it, the text does not divide teaching elders from ruling elders. It does not distinguish pastors from bishops, or either of these from elders. The unity of the office of elder implies that all pastors really are equals in some very important ways.

Within a congregation, all pastors are equally pastors. One may be designated as a senior pastor, another as an assistant pastor, and still another as a youth pastor. In all of these cases, however, the operative word is *pastor*. Each bears full responsibility to meet the qualifications and to perform the functions of the pastoral office.

All pastors are leaders. Furthermore, all pastors lead in the same way, namely by their teaching and their example. The work of a pastor is to teach the Scriptures. Whether this takes place in the pulpit, in the youth room, directing the choir, or in the context of personal discipleship is not the issue. The substance of pastoral leadership is teaching, and a pastor who does not teach is not fulfilling his primary pastoral duty.

All pastors hold their office by virtue of the congregation's call. The New Testament does not recognize pastors who appoint themselves. It does not recognize pastors who are appointed by committees. It does not recognize pastors who are appointed by other pastors. In a genuinely Baptist church (i.e., a church that follows New Testament order), the only way in which one becomes a pastor is by consent of the congregation. When a church has multiple pastors, a candidate may and should be examined and recommended by the other pastors. The final decision, however, is the church's. If the church has not expressed its consent, then a man is not a pastor.

Each pastor holds his authority from Christ through the call of the church. Even an assistant pastor or youth pastor is still a pastor. He is called by and accountable to the church. His is not merely an extension of the senior pastor's ministry, though he should conduct himself in such a way that his ministry supports and complements that of the senior pastor. If he needs to be removed from the pastorate of the church, the decision must be made by the congregation and not merely by the other pastors or even the senior pastor.

Pastors have an equal right to expect financial support from the congregation. The apostle Paul made an extended case in 1 Corinthians 9:3–14 that those who preach the gospel should normally make their living from the gospel. In other words, the norm is for a church to provide whatever financial support is necessary for each pastor to care for himself and his family. While Paul personally declined to exercise this right, he also made it clear that others used it (v. 4). Under usual circumstances, a pastor will be effective only as he has time to put into the labor of ministry. By working an outside job to support himself, he is deprived of much of that opportunity. Granted, if he has good reasons, a pastor may forego the compensation that a church owes him. It is not the church's place, however, to refuse to pay its pastors. A church that deliberately tries to build its pastoral staff by using volunteer elders who have no hope of leaving (and often no desire to leave) their outside employment is acting presumptuously.

In all these ways, pastors or elders who labor together in a local church are genuinely equals. Consequently, there is no room for one pastor to behave dismissively or arrogantly toward other pastors. A situation in which one pastor sees himself as the boss and the others as lackeys is always out of place. The pastors must pray together, plan together, worship together, and fellowship together. Their spirit should always be one of collegiality in which even the most junior pastor is heard and respected by the others.

Nevertheless, pastors within the same church are not equal in every way. They are not equally gifted. They are not equally devoted to their work—depending upon their stages of life, the attention of some may be drawn away by family interests or by heath concerns. They are not equally knowledgeable in the Word or equally skilled as shepherds. Because of these and other inequalities, some pastors will minister more effectively than others.

A pastor who engages faithfully in his duties may be leading (ruling) adequately, even if he endures many distractions. Such a pastor should be honored, as should all pastors who fulfill their duty. To discharge the responsibilities of a pastor dependably is an accomplishment of no mean quality. Yet some pastors are able to do more. Perhaps because of their stage in life, or perhaps because of their singular focus, they are able to give themselves to the ministry. They labor in preaching and teaching. They do not simply rule or lead: they rise above the level of adequacy to lead well. According to the apostle Paul, such pastors are worthy of double honor (1 Tim. 5:17).

The word that is translated *honor* is a fairly flexible term. It can also be translated by words like *respect, reverence, esteem, rank, dignity,* or even *compensation.* The point of what Paul is saying is that all elders are not to be treated equally. All are to be honored, but some are to receive more honor than others. In other words, within a local church some pastors ought to be more respected than others. Some should occupy a higher rank or receive greater dignity than others. Probably Paul is even suggesting that some ought to receive greater compensation than others. The honor that they receive should be proportioned to the effectiveness with which they minister.

The notion of "double honor" can be illustrated from the example of James in relation to the other elders in the Jerusalem church. We have already seen that Jerusalem had multiple elders. Yet at a crucial moment in the church's history, James was the one who stepped forward with a Biblically supported solution to a doctrinal problem (Acts 15). James was obviously the most effective elder or pastor within the Jerusalem church. Consequently, it is no surprise that when Peter was miraculously delivered from prison, he specifically asked for James to be notified (Acts 12:17). Paul narrated how, early in his ministry, Peter and James were the two individuals he sought out at Jerusalem (Gal. 1:18–19). Later James was one of the three who, together with Peter and John, extended the right hand of fellowship to Barnabas and Paul, recognizing their ministry to the Gentiles (Gal. 2:9). At the end of Paul's missionary travels, James was the one whom Paul went to visit, though the other elders were present (Acts 21:17–18). Evidently, James was widely recognized as the leader of the church at Jerusalem.

Even churches that aim for strict equality among their pastors usually end up with somebody like James. One elder will possess such exceptional gifts, or will evidence such exceptional dedication, or will grasp the Scripture so profoundly, or will minister so effectively that even the other elders will begin to look to him for leadership. Virtually every church, whatever its official polity, ends up de facto with a senior pastor.

Baptists believe that this is precisely what Scripture intends. When a church has more than one pastor, one will unavoidably be honored more than another. This additional honor is right. It is Biblical. All elders should be honored, but some should be honored more than others.

Recognizing an order among pastors does not make the senior pastor the head of the church. New Testament churches have only one head—Jesus Christ. His authority is mediated through the congregation in its decision-making process. A pastor's authority within the church consists in his teaching of the Word and his example of godliness. This appears to be the only authority that is lawfully available to him, even in his relationship with other pastors.

What can be said about a pastor's teaching authority in the church, however, can also be said about a senior pastor's authority among the other pastors. Someone is going to have a stronger voice in deciding what should be taught in the church, when it should be taught, and by whom it should be taught. Certainly the pastors of a church will consider these matters together, and most likely each will exercise an individual sphere of authority. Nevertheless, the senior pastor does have a duty to comprehend the entire teaching ministry of the church and to understand the direction in which the whole needs to move. Even though his leadership is moral and not fiat, he does need to instruct and even direct the other pastors in the exercise of their ministry. For their part, they (along with the rest of the congregation) owe him double honor, deference, respect, and esteem.

In sum, the primary relationship between members of a pastoral staff ought to be collegial. Matters of pastoral interest should routinely be discussed among all pastors, and the counsel of each should be weighed by all. When a consensus is not evident, decisions should become matters of earnest prayer and conversation. Still, an order is and ought to be present among the pastors of a church. Maturity, knowledge, dedication, and skill should lead the church to extend to some elders greater respect and deference than they extend to others. In fact, while the church should normally pay all of its elders at least a token compensation, it should pay some elders more than others.

The elders need to maintain proper attitudes among themselves. Senior pastors must never view themselves as bosses and their fellow-pastors as lackeys. Those who are less honored must never allow jealousy, pride, or ambition to creep into their relationship with the other pastors. Under all circumstances the pastors must support one another, pray for one another, help one another, and, when necessary, confront one another. Since they are under-shepherds of the same flock, division among them will necessarily produce division in the church.

Women as Pastors and Preachers

The question of whether women may preach or pastor is an old one. It has gained new traction recently, as women have been welcomed into more and more fields that were once closed to them. Vocational ministry is about the only field in which women's participation remains controversial. Contemporary evangelicals are divided on the question, with organizations like Christians for Biblical Equality favoring the participation of women in vocational ministry, and organizations like the Council for Biblical Manhood and Womanhood opposing it. The arguments are complex and far too detailed to explore in this context. However, one key text is worth examining. It appears to be the text that most directly aims to answer the question. Consequently, it should take precedence over other texts that touch on the issue more tangentially.

The text is 1 Timothy 2:11–15, and while a detailed exegesis of the passage goes beyond the purpose of this discussion, an examination of this text in its context provides a convincing answer to the question of whether women should become preachers and pastors. Broadly, the context begins in 1 Timothy 1, where Paul made it clear that one of his concerns in writing to Timothy was the presence of false doctrine in the church (vv. 3–7, 18–20). In the opening verses of chapter 2, Paul expressed God's desire for all to be saved (v. 4). To that end, Paul encouraged the offering of prayers for all, but especially for civil officials whose governments permit Christians to live peaceful and orderly lives (vv. 1–3). He also reviewed God's gracious work in making salvation possible and in sending Paul to preach the gospel (vv. 5–7).

In a transitional verse, Paul expressed his purpose that all men everywhere should pray (v. 8). This verse obviously looks back to the opening verses of the chapter with its emphasis on prayer. It also introduces a new element, however. The word for "men" does not designate generic humanity, but specifies adult males. Paul's purpose was for grown men to give themselves to prayer. Very likely, he was thinking about prayer in the public assembly rather than in private devotion.

In the next verse, Paul shifted the focus from men to women, probably still within the context of the public assembly (vv. 9–10). These verses reveal that Paul was concerned not only with the men's praying, but also with the women's adornment and deportment. Paul essentially forbade the women from putting themselves on display. He wanted them to avoid ostentation in their dress and grooming. In their behavior they should be self-possessed and orderly, for if they were to attract attention at all, Paul wanted it to be on account of their good works.

While some of what Paul confronted (e.g., braided hair and jewelry) arose from a specific situation and was the result of specific disobedience, his remarks about women in these verses are, in principle, equally applicable to both men and women at all times. The attitudes of sobriety and modesty that Paul described are virtues that will adorn the character of any Christian, whether male or female. The good works for which Paul called are just as suitable for either sex.

Much attention is often focused on the next verse, where Paul commanded women to learn in quietness and all submissiveness (v. 11). The qualifiers must not be allowed to obscure the fact that the primary command is for women to learn. Paul placed no limits upon the learning that should be made available to women. Apparently, even the deepest and most technical Biblical and theological matters are open to them. While they learn, however, Paul wanted them to maintain quietness and submissiveness. The word for *quietness* (*hesuchia*) is not a word that denotes absolute silence, but rather a term that connotes a quiet and submissive demeanor. Coupled with his reference to submissiveness, Paul appears to have been describing the virtue of teachability (the classical word for this virtue is *docility*). This virtue is also good counsel for men as well as women. Paul certainly was not forbidding women ever to say anything in the public services of the church.

Paul then focused directly upon the distinct role that women have in the church (v. 12). The verse contains two prohibitions and one direct command. The positive command is that they are to be quiet. The prohibitions are, first, that women must not teach men, and, second, that they must not exercise authority over men. These prohibitions are the heart of the contemporary controversy over women in vocational ministry. Women are not supposed to teach which men? Where should they not teach them? What kind of teaching are they not supposed to do? What sort of authority are they not supposed to exercise? Are these commands absolutes that apply to every circumstance, or are they restricted to particular settings?

To get correct answers to these questions, the context must be allowed to speak. So must other Scriptures in which women are depicted as functioning commendably in the church. With these matters in mind, certain conclusions can be drawn.

First, 1 Timothy 2:12 does not forbid women from teaching or even discipling men outside of the public gatherings of the church. The context is most likely concerned with public assemblies, not with private conversations. Moreover, Priscilla was a commendable example of a woman who actively challenged and instructed a male teacher, Apollos (Acts 18:24–26). Theologically perceptive women may have much to say to men about the Bible's teaching.

Second, 1 Timothy 2:12 does not forbid women from teaching children or other women within the public assembly. While the age-and-gender-segregated Sunday School is a modern invention, the early churches doubtless incorporated occasions for offering separate instruction to women and children. Nothing in this verse bars a woman from teaching children or other women at the most sophisticated levels.

Third, the verse forbids a kind of teaching that is tied to exercising authority. Probably the authority in view is the sort of authority that would be exercised by an elder. Even within the church, occasions exist when men may learn from women, provided the women do not attempt to teach as if they hold official authority within the church. In the New Testament, women both prophesied and prayed in public (1 Cor. 11:5), but they did it while demonstrating appropriate tokens of submission to legitimate authority. In today's environment, many churches are blessed by the testimonies and even exhortations of female missionaries. Nothing in this verse forbids women from doing that kind of teaching.

Fourth, this verse has nothing to say about women exercising non-ecclesiastical authority in non-church settings. Other passages in the New Testament do emphasize a woman's submission to her husband (Eph. 5:22–24, 33; Col. 3:18). Otherwise, the New Testament contains no hint that women are excluded from areas such as commerce, the learned professions, or even statecraft. Christian women are not supposed to submit to all men at all times everywhere.

Nevertheless, 1 Timothy 2:12 clearly forbids several roles to women. Women must not preach to audiences that include adult men. Women must not authoritatively teach the Bible to men or to mixed audiences in a church setting. Furthermore, and apropos of the present discussion, women must not exercise the authority of a pastor-bishop-elder. This verse definitely does restrict the pastoral office to men.

Some have objected that 1 Timothy 2:11–15 is simply addressing a local situation in Ephesus and is therefore inapplicable to churches in general. Paul, however, grounded his commands, not in some transitory situation, but in the order of creation (vv. 13–14). Adam was formed first and then Eve. The man was not deceived, but the woman was. Clearly Paul thought that these considerations ought to be persuasive, but why?

The order of creation is relatively easy to understand. Adam was created first out of the dust of the ground. Eve was created later out of Adam's rib. She was created to be a helper like him (Gen. 2:18). An order of authority was already present in creation. Male headship has always been part of God's plan, even before the Fall.

What about the order of the Fall? What did Paul mean when he pointed out that Eve, not Adam, was deceived? Certainly he was not suggesting that women are intrinsically more gullible than men. Rather, he was thinking about the events that occurred in the temptation and Fall. Eve was not alone at the time of the temptation. The man was with the woman while she was being tempted (Gen. 3:6). When the serpent singled out Eve, she might have deferred to Adam. Instead, she chose to answer for them both, and Adam apparently acquiesced. This constituted a reversal of the creation order: Adam should have stepped forward and taken responsibility, and Eve should have waited for him to do so. The order was reversed, however, and the results were calamitous. This is all the evidence that Paul needed to insist that women should not exercise spiritual authority over men in the church.

Does this mean that women are now deprived of some particular blessing or opportunity to serve the Lord? Paul did not think so. He emphasized that women will be saved in childbearing (1 Tim. 2:15). While this verse mystifies a great many interpreters, it actually contains a powerful truth. In verse 15, Paul was drawing upon the doctrine of calling.

The doctrine of calling begins with the recognition that Christians find themselves in different stations of life. Some are young and others are old. Some are married while others are single. Some live in one nation and some in another. Some earn a living one way and others in a different way. In the New Testament, each of these stations represents a calling (1 Cor. 7:17–32). Each includes its own opportunities to serve God and to bring glory to Him. All Christians put their salvation on display in the way that they fulfill the callings in which they find themselves.

Ministers have a calling. If they pursue their ministry well and faithfully, then they have a wonderful opportunity to exhibit the grace of salvation at work in their lives. Farmers, shopkeepers, mechanics, and physicians also have callings, for callings are simply the stations of life in which God places believers. Like the pastor, all Christians have the opportunity to put the grace of God on display by demonstrating how salvation is worked out in their individual callings.

What Paul was saying in 1 Timothy 2:15 is that domesticity and maternity are callings. The woman who fulfills her calling as a wife and mother has the opportunity to exhibit the grace of salvation through her faithful activity. She can show others what salvation looks like when it is worked out in the context of motherhood. True, she cannot be a pastor. The pastor, however, cannot usually be a physician, and the physician cannot be a sous chef. The doctrine of calling teaches that these callings—and an immeasurable variety of others—are equally valuable and equally dignified in the sight of God. Each has the same opportunity to magnify God by exhibiting His grace in salvation. The stay-at-home mom can make as much difference for God as the internationally known pulpiteer.

Some people insist that women have a right to be pastors. They believe that denying the pastoral office to women is a slight against women's value or abilities. Actually, their position is a slight against the value and dignity of motherhood. Biblically, a woman who devotes her life to maternity and domesticity has the opportunity to accomplish something of eternal value, and this is not a matter to take lightly.

Deacons Serve

The office of deacon stands alongside that of pastor-bishop-elder as one of two that were instituted by Christ within the church of the New Testament. Because theirs is a divinely ordained office, deacons should never be held up to contempt or ridicule, as too often occurs among certain kinds of pastors. Rather, pastors should labor to equip deacons so they can fulfill their God-given responsibilities within the local church. A church must have properly functioning deacons if it is going to thrive.

Qualifications for Deacons

The Biblical qualifications for the office of deacon are virtually identical to those for the office of pastor (1 Tim. 3). The only functional qualification that is exclusive to pastors is that they must be skilled teachers (v. 2). Though deacons may teach, that is not their primary duty. They must, however, possess a serious knowledge of doctrine and practice, and their lives must conform to what they know (v. 9). In every other way, what we say about the qualifications for deacons will also be true of the qualifications for pastors.

The fundamental qualification for both bishops and deacons is that they must be blameless. Of course, *blameless* does not mean *sinless*. What is does mean is that no one can level a credible charge of scandalous conduct. Both pastors and deacons must live their lives with such transparency and care that any accusation of scandal is virtually self-defeating.

Questions are sometimes asked about the pastors' and deacons' family requirements. They text assumes that they are married and have children, and some have deduced that both marriage and children are a Biblical requirement for both offices. The majority view is that marriage and children are not necessary requirements to be a pastor or deacon, though they are obviously very desirable. If a pastor or deacon is married, however, and if he does have children, his relationship with his wife and children definitely constitutes part of his qualifications. He must be absolutely faithful and devoted to his wife— not only adultery, but flirtatiousness is a disqualification from both offices. His children must be faithful in the sense that their lives are free of scandal—as Paul wrote to Titus, they cannot be open to the charge of debauchery or rebellion (Titus 1:6). If a pastor or deacon has children, they must be under control as long as they are in his household.

Sobriety and dignity are essential for both deacons and pastors. They bear a heavy responsibility—to care for the church of the living God. They must take this responsibility seriously, just as they take life seriously. This does not mean that they must be devoid of humor—indeed, a good sense of self-deprecating humor is a significant asset for a pastor or deacon. But life cannot be a joke to them. They have to be serious about God, about Scripture, about ministry, and about personal holiness. If they lack this quality, they are not suited to the offices.

Both pastors and deacons must be self-possessed and under control. They must not be the kind of people who will abandon themselves to alcohol (or to other substances, for that matter), to money, or to fits of temper. Steadiness and constancy in the face of temptations and afflictions are crucial to these offices.

Hospitality is mentioned as a qualification for bishops. While it is not re-peated for deacons, the New Testament says enough elsewhere concerning hospitality that it should be seen at least as a virtue for deacons (3 John 5–8). As the word is used in Scripture, *hospitality* means more than occasionally having friends in for a meal. Hospitality entails a genuine openness of heart and home, a willingness to share whatever one has, sometimes even with strangers. Pastors must, and deacons should, be generous individuals.

Besides discussing qualifications for pastors and deacons, the text also de-tails qualifications for deacons' wives (1 Tim. 3:11). Certainly what is said of them ought to be true of pastors' wives as well, and indeed of all mature women in the church (Titus 2:3). These women should evidence the same kind of so-briety and self-control that must characterize pastors and deacons.

The word translated *wives* in 1 Timothy 3:11 could also be translated *women*. Some have suggested that perhaps the word refers not to the deacons' wives, but to female deacons or deaconesses in the church. Sometimes Phoebe is pointed out as an example of a female deacon (the word translated *servant* in Romans 16:1 is also translated *deacon* in other passages). While these references constitute slender evidence upon which to establish women in the office of deacon, some Baptists churches do have deaconesses who minister specifically to the needs of women in the congregation. In churches that do not have deaconesses, the deacons' wives typically assume similar duties. The notion of women as deacons would probably seem less jarring if the office of deacon were properly understood in terms of service rather than leadership.

The Function of Deacons

Baptist churches use deacons in a variety of ways. In some churches they constitute a virtual governing body, and it is common to hear Baptists refer to the "deacon board." Sometimes they see themselves as watchdogs over the pastor, while in other churches they function as the pastor's eyes and ears within the membership. Unfortunately, it is fair to say that many Baptists have borrowed their notion of deacons from other kinds of churches or even from models in the business world. What, then, is the Biblical function of deacons?

Negatively, Biblical deacons are not rulers or governors over the church. They do not constitute a board. A board is a governing body that has authority to make binding decisions on behalf of an organization. In a Baptist church, however, all decision-making authority is rooted in the congregation. The congregation may delegate certain decisions to pastors and deacons, but it always reserves the right to call its officers into account. Baptist churches are congregationally governed, not diaconally governed. In New Testament churches, deacons never constitute a board, and Baptists would do well to banish this word from their vocabulary. Rather than talking about the "deacon board," we should simply say, "the deacons." Instead of discussing the "chairman of the board," we should just say "the chairman of the deacons" or even "the deacon chair." This shift in language would go far toward eliminating a false concept of the function of deacons.

Positively, New Testament deacons are servants of the congregation and the pastors in order to accomplish the God-given purposes of the church. The best example of the work of deacons probably comes from Acts 6:1–7, though not everyone agrees that deacons are in view in this text. If (as most think) they were deacons, their office was created to administer the material affairs in the church. This passage indicates that deacons are over the distribution of benevolence. They care for the needs of members. They administer the material property of the congregation. If they fulfill this task well, then the spiritual leaders of the church gain the opportunity to devote themselves to Scripture and to prayer—their real concerns.

In other words, the office of deacon is primarily a position of service and not of leadership. Effective deacons are aware of the needs of the church's members, and they labor to meet those needs. Effective deacons care for the business matters of the church, ensuring decency and order in the care of resources. By taking these burdens out of the hands of pastors, they liberate the church's spiritual leadership for their specific tasks of ministry.

Of course, a form of leadership is implicit in the deacons' responsibilities. Deacons do manage material affairs, which, in the twenty-first century, will include matters like banking, record keeping, legal matters, buildings, and properties. While they do not make unilateral decisions in these areas, deacons must have the ability to act reasonably on behalf of the congregation. Deacons also minister to the material needs of church members, and it is natural for those members to look to their deacons for spiritual counsel. Deacons who spend hours helping people with their needs will certainly develop spiritual influence within the church.

Such influence is not wrong, and wise pastors will not feel threatened by it. Pastors should not grasp for power, but rather should aim to distribute power as widely as possible throughout the church. When power is clutched, it chokes and dwindles. When power is shared, it multiplies, and the overall energy of the congregation blossoms. A wise pastor will delight in having deacons who are strong and vigorous, for their power can be used to bring great glory to God.

For themselves, deacons must be sure that their use of power conforms to the nature of their office. Theirs is not the power to control, but to facilitate. They are helpers and servants, first, to the congregation, and second, to the pastor. By meeting the material needs of church members, they liberate their pastors to excel in spiritual oversight. Because they are close to the congregation, they may become aware of spiritual needs before pastors know of them. They can often meet these needs through member-to-member ministry, or, if necessary, they can bring a pastor into the situation. Strong deacons who use their power wisely are a great blessing in the work of the local church.

One area in which deacons typically serve is in the administration of the ordinances. Deacons and their wives usually help to prepare candidates for baptism. They are usually responsible for the preparation of the elements and table for the Communion service. While these responsibilities are not specifically assigned to deacons in Scripture, they are part of the material organization and welfare of the church. In the absence of a pastor, nothing in Scripture prevents the church from asking a deacon to baptize or to administer the Lord's Table. If pastors would train deacons to conduct the ordinances, some churches might be spared a bit of embarrassment when they are without a pastor.

Deacons and Other Offices

The New Testament defines two offices for the church: pastor-bishop-elder and deacon. To be fully organized, a New Testament church needs at least one pastor and at least two deacons. Often a church will find it useful to have more than one pastor or more than two deacons. Sometimes, however, an odd phenomenon occurs. A church will choose to have only one pastor when it actually wishes to grow a ministry that requires more than one. Rather than calling another pastor, it will begin (deliberately or inadvertently) to assign pastoral responsibilities to deacons. When this phenomenon occurs, deacons will begin to absorb more and more of the spiritual leadership of the church. In extreme forms, this trend can lead to situations in which vigorous deacons actually overshadow the spiritual leadership of the pastor.

While this phenomenon is understandable, it is also fraught with hazards. Pastors and deacons do not fulfill the same responsibilities. Certain pastoral responsibilities cannot rightly be met by deacons. Furthermore, if deacons are busy absorbing pastoral responsibilities, then they are likely to leave their diaconal responsibilities unfulfilled. Churches then begin to invent new and extra-Biblical offices to cover the areas that the deacons are unable to manage. The situation becomes truly alarming when the qualifications for these humanly invented offices are kept lower than the qualifications for the Biblical office of deacon. In the worst cases, either pastoral or diaconal oversight (or both) is taken over by church committees that may or may not be composed of qualified individuals.

An example of a humanly invented office is that of trustee. Many churches choose to incorporate, and a corporation legally must appoint trustees. In itself, that is not a problem, for what trustees are supposed to do legally is exactly the kind of thing that deacons are supposed to do Biblically. In many churches the deacons—or some of the deacons—actually serve as trustees. Other churches choose to distinguish their trustees from their deacons. Making that distinction may not pose too great a problem as long as both trustees and deacons are held to the same spiritual standard. In many of these churches, however, deacons are seen as an office for spiritual leadership while trustees are seen as an office that is concerned with the material affairs of the church. In other words, the distinction that these churches draw between deacons and trustees is almost exactly the distinction that the New Testament makes between elders and deacons.

Sadly, in some of these churches, trustees are held to a lower spiritual standard than deacons. Some churches use the office of trustee as a training position for future deacons. Other churches will knowingly appoint individuals to act as trustees who would not be qualified to serve as deacons. Consequently, the deacon-trustee distinction becomes a mechanism for skirting the Biblical qualifications (seen by some as onerous) for deacons. One hardly need wonder that such churches often become hotbeds of political gamesmanship.

The creation of functions such as trustee or Sunday School superintendant is not in itself wrong or bad. However, to the extent that these positions reflect either pastoral or diaconal responsibilities, they should be filled by pastors or deacons. If that proves impossible, then at minimum the individuals who fill these positions should meet the qualifications for the Biblical office whose functions they reflect, and they should always be answerable to the Biblical officers.

Church Unity

The picture that emerges from the New Testament is of autonomous churches governed by their congregations, led by their pastors, and served by their deacons. This situation creates more than one locus of authority in the church. Congregations have a rightful sphere of authority, but so do pastors. New Testament deacons do not exercise official authority, but they do gain significant influence through their ministry (1 Tim. 3:13). Given this dispersal of both de jure authority and de facto power, how can a church maintain its unity?

The Nature of Unity

Unity is always a function of that which unites. Furthermore, it always reflects the character of that which unites. A church that unites around a pastor or a program will reflect the character of that pastor or program. Genuine spiritual unity, however, cannot be contrived. It cannot be imposed from outside, but must grow up from inside. The apostle Paul referred to this authentic unity both as the unity of the Spirit (Eph. 4:3), and as the unity of the faith and the full knowledge of the Son of God (Eph. 4:13).

The fundamental unity of the church is produced by the Holy Spirit, Who unites all of the members to Christ and consequently to one another (1 Cor. 12:13). Church unity is created and advanced when the individual members of the church follow Jesus' voice, trusting Him more implicitly, knowing Him more fully, loving Him more completely, and obeying Him more perfectly as sheep of His flock (John 10:4–5, 16; Eph. 4:13). Unity also increases as the church advances further and further into the faith, that is, the body of teaching and practice that was revealed by Christ through His apostles and committed to His church for safekeeping throughout its generations (Jude 3).

All this means that church unity cannot be aimed for directly. It is a by-product of something else. As the members of a church draw close and closer to the center of the faith, the whole counsel of God, they will necessarily draw closer to one another. As they approach nearer and nearer to Jesus Christ and advance in their conformity to His character, they will necessarily draw nearer and nearer to one another. The responsibility of the church's leaders is not to grow unity, for they have no power to do that. What they can do, however, is foster the conditions that permit its growth.

The best environment for the advancement of unity is one that is strongly committed to the glory of God through the exaltation of Christ. It is one that centers upon the cross of Christ and His triumphant resurrection. It is one in which men and women are drawn into God's presence through the mediation of the Word and the Spirit. It is one in which lives are being transformed as people constantly gaze into the face of Christ and yearn to be like Him.

Creating such an environment is the responsibility of the spiritual leaders of the church. This area, more than any other, is where pastors must lead by their example and character. They will experience constant temptations to divert the attention of the church toward lesser matters, but they must maintain an un-swerving focus upon God in Christ. When pleasing Christ stops being a cliché and becomes the priority of the church, real unity can begin to emerge. Apart from such a Christ-focused environment, all attempts at church unity will feel contrived and manipulative.

Instructed, Mature Congregations

All believers, even the most humble, have been given spiritual wisdom. Without that assurance, congregational polity would be a frightening prospect indeed. Yet some believers are more mature than others. They understand the Scriptures better. They are capable of greater discernment and therefore of mak-ing better decisions (Heb. 5:13–14).

A pastor who wants the church to make wise decisions must labor for the maturity of the flock. Indeed, maturity is one of the marks of a successful church (Eph. 4:13). A wise pastor works to bring the entire flock into spiritual adult-hood so that each member, arriving at a level of stability, is able to offer his or her fitting contribution to the entire body (Eph. 4:14–16). Congregational polity will work only in a church that is being instructed and is growing in knowledge and virtue.

This reality must shape the pastor's ministry. While quick, deeply emotional decisions may be spectacular, they seldom provide a good foundation upon which to build spiritual stability. A manipulative pulpit ministry may produce visible results rapidly, but people are soon fatigued by frenetic emotional appeals. Such a ministry begins to pall, and soon saints will either fall away from the church or fall out with one another.

The only ministry that can build the required maturity is a ministry of patient teaching and example. The pulpit is not a place for a pastor to announce his private opinions, however salutary they might be. It is the place to open God's Word and to help God's people understand Who He is, what He has done in Jesus Christ, and what He now wants of them. Every sermon and every lesson should ask people to change. These changes may not be large—in fact, they will generally be relatively small. Over time, however, a constant stream of small changes can add up to genuine transformation.

Maturity also comes as pastors instruct church members in the details of church life. Christian instruction must not remain at the level of platitudes. Church members need to know why the church operates in the way it does. They need to have a clear understanding of the church's priorities, its decision-making procedures, and the obligations that they bear as members of the church.

The best time to do much of this instruction is actually before people become members. For this reason, joining a Baptist church should not be easy. Prospective members should bear testimony of their conversion and baptism, and in their testimonies the truths of the gospel should be clear. Prospective members should understand just what they are getting into when they join the church, and their commitment to uphold its covenant and doctrines should be more than tacit. Ideally, each prospective member should complete a detailed application and should be taken through a discipleship course that covers both the basics of the Christian life and the particularities of the given congregation.

Instructed church members also need to know the nuts and bolts of congregational living. They need to know how to address conflicts. They need to know what loving confrontation looks like and feels like, both in terms of confronting and being confronted. They need to know how to deal with a soul about salvation. They should know how to offer the basic forms of counsel, encouragement, and warning. They should know how to read the Bible and understand it for themselves, and they should know how to pray effectively.

Activities like confronting, counseling, encouraging, and warning are not the sole responsibility of spiritual leaders. These are the things that ordinary saints should learn to do as they progress toward maturity. A congregation that is going to govern itself must be populated with members who are advancing in these skills as they grow in grace and knowledge. Pastors lead by teaching God's people about such things, by modeling these things, and by drawing church members into circumstances where they will have occasion to practice these things.

Instructed, Skilled Deacons

In a healthy church, pastors must not only train the congregation but also train the deacons. To meet the Biblical qualifications, deacons must be both men of great character and men with a considerable understanding of the Scriptures (1 Tim. 3:1–13). Paul insists that they must hold the mystery of the faith with a clear conscience, which indicates an advanced level of spiritual understanding and maturity. The "mystery of the faith" is probably the same thing as the "mystery of godliness" (1 Tim. 3:16), which, stated simply, is the gospel with its implications. Those implications are so profound, however, that the best theologians have struggled to comprehend them. The overall picture is that, even though deacons are not the teachers of the congregation, they do have a responsibility for a certain level of Biblical and doctrinal knowledge. The fact that they must hold this knowledge with a clear conscience indicates that they must also be spiritually mature men who have attained a level of piety.

Part of the job that pastors must do is to prepare Christian men to serve as deacons. Ideally, every man in the congregation should be advancing toward this goal, though not all will otherwise be qualified to serve. Men who are already deacons should continue to advance in their knowledge of the faith and in the clarity of their consciences. They may also assist pastors in the practical equipping of future deacons. While their office is not formally one of spiritual leadership, many deacons will become informal leaders by virtue of their service, their sobriety, and their maturity.

Such individuals are extremely valuable both to churches and to pastors. By their public actions and their personal interactions they can contribute much to the unity of the congregation. The original deacons (if such they were) of Acts 6 were chosen in order to resolve a conflict within the church at Jerusalem. When deacons are well equipped for their role, their activity should head off many church conflicts before they even begin.

Structuring Conversation and Decisions

Baptist churches are congregationally governed. The church's decisions must eventually be made by vote of the congregation. Pastors and churches can do much to ensure that decisions are reached in a way that promotes unity rather than undermines it.

To make good decisions, people require full information. Consequently, rather than attempting to limit the flow of information within the church, pastors and deacons should facilitate it. Information is especially important when the congregation is asked to make important or controversial decisions. Except under rare circumstances (such as when confidences must be honored), the congregation should have access to all information that affects a decision.

Part of the information that people need is intangible. They need to know what others think and, just as importantly, how others feel about the decision. They need to have some sense of how the decision is likely to affect their brothers and sisters. The only way that they can get this information is by talking to one another, which is what they should be encouraged to do. For church members to discuss their decisions among themselves does not constitute gossip; it is a way of taking counsel together. This behavior is not to be feared but fostered. Under most circumstances, pastors and deacons are well served to let their guard down and to freely interact with members of the church informally, just as the members will be interacting among themselves.

Good decisions also require good counsel. During the decision-making process of the local church, the members must take counsel with one another. Important decisions require deliberation, not for the sake of parliamentary procedure, but for the sake of wisdom. In the deliberations, every member is entitled to speak. Some will be heard more receptively than others, of course, but church members should never feel that they have been denied the opportunity to share their perspectives on the church's decisions.

Many of the church's decisions are pedestrian in nature, and such decisions may require little by way of information and deliberation. They can often be made almost as a matter of form. When the congregation has to make a significant decision, however, the process of information and deliberation is likely to consume a good bit of time. Very often, people will wish for time to digest the information and to weigh the counsel that they have heard. Furthermore, they will want to devote themselves to serious prayer before important decisions. For that reason, the church's leadership may wish to separate the time for deciding from the time for information and deliberation. While additional meetings do consume more energy and time, the resultant unanimity is often worth the investment.

Churches do not need to vote unanimously in order to act. Because people of good will sometimes see matters from different perspectives, they can believe that different decisions are right. A divided decision is not necessarily a sign of spiritual illness or bad faith on the part of the church. If a vote is very close, however, and if the decision is very important, a church might be wise to engage in further prayer and deliberation before moving ahead. This is especially true when members of the congregation feel very strongly about the matter.

Once the decision has been made, however, deliberation should end. All members (including pastors and deacons) are under the authority of the church. All members have a duty to support the decisions of the body. Unless unforeseen considerations arise, constantly revisiting or attempting to renegotiate the decision will often harm the unity of the church. This is the door to the kind of partisan political maneuverings that have plagued churches ever since Paul rebuked the Corinthians.

Conclusion

The governing authority of New Testament churches rests with the congregation. Congregations, however, must be led by pastor-bishop-elders who give themselves to teaching the Word and modeling godliness. Both churches and pastors must be served by spiritual deacons who bear responsibility for material concerns. As congregations grow in unity through their commitment to Christ and to Scripture, and as they heed the Scriptural counsel of their pastors and the concerns of their brothers, they will be able to make wise decisions that will honor Jesus Christ, Who alone is the head of the church.

6 Separation of Church and State

EARLY CHRISTIANITY quickly became an illegal religion in many parts of the Roman Empire. At times it was universally prohibited. The emperor Diocletian was so successful in his persecution of Christianity that he thought he had annihilated it. His successor Constantine, however, formally declared Christianity to be a legal religion in 313, and himself converted to Christianity. Soon he became a patron of Christianity, building churches and exempting the clergy from taxes. In return, he claimed the right to supervise church affairs, acting as judge in the Donatist controversy and calling the Council of Nicea to deal with Arianism. Over time he extended greater privileges to Christianity. When he built the city of Constantinople, only Christian churches were allowed within the city walls, and these were constructed with taxes levied upon pagans. By the end of his life, Constantine had effectively made Christianity a department of the Roman government.

Constantine's merger of church with state remained virtually unchallenged for more than a millennium. The balance swung in different directions, sometimes with civil rulers exerting authority over churches, and other times with church leaders (especially popes) exercising lordship in civil affairs. Different branches of Christianity would use the power of government not only to persecute pagans but to torment other Christians. Hardly anyone, however, could imagine trying to disentangle church and state.

The major Reformers (Luther, Zwingli, Calvin, and Knox) appealed to the power of the state. They continued to use governmental authority both to defend Christianity and to persecute heresy. Far from abandoning the union of church and state, they embraced it.

That situation changed in the wake of the Reformation. Through their study of the Word of God, some of the younger Reformers concluded that only believers should be baptized. They saw their infant baptism as invalid, so they began the practice of rebaptizing (or, as they saw it, baptizing for the first time) those who professed faith in Christ. Because of their practice of rebaptism, these people were called Anabaptists.

Anabaptists came in different varieties. Some of them believed that God was giving them new revelation. Some of them were political radicals who tried to establish a utopian society by force. Nevertheless, the mainstream of the Anabaptist movement (represented by leaders like Conrad Grebel, George Blaurock, Felix Manz, Michael Sattler, Balthasar Hubmaier, and, eventually, Menno Simmons) remained strictly biblicist.

The problem that the Anabaptists faced was not only theological. In countries that had united church and state (an arrangement known as *Christendom*), baptism was not merely a religious act; it was also a political rite of passage that marked one as a citizen. To submit one's self to rebaptism or to fail to baptize a baby was, in effect, to commit treason. Nevertheless, convinced that Scripture authorizes only the baptism of believers, these younger Reformers refused to allow their babies to be baptized.

The consequences for them were often calamitous. The governments of Christendom hounded the Anabaptists, who were beaten, tortured, and banished. Felix Manz was drowned in the Zürichsee. George Blaurock and Hans Langegger were burned at the stake. Balthasar Hubmaier was burned, and his wife was drowned in the Danube. Michael Sattler had his tongue cut out, then pieces were torn from his body with red hot tongs. Finally he was burned, the men in his church were killed with swords, and the women were drowned.

The Anabaptists eventually responded by renouncing all involvement with the state. They refused to take oaths, to hold office, or to serve in the military. Many of them became pacifists. They did not dishonor or rebel against civil authorities, but they practiced a complete separation of Christians from all participation in government and civil affairs.

A century after the first Anabaptists, a parallel movement arose in England. It began as an offshoot of English separatism, which was itself an offshoot of Puritanism, a branch of the English Reformation. This new movement did not trace itself directly to continental Anabaptism, though some attempts were made to establish ties. Rather, it arose when some theological cousins of the Pilgrims (English separatists who fled to Holland, then to America) concluded that the New Testament authorizes the baptism of believers only. Like the Anabaptists, this new movement in England began to rebaptize professing believers who had been baptized as infants. In England, however, they came to be known simply as *Baptists*.

Early Baptists in England and America faced many of the same difficulties that continental Anabaptists had already encountered. They were not burned as often, but they were imprisoned, fined, whipped, and sometimes hanged. In the American colonies, Roger Williams was banished from Massachusetts Bay in the middle of the winter. His condemnation to the wilderness was meant to be a death sentence.

Like the Anabaptists, the English and American Baptists began to articulate a complex of ideas that would become known as the separation of church and state. Roger Williams in particular became notorious for writing against the use of governmental force to regulate matters of religious conscience. While he remained a Baptist only briefly, he never gave up his commitment to complete religious freedom. When he established the Rhode Island Colony, it became the first of the colonies to incorporate full religious freedom as a matter of principle.

Unlike the Anabaptists, however, English and American Baptists did not renounce all participation in civil affairs. Nor were they pacifists. When permitted, they were willing to serve in the military and to hold public office. They had no difficulty swearing oaths. They saw no necessary contradiction between their commitment to Christianity and their participation in affairs of state.

Baptists have been identified by their insistence upon the separation of church and state. Their position has been characterized by two elements. First, Baptists believe that the coercive power of the state must not be used to enforce matters that should be left to the conscience before God. Second, Baptists believe that Christianity should not appeal to the state for support or advantage. In short, from a Baptistic point of view, the best attitude of the state toward matters of religion is simply to ensure that people have liberty to worship God according to the dictates of their own consciences. The state has no right either to establish a religion or to prohibit its free exercise.

The Nature of True Devotion

Why are Baptists so strongly committed to the separation of church and state? Their first reason derives from the nature of true worship. Baptists believe that any devotion offered to God must come from the heart to be acceptable. Merely formal religious exercises are an offense to God and merit only judgment for those who practice them.

Jesus emphasized the necessity of inner religion in His conversation with the Samaritan woman (John 4:1–26). Brought under conviction of sin, she attempted to divert the conversation by raising a question about the proper location from which worship should be offered (v. 20). Jesus' reply shows that the external circumstances of worship matter far less than the heart of the worshiper (vv. 23–24). He grounded His observations in the very nature of God Himself. Since God is a Spirit, true worship must be offered in spirit and in truth. God is looking for people to offer that kind of worship.

Coerced worship is not offered in spirit and in truth. People who are being coerced neither believe in what they are doing nor wish to participate in it. Since their hearts are not in what they are doing, their hearts are far from God. External forms of worship and outward exercises of devotion can never please God when they are not backed by a faithful heart.

People can seem very religious by engaging in all of the external exercises that are supposed to reflect devotion. They can give to the poor, they can engage in prayer, and they can fast, but all to no avail (Matt. 6:1–18). As long as they engage in these practices in order to gain human recognition, they already have their reward. God, on the other hand, is neither impressed nor pleased.

Jesus made the same point in His denunciation of the scribes and Pharisees (Matt. 15:1–9). He cited the prophet Isaiah to the effect that such people may worship God with their mouths, but their hearts are far from Him. Jesus called this kind of worship hypocrisy, and declared that in God's eyes it is worthless (Matt. 15:7–9, cf. Isa. 29:13). Indeed, it is worse than worthless, for in the passage that Jesus cited, Isaiah actually went on to pronounce judgment against such false worshipers (Isa. 29:14).

Isaiah opened his prophecy by excoriating formalistic religion (Isa. 1:10–16). Though the leaders of Israel were fully engaged in the prescribed forms of temple sacrifice and worship, Isaiah made it clear that their activity brought only disgust to God. God repudiates external worship when it conceals a rebellious heart. The only worship that God finds acceptable is worship that flows out of genuine devotion.

Governmental threats can enforce external conformity, but they cannot secure the heart's allegiance. Under coercion, people may go through the expected external rituals, but inwardly they remain hardened and unchanged. God is not impressed by such external displays. In fact, they are an offense to Him. If it is wrong to engage in empty, formalistic, external religion, then it is wrong to encourage empty, formalistic, external religion. It is simply outrageous to use the threat of imprisonment or death to compel empty, formalistic, external religion.

The Precedent of the New Testament

Does Christianity have a right to rely upon the civil authority for support? Certainly the New Testament never makes such a declaration. Nowhere do the apostles appeal for special privileges in the public square, and nowhere do they appeal for special treatment for churches.

The pattern of the book of Acts is instructive in this regard. Early on, the Christians in Jerusalem ran afoul of the Sanhedrin, which was a Jewish religious court that exercised some civil authority (Acts 4:1–22; 5:17–42). This court used its power to oppose, threaten, and eventually persecute the apostles and the early believers. In response the apostles made it clear that their authority did not come from the Sanhedrin. They rejected the power of the court to govern their message.

Before long, Herod interjected himself into the situation (Acts 12:1–19). First he killed James, then jailed Peter with the intent to execute him. When an angel subsequently delivered Peter from prison, Peter did not linger on death row out of respect for Herod's authority. Herod's relationship to Christianity was entirely hostile.

Paul and Silas found themselves jailed for their preaching in Philippi (Acts 16:16–40). After they were miraculously freed, the *strategons,* or governors of the city, told them to leave town quietly. Paul and Silas refused. In their refusal they did not plead that they were Christians, apostles, or bishops. Instead, they pleaded the rights of Roman citizens, which had been violated by the collapse of due process. At no point did Paul and Silas indicate that either their faith or their ecclesiastical position might exempt them from state interference. Their Roman citizenship was what protected them.

The episode was nearly repeated a short time later in Thessalonica (Acts 17:1–9). Paul escaped violence only when the mob could not find him. Instead, it seized Jason and dragged him before the *politarchs* or city officials. The sole response of the government was to require a good-conduct deposit from Jason. Christians again made no attempt to secure any special position or favor from the civil authorities.

Paul found himself in court again in Corinth (Acts 18:12–17). The Jewish leadership in that city attempted to have him prosecuted for (as they saw it) false doctrine. The proconsul, Gallio, refused even to hear the case. He distinguished wrongdoing and criminal activity from religious questions, denying that the latter were within his purview. If Paul thought that Christianity actually had a moral right to rely upon the support of the state, this would have been an ideal opportunity to say so. Instead, he (and Luke, the narrator of the episode) seems to have been content with the outcome.

A series of observations can be offered in connection with Paul's imprisonment and trials in Cesarea. First, according to Claudius Lysias, who was the commander of the Roman garrison in Jerusalem, Paul was under protective custody (Acts 23:23–35). The Roman official distinguished crimes, which were a matter for his concern, from theological disputes, which were not. He had no interest in addressing religious accusations, but he did use his authority to protect a citizen from religious coercion.

Second, when Paul defended himself before Felix (Acts 24:1–27), he did not ask the court to recognize or establish the truth of Christianity. He did acknowledge that certain religious points were in dispute, but he denied that these constituted any criminal activity. The clear implication was that Felix had an obligation to release him if the only complaint was religious in nature.

Third, Paul's defense before Festus was succinct (Acts 25:8–11). In no sense did Paul appeal to any ecclesiastical privilege. He simply argued that if he was a criminal, he was willing to accept the penalty. No criminal charge could be proved against him, however, so he ought to be freed. The implication is that civil authorities simply do not have the right to decide questions over religious matters. In the long run, Agrippa agreed with Paul (Acts 26:30–31), but by that time, Paul had already appealed to Caesar.

The picture that emerges from the book of Acts is that the churches of the New Testament neither expected nor received any form of support from the state. Under the best of circumstances, civil authorities refused to render judgments on religious matters. Neither the New Testament churches nor their leaders ever asked for any special favor, recognition, or assistance from the governments of their day.

Some have suggested that this apparent refusal of state support was necessary while Christianity was an infant religion in a hostile environment. When Christians grew numerous and powerful—so the argument goes—they would be in a position to do what the apostolic churches could not. They would be able to claim their rightful role in manipulating the civil power to the advantage of Christianity.

The suggestion rings hollow. One searches the New Testament in vain for any indication that any union of church and state would ever be desirable. The New Testament contains no agenda for churches to dominate the political process. It contains no strategy for employing civil power to enforce matters of conscience. It contains no instructions for gaining or deploying the support and assistance of governments. Church and state appear as distinct institutions, independent of one another, each with an assigned role, neither interchangeable with the other. While Christians are instructed to submit to the state, owing respect and paying taxes (Rom. 13), the state is nevertheless constantly viewed as potentially hostile and not as a source of support.

The only Biblical argument that can be used to justify the union of church and state is to appeal to the example of Old Testament Israel. Some Christians (the Puritans, for example), assuming that the church somehow replaces or continues Israel, have believed that the pattern of Israelite theocracy can be transferred directly to the church. This is an argument that Baptists have consistently rejected. While they have not agreed among themselves about the relationship between Israel and the church, they have agreed that the pattern of order for God's work in the world changed between the Old Testament and the New. Baptists have insisted that the New Testament is the absolute authority for the faith and order of the church. The appeal to the pattern of Israel is illegitimate.

Baptists and Civil Authority

Related to the problem of church and state is the question of how individual Christians should view their governments. Anabaptists have generally taken a pessimistic view of human government and have refused to participate in civil affairs. Baptists, however, have held a more positive perspective. They have been willing to serve in the military and to hold public office. In some instances Baptists have also been willing to engage in overt civil disobedience, and not always for reasons related to freedom of religion. The following sections will attempt to detail the attitude that Baptists normally hold toward their governments, as well as the circumstances that may give rise to exceptions.

Submission and Participation

In understanding their relationship to the state, Baptists have relied upon a network of New Testament passages. One of the earliest (at least in terms of the events that it mentions) involves the response of John the Baptist to repentant publicans and soldiers recorded in Luke 3:12–14. Publicans were tax collectors, minor officials in the Roman governmental system. They had a nefarious reputation for abusing their office to extort money. John did not instruct these repentant publicans to leave office, but he did tell them to collect only what they were authorized. Similarly, soldiers often exploited their position to threaten people and extort money. John did not instruct repentant soldiers to abandon the army, but he did tell them not to intimidate people through fear of force or false accusation, and to be content with their wages.

In his first epistle, the apostle Peter commanded Christians to be subject to every human institution, specifically to kings and governors (1 Pet. 2:13–17). Such individuals, said Peter, are sent by God for the punishment of evildoers and the rewarding of those who do good. For Peter, fearing God and honoring the king were perfectly compatible activities.

The apostle Paul commanded Titus to remind believers that they must submit obediently to the "principalities and powers," two of his terms for civil authorities (Titus 3:1). Paul also urged Christians to pray for kings and others who occupy high positions (1 Tim. 2:1–4). These prayers are to be offered so that Christians might be able to live quiet and peaceful lives that are godly and dignified. In the flow of Paul's thought, this kind of life apparently enhances evangelistic effectiveness.

In his most protracted discussion of civil authority (Rom. 13:1–7), the apostle Paul echoed and expanded upon these instructions. Every Christian, he wrote, must be subject to civil rulers, for these authorities have been ordained by God (v. 1). Those who resist the authorities are resisting God's ordinance and can expect judgment (v. 2). As a general principle, rulers do not strike terror into the hearts of people who are doing nothing wrong, but rather into the hearts of evildoers (v. 3). Consequently, Christians ought to behave well so as to gain the approval of the civil authority. Governors are actually serving God and promoting good for Christians, but workers of calamity should be afraid. God has committed to the state the prerogative of capital punishment, which would imply the prerogative of lesser punishments (v. 4). Consequently, submission to governments is based upon two powerful motivations: first, the desire to avoid judgment, and second, the yearning for a clear conscience (v. 5). Christians are obligated to pay their taxes (v. 6) and to render such tokens of respect and honor as are due to the authority (v. 7).

Baptists have taken these teachings very seriously. For example, the London Confession (1644), popularly known as the First London Confession, was drafted during a period when Baptists could still be persecuted in England. The confession recognized the king and Parliament as the supreme authorities in the realm and exhorted Christians to maintain and defend the laws of the land. Yet the confession also insisted that Jesus Christ is the only lawgiver in matters concerning the worship of God. Magistrates have the duty to guard the liberty and conscience of the people and to protect them from injury and oppression.

In matters of worship, Christians are responsible to be fully convinced that their actions accord with Christ's laws, neither neglecting what He commanded nor doing what He forbade. If the government requires Christians to violate their consciences, then they should "yield our persons in a passive way to their power, as the saints of old have done."[1] Even if the magistrate proved to be hostile, obedience to Christ must not be abandoned.

The First London Confession also dealt with Christian involvement in the affairs of government. It specified that Christians could hold public office and swear oaths. These permissions distinguished Baptists both from their Anabaptist cousins and from the Quakers, a religious sect that had become a significant problem during the middle of the seventeenth century. Followers of George Fox, the Quakers were pacifists whose refusal to take oaths of loyalty barred them from public office. Baptists believed that both oaths and offices were perfectly permissible.

The First London Confession was prepared by Particular Baptists, one of two important Baptist groups in England. The other group was the General Baptists, who produced their own statement, known as the Standard Confession (1660). The political atmosphere was rife with intrigue, including speculation that Baptists were renegades and that they wished to use liberty of conscience as a pretext to dismantle civil order. Parts of the Standard Confession were meant to allay these fears without surrendering the Baptist position. On the one hand, the Confession insisted that everyone should have liberty of conscience in all matters of worship and religion, without oppression or persecution (article 24). On the other hand, it recognized the necessity of civil magistrates to punish all "fleshly filthiness" and "wicked lewdness" without respect of religion (article 25). The confession explicitly denied the authority of civil powers to impose obedience in matters of religion, recognizing the necessity of obeying God when government overstepped this boundary.

In 1678, a group of General Baptist churches in the Midlands of England published what they called the "Orthodox Creed." The creed included an article on the civil magistrate (45), recognizing the right of Christians to hold office and even to wage war. It also enjoined submission to magistrates "in all lawful things." The next article (46) dealt with liberty of conscience, denying that humans had the right to bind the conscience contrary to the Word of God. A later article (48) allowed for the swearing of oaths by Christians.

---

1. London Confession (1644), Articles 49–51. In the second edition (1646), Articles 49 and 50, modified somewhat, become a note to Article 48. This quotation is taken from the 1646 note.

Perhaps the best-known Baptist statement of faith is the Baptist Confession of Faith (1689), popularly known as the Second London Confession. It reiterated many of the themes that had been developed by both Particular and General Baptists. By the time of its adoption, persecution was much less likely. The chapter dealing with obedience to civil authority (chap. 24) was correspondingly shorter, omitting the mention of limitations upon the state's authority in matters of conscience. Like the Orthodox Creed, it defended the right of Christians to hold public office, even specifying their right to wage war "upon just and necessary occasions" (24.4). A separate chapter (23) recognized lawful oaths as part of religious worship, and it actually regarded them as obligatory under certain circumstances.

The wording of the Second London Confession was reproduced by the Philadelphia Confession (1742), perhaps the most famous Baptist confession in America. The other major confession adopted by American Baptists was the New Hampshire Confession (1833). The New Hampshire Confession was much later and rather shorter than the earlier statements. It has been widely copied (sometimes in revised form) by Baptists down to the present day. It contains only one article on civil government (article 16), in which it states that government is to be obeyed except in "things opposed by the will of our Lord Jesus Christ."

Taken together, these statements paint a clear picture of the Baptist understanding of church and state. This understanding comprises three elements. First, God has appointed civil authority, to which Christians must submit in civil affairs. Second, in matters of conscience, the state possesses no authority; and Christians must obey God. Third, Christians may participate in civil affairs, swearing oaths when required to do so, holding office when called, and even waging war when necessary.

Civil Disobedience

While the general approach of Baptists has been to recognize and submit to the authority of civil government, exceptions do exist. For example, some Baptists were among those who supported both the American War of Independence and the Confederacy during the War between the States. At first glance, this participation in secessionist wars seems incompatible with the general Baptist attitude of submission to civil authority. How can this anomaly be reconciled?

The Bible allows for two situations under which civil disobedience can be morally justifiable. The first and most obvious is that civil disobedience is not only permissible but obligatory when a moral imperative is at stake. When the state requires people to violate God's laws, Christians are obligated to disobey. Civil authorities have no right to forbid what God commands or to demand what God forbids. When government crosses this line, our refrain must be that of the apostles: "We ought to obey God rather than men" (Acts 5:29). When the state demands that its citizens disobey God, even the normal tokens of respect to government should drop away. When God's people face a choice between loyalty to God and loyalty to the state, they must express their decision in blunt terms (Dan. 3:16–18).

Respect for divine authority demands freedom of conscience, which civil government is obligated to protect. Of course, the appeal to conscience opens the possibility that someone might disobey the government over a personal preference or matter of convenience rather than over a genuine divine requirement. This places a heavy burden upon Christians. If they are going to disobey the government for the sake of conscience, they have a duty to be sure that some divine commandment really is at stake. Baptists especially should be wary of claiming freedom of conscience or separation of church and state over activities that are not clearly required by Scripture. These claims should never be used as a ploy to avoid those responsibilities that rightly pertain to all citizens. Unless a clear Biblical principle is at stake, believers are obligated to obey the law. To do otherwise is to risk the displeasure of God Himself, for God is the One Who has ordained civil authorities.

Besides obedience to God rather than humans, the Bible also teaches a second rationale for civil disobedience. This rationale is less obvious, but equally legitimate. It can be inferred from the Jews' appeal to Darius in Ezra 5. The Jews in Jerusalem had begun to rebuild the temple, an act that violated a decree in which Darius commanded that work on the temple should cease. In other words, the Jews were engaged in civil disobedience. When challenged, however, they did not appeal to God's command (though they were obeying God). Instead, they appealed to Persian law. They claimed that they had been granted legal authority for their work by an earlier decree in which Cyrus had commanded the rebuilding of the temple. Under the law of the Medes and the Persians, the later emperor Darius had no authority to annul the decree of Cyrus. In other words, the decree of Darius was actually illegal. By resuming their work of rebuilding the temple, the Jews were obeying the earlier decree that had come from Cyrus. Eventually, Darius himself agreed that they were correct and that building the temple was their duty.

A similar circumstance can be found in Acts 16. In this chapter, the civil authorities of Philippi acted illegally by throwing Paul and Silas into jail without respecting their legal rights as Roman citizens. Later, the authorities issued orders that the two missionaries were to leave town quietly. Paul refused, using terms that were blunt to the point of defiance (v. 37). He insisted that the authorities themselves had violated the law. Furthermore, he demanded at least a token restitution. When the rulers of Philippi learned that they themselves were the ones who had broken Roman law, they hurriedly made amends. Since Philippi was a Roman colony, their miscarriage of justice could have landed them in serious trouble.

In both of the above circumstances, the civil authorities were forced to bow to the rule of law—that notion that ultimate authority does not rest personally in the rulers of a society, but in that society's laws. The rulers themselves are subject to the law of the land. When they act contrary to the highest laws, issuing decrees and making laws that conflict with them, they may rightly be disobeyed. In fact, they can be forced to obey the laws of the land.

This understanding of civil disobedience is sometimes captured in the expression *Lex, Rex,* "the law is king." Over every civil order exists some legal code, the maintenance of which is equally obligatory for both those who govern and those who are governed. If the rulers seek to overturn this code, those who are ruled may rightly reject their authority in favor of the authority of the law. In such instances, the rulers, and not the ruled, are the rebels, because the rulers are the ones who despise the just authority of the law.

The principle of "rule of law" still holds true. Civil governors do not have the moral prerogative to act contrary to law. If they do, then the governed may rightly reject their demands and take whatever measures are necessary to restore the rule of law. These measures may even include the toppling of lawless rulers. Christians have no moral obligation to obey officials whose demands violate the law. They have no responsibility to obey lower laws that violate higher ones. They need not obey any decree, directive, order, or legislation that conflicts with the highest law of the land.

Scripture presents two possible rationales for civil disobedience. The first is that citizens must disobey the law when it either requires them to do evil or forbids them to do good. The second is that they may disobey the law (though they are not required to do so) when a particular law or directive violates the higher laws of the land. These two reasons place a responsibility upon Christians to be wise and knowledgeable citizens. They must know what the law of their land is, what it requires, and what it allows. If they are going to disobey any law, they must be sure that it genuinely conflicts either with a moral imperative or with a higher law. Only under these circumstances may they justly engage in civil disobedience.

In recent years, Christians have been confronted with increasingly complicated issues. Great evils are being done in Western societies. For example, millions of unborn babies have been murdered by abortion. Because these societies are governed representatively, many Christians feel a degree of responsibility for challenging these atrocities. Some Christians have responded by breaking property laws in order to protest, by damaging the property of abortion clinics, and even by assaulting those who perform abortions. Are Christians permitted to resort to these means? Might such tactics even be obligatory for Christians? Three Biblical principles help to clarify the answer to these questions.

The first principle is that Christians have no Biblical obligation to halt all immoral practices in their societies. The New Testament never charges Christ's church with the duty of establishing righteousness through legislation, let alone through civil disobedience. Very few Christians wish to see people made to conform to all of Biblical morality through the use of force. Even if the government were run exclusively by Christians, most of them would rightly resist any attempt to make Christianity obligatory. They should also resist the attempt to legislate any moral principle that cannot be justified through appeal to the natural order. Virtually all Christians recognize that, even in the absence of special revelation, common grace makes decency possible. Christians are not obligated to impose more than that level of decency within the public square.

Unfortunately, Christians frequently try to justify moral legislation by appealing directly to Biblical revelation rather than natural revelation. This appeal often renders their arguments suspect in the eyes of non-Christians. Of course, Christians can and should develop their own morality by appealing to Scripture. When they enter the public square, however, they are obligated to justify civil laws by some appeal to natural order. This takes hard thinking and careful argument. The failure to do this thinking and to make these arguments is a species of intellectual laziness.

The second Biblical principle pertinent to civil disobedience in the contemporary moral climate is that Christians must submit to all just laws. This is the clear message of Romans 13:1–7. Believers owe this duty to the civil authority, for the authority stands as a minister of God for good. If under any circumstances Christians subvert just laws, they are subverting the very possibility of the kind of ordered society within which Christianity can exist peacefully.

Too often, civil disobedience is employed not to avoid evil but as a form of protest and a way of making political statements. It has become an assertion of power against power, a means of demanding recognition without the trouble of gaining reasoned consent. In the atmosphere defined by unjustified civil disobedience, self-assertion takes the place of civility and reason. At some point, civility collapses and nothing remains but the will to power. At that point, the only way to avoid anarchy is through a totalitarian state. Western civilization has descended far along this path. Baptists must not be among those who hasten the decline.

The third Biblical principle that informs a Christian understanding of civil disobedience in a morally drifting culture is that laws that protect property from trespass are just laws. They protect a fundamental, God-given right, namely, the right to property. To deprive persons of their property without due process is to violate the eighth commandment (Exod. 20:15). To deny persons the use of their property is, in effect, to deprive them of the property itself. Protestors that break trespass laws are guilty of violating both human and divine requirements.

This is no incidental matter. The rights to life, liberty, and property ultimately stand or fall together. To assail any transcendent right is to assail them all. This implies that nonviolent civil disobedience is not qualitatively different from violent resistance. To deny persons the use of their property is to steal from them. Simply because the theft is not conducted at gunpoint does not mean that it is not a theft. The evil of stealing is not negated by the intention of the thieves to prevent a greater evil. In other words, whether someone blocks the entrance to an abortion clinic or sets off a bomb in its lobby, that person is essentially committing the same act, different only in degree. At minimum such a person is violating the eighth commandment, and the theft is rightly condemned by just laws.

In sum, Christians are not permitted to break just laws in order to challenge injustices. Evils such as abortion are certainly unjust, and Christians should strive to alleviate them. Nevertheless, civil disobedience is not the answer.

Churches, Pastors, and Politics

Throughout their history, Baptists have been strongly committed to the separation of church and state. At the same time, they have supported the rightness of the individual Christian's involvement in governmental affairs. Their support has been more than theoretical: Baptists have often served in the military or held public office. Many Baptists think that voting for the correct political candidates is almost a moral obligation. Yet this willingness to become involved in public affair raises potential problems for Baptists, who must decide what boundaries are appropriate for political involvement by individual Christians, for Christian leaders, and for Christian churches.

The Mission of the Church

For Baptists seeking to understand their relationship to the state, a solid understanding of the church's mission is foundational. Like some other Christians, Baptists typically distinguish the mission of the church *as the church* from the obligations of Christians as private individuals. They have often defined the mission of the church by appealing to the Great Commission (Matt. 28:19–20). In this text, the risen Lord Jesus commanded His disciples to make disciples of all nations by baptizing them and teaching them to observe all the things that He has commanded. If these verses can be rightly applied to the church (as most Baptists think they can), then the mission of the church is decidedly spiritual.

Another Biblical text that is important for understanding the mission of the church is Ephesians 4:11–16. In this text, the apostle Paul articulates four tests that can be used to determine the health and success of a church (Eph. 4:13). These tests include unity of the faith, unity of the full knowledge of the Son of God, mature spiritual manhood, and conformity to the full character of Christ. Since these tests define church success, they also define the church's mission. Once again, the church's mission is spiritual.

The New Testament assigns no political mission to the church. Nowhere is the church asked to reform civilization or to capture the social order. Nowhere is it given the job of dominating the political process. The church *as the church* has no political responsibility.

The church does, however, bear a moral responsibility to the world at large (Eph. 5:3–14). The apostle Paul commanded churches not to participate in the works of darkness, but to reprove them (v. 11). These works include sexual immorality, impurity, greed, filthy behavior, foolish speech, and coarse joking (vv. 3–5). Whether through conduct or direct confrontation, Christians are obligated to let the world know what God thinks of such behaviors. God uses this exposure to bring conviction of sin to worldly people and to prepare the way for the proclamation of the gospel (v. 13).

The ministry of exposing the works of darkness may be similar to the phenomenon that Paul mentioned in 1 Corinthians 14:24–25. There he pointed out that unbelievers may be brought under conviction of sin by hearing prophecies in the church. This occurs, he said, when the secrets of their hearts are made obvious so that they feel themselves convicted and called into account.

The gift of prophecy is no longer being given within the church, but the duty to expose and even reprove sin remains. Part of this exposure certainly depends upon Christians living their lives differently from the unsaved around them. Christians must not participate in the works of darkness. Part of this exposure may also involve deliberate verbal rebukes and challenges. Specifically, the ministry of church leaders involves an element of reproving, rebuking, and exhorting—and they are to persevere in this ministry whether it seems to be welcome or even effective (2 Tim. 4:1–5).

In sum, the mission of the church is spiritual in nature. It centers upon the proclamation of the gospel, which is clearly an element in making disciples. It involves observing the ordinances and teaching believers. But it also includes proclamation of all the counsel of God (Acts 20:27), including the exposure of those works that God considers sinful.

Thus, while the church is not called to a political mission, it is called to a moral mission. Sometimes unsaved people prefer wickedness to morality. Sometimes they write laws to protect their immoral conduct. Sometimes politicians are willing to curry favor by passing immoral laws. Under such circumstances, the church's ministry of moral reproof will certainly run afoul of powerful political enemies. When that happens, the church must not be intimidated into abandoning its proclamation of God's displeasure with the works of darkness. Churches and pastors must continue to treat the ministry of exposure and reproof as part of their mission. Preaching morality is not preaching politics, even when morality is being undermined within the political sphere. The church as a church may and should rebuke governors and oppose laws that are at odds with true Biblical morality.

Christian Political Responsibility

The prophet Daniel provides an example of a man of God who served within the government of unbelieving Gentile kings. Many lessons can be drawn from the nature of his service, but one in particular stands out—God judges kings, even unbelieving kings of pagan nations. When Nebuchadnezzar became proud and tried to claim credit for his own accomplishments, God broke his pride by reducing him to insanity (Dan. 4). When Belshazzar in his arrogance defiled the vessels from the temple, God immediately pronounced and executed judgment (Dan. 5). God holds kings accountable for their actions whether they are believers or not.

The obligations of Christian citizens will vary depending upon the nature of the societies within which they find themselves. Believers living under repressive and authoritarian governments may have little opportunity to influence the political process. The Western democracies, however, are constructed around the notions of limited government, separation of powers, checks and balances, and the popular election of officials. Western governments are bound by constitutions and are ultimately answerable to their citizens. This complex of political arrangements means that average citizens exert a direct and substantial influence over national policy. In these nations, votes matter because ordinary citizens, working together, have the power to reshape the entire national direction. Such citizens are not merely the ruled, but also the ultimate rulers.

If God held kings accountable in Biblical times, then He certainly must hold presidents, prime ministers, parliaments, congresses, and courts accountable today. More than that, he must hold individual citizens responsible to execute their political responsibilities rightly, for in the long run, officials can govern only as the people allow. Even the unsaved are accountable, but Christians, who ought to understand God's design for nations, have a special responsibility. Even if they are a minority, they must use their influence within the public square to move their government as far as possible toward just policies—and that means policies that are just as God understands justice.

How should Christians influence their governments? The first and most obvious way is through the proclamation of the gospel. The gospel is the power of God to salvation for everyone who believes (Rom. 1:16). The gospel transforms those who receive it, altering their identity and progressively remaking them in the image of Christ (2 Cor. 5:16–21; Col. 3:8–17). This transformation affects not only the inner life of believers, but also their social relationships (Col. 3:18–25). When the gospel begins to transform enough people within a single society, the society itself will necessarily be altered.

Preaching the gospel is the single most important way in which Christians can influence the civil order, but it is not the only way. Part of the Christian mission involves exposing and even reproving the works of darkness (Eph. 5:3–17). This ministry is not merely the business of the church, but also of individual Christians. Whether through word or deed, Christians have a responsibility to remind the unsaved world that certain ways of living are futile and destructive.

Some ministry of exposure and reproof must precede effective efforts at legislation. In Western societies, laws ultimately depend for their enforcement upon the consensus of the governed. A law that is held up to contempt will eventually be overturned, and those who try to maintain or enforce it will be viewed as oppressors. If they intend to influence society, individual Christians must capture hearts and imaginations as well as legislatures and courts. Moral reality has been worked into the very nature of the created order. Certain patterns of conduct will inevitably produce disastrous consequences for the society that tolerates or encourages them. As citizens, Christian individuals have a duty to point out these consequences and the behaviors that lead to them, showing people the connections and persuading them of the necessity of civil order in these areas.

Beginning with the United States, the Western democracies have chosen a form of order in which government is genuinely "of the people." Consequently, to some extent, every citizen is a ruler. Those who rule cannot escape their duty by simply choosing not to pay attention to their obligations. In other words, in those nations that are governed by participation of the populace, Christians have a duty to use their voice and influence. Because they bear some responsibility for public affairs, they have a duty to seek public justice.

What can Christians do? At the least, they should refuse to support any unjust policy, even (and perhaps especially) when the policy seems financially advantageous. Second, they should consistently exercise their vote—which is not necessarily the same as voting. If no suitable candidate is available, Christians may sometimes choose not to vote, but refusing to vote should be a choice and not mere negligence. Third, many should become involved in the political process by attending their local precinct caucuses. Fourth, some might join the campaign staff of a particularly desirable candidate. Fifth, some may even choose to run for public office. Baptists believe that these are all legitimate areas of Christian involvement.

Often, questions are raised about whether pastors should become active in politics. Such questions may lead to different answers depending on the circumstances. On the one hand, pastors are also citizens and bear the responsibilities of citizens. They are not Scripturally forbidden from voting, campaigning, or even holding office. On the other hand, a couple of warnings should be issued about pastors and politics.

The first and most obvious is that pastors bear a greater responsibility than temporal government. They lead the church of God. This leadership places the care of souls upon their shoulders. They must not allow temporal concerns to blur their focus or diminish their effectiveness as shepherds of God's flock.

Second, when pastors speak to political questions, they must do so as citizens and not as pastors. They must not carry questions of mere politics into their pulpits or ministries. Nor may they attempt to leverage their pastoral prestige into political influence. The fact that a man is a pastor gives him no right whatever to be heard on merely political issues. If pastors try to convert their pastoral authority into political prestige, they may gain a brief increase in civic influence, but they will also dilute the authority of their office, for a pastor *as a pastor* possesses only the authority to explain and apply the Word of God. The moment he begins to exploit his pastoral influence for the purpose of political persuasion, he demeans the Scriptures and damages the true authority of his office.

Of course, pastors have a perfect right and even a duty to address moral questions, even when those questions also happen to be political. Moral instruction is certainly under a pastor's purview, and it is a necessity if the members of his flock are to understand their civic responsibilities. The moral preparation of God's people may be a pastor's single greatest contribution to their civil effectiveness.

Other Civic Activities

Christians, and especially pastors, are often asked to participate in civic events such as offering prayers or delivering addresses at baccalaureate services, official meetings, and public holiday observances. Baptists have rarely thought that these events violated the separation of church and state, though not all pastors are equally comfortable participating in them. As a rule, Baptists have seen these occasions as community activities for which God's favor may be invoked without compromise of the Christian message, even though non-Christians participate in them.

The same may be said of military chaplaincy. Many Baptist ministers have worn their country's uniform as chaplains. Chaplains are noncombatants whose presence in the military is explicitly for spiritual and moral ministry to the troops. While they learn military customs and courtesies, and while they hold military rank, chaplains do not fight and they do not command. In the United States, they are paid by their government, but in effect, they work for the ecclesiastical bodies that endorse them. The military cannot force them to disregard the directives of their endorsing bodies. In other words, they have liberty to serve the Lord without any necessary compromise of their theological beliefs and practices.

Increasingly, however, new pressures are being applied both to military chaplains and to ministers who participate in civic events. They are being asked to keep their prayers and remarks very generic (the code word is *nonsectarian*) so as to avoid giving offense to people of other faiths. For example, Christian ministers are asked not to pray in the name of Jesus. This push toward a generic nonsectarianism is being done in the name of pluralism. Christians in general, and Baptists in particular, are going to have to decide how they will respond to such requests.

From a traditional point of view, a version of nonsectarianism made a measure of sense. Historically, the culture of most Western nations was strongly Christianized. The main debates were between varieties of professing Christianity. In such a situation, words like *God* and *Christ* meant just about the same thing to everybody. Prayers could be offered and general remarks delivered without focusing on the minutiae of the differences between the groups.

That consensus no longer exists. The Western nations have witnessed a sharp increase in the number of adherents to non-Christian religions such as Buddhism, Hinduism, and Islam. They have seen a significant increase in the number of people who, while religious, profess allegiance to no traditional faith or theology at all. They have also experienced a surge in atheism and agnosticism, frequently in quite hostile forms. As a result, the meanings of the most basic terms—words like *God*—are now subject to debate. While Christians still hold a plurality in some places, they cannot assume that they share a common vocabulary with many other people in their societies.

Increasing diversity and increasing hostility to religion have resulted in an impulse to limit all religious expression and conviction to the private sphere. For the moment, individuals are still permitted to hold their private beliefs, but they are pressured not to allow these beliefs to show up in their public lives. To the extent that any public religious expression is offered, it is expected to be kept in the realm of hazy platitudes. Any expression specific enough to offend the adherents of other religions is strictly forbidden. This is the contemporary vision of pluralism.

Baptists have always believed in pluralism, but they have understood it differently. According to their view, religious faith is far too important to be confined to one's private life. Whatever people believe will determine their values and, ultimately, their choices. Baptists have insisted upon the right of soul liberty, even for their theological opponents. They have objected to the use of governmental force in matters of conscience. This means that they have envisioned a civilization in which different religions could exist side by side, each relying on only its powers of persuasion to capture people's belief and loyalty. Baptists have also insisted that all persons must have liberty to express their convictions, whether in private or public. Any attempt to confine religious expression to the private sphere is, in effect, a form of tyranny.

This form of pluralism gives all members an equal right to express their convictions, both privately and publicly. People who pray in public should pray according to the dictates of their faith, not the dictates of an insipid and false pluralism. When rabbis are asked to pray, they should pray like rabbis. When Buddhists pray, they should pray like Buddhists. Muslims should pray like Muslims. Baptists should pray like Baptists—and, with all Christians, Baptists believe they have the right to approach God only in Jesus' name (John 16:23–27).

Of course, no one is so naïve as to think that the phrase, "In Jesus' name, Amen," can simply be tacked onto the end of a prayer like a kind of talisman. The words themselves contain nothing magical. Nevertheless, no one has the right to approach God outside of the authority and name of Jesus Christ. To pray in Jesus' name or some equivalent expression is the appropriate recognition of our authority to address God. (Incidentally, the expression "In *Thy* name," is not equivalent to "in Jesus' name," for Christians do not approach the Father in the name of the Father, but of the Son.) To demand that Christians not pray in the name of Jesus (or equivalent language) is precisely the same as demanding that they not pray at all.

The Baptist understanding of pluralism requires Christians to extend to other religions the same rights that they themselves claim. If Baptists want to pray in Jesus' name, then they cannot object if Muslim imams are asked to pray on civic occasions, nor should they complain when those imams pray like Muslims. While Christians cannot agree with Islam as a system, they can and should respect the right of Muslims and other groups to practice their faith freely, both in private and in public. Genuine pluralism does allow differences and even disagreements, but it insists that disagreements ought to remain respectful.

Difficult Judgments

According to the Baptist understanding of the New Testament, church and state ought to be distinct and separate entities. Churches should rely upon the government for neither enforcement of their position nor support of their institutions. Governments must not use their coercive power to enforce religious matters. Individual Christians are fully entitled to involve themselves in civil affairs, but the concerns of churches are spiritual and moral.

This theory sounds compact and clean, and for the most part it has been. Increasingly, however, the boundaries between state authority and religious freedom are being challenged. While these challenges may sometimes be the result of ill-will on one side or the other, mostly they arise from the changing situation in which Christians find themselves. Baptists of the future will have the responsibility of working through these challenges thoughtfully and carefully.

Government Regulation

Contemporary governments are assuming a larger and larger role in propagating regulations that are intended to promote health, safety, and security for their citizens. Whether enacted as laws or imposed as rules by governmental agencies, these regulations become public policies to which citizens and organizations must conform. The question is to what degree churches must also conform to regulation and public policy, and to what degree they ought to claim exemption as a matter of religious freedom.

Some regulations, such as fire and building codes, are necessary for public safety. The state has an obvious interest in protecting its citizens from predators and bumblers in these matters. It is difficult to imagine how churches could object to being brought under the same regulations as other organizations. For the government to impose these codes is normally no infringement upon the free exercise of religion.

In some instances, however, municipal codes can mask an attack upon churches and religions. Officials can use zoning codes to try to keep some kinds of religions out of their communities. They can also use the permitting process to shut down nearly all construction of churches or other tax-exempt entities. These are abuses of authority that every Baptist should be prepared to challenge, even when they are directed against non-Baptists or even against non-Christians.

Baptists who believe that the office of pastor (and perhaps other positions) should be restricted to males will find that their conviction runs afoul of the spirit of the age. Depending upon how this conviction is articulated and where it is implemented, it may also run afoul of laws and public policies against discrimination. Increasingly, homosexuals are also being granted special legal protections. The responsibility rests upon churches and other religious organizations to raise their voices so that these laws and public policies, if enacted at all, include religious exemptions. Churches and religious organizations must also ensure that they comply with the exemptions in responsible ways.

In general, governments are not violating the separation of church and state when they apply the same regulations to churches that they apply to other organizations, as long as those regulations do not in themselves violate religious convictions. Indeed, it could be argued that for the state to make exceptions for religious organizations would involve granting them a special status. As a rule, churches should seek to conform to regulations that are designed to protect any area in which the state has a legitimate interest as a part of its God-ordained role.

Religious Sedition

Governments have an obvious interest in preventing sedition. The Western democracies guarantee freedom of speech to varying degrees, but they do not guarantee the right to incite or commit acts of violence against lawfully consti-tuted authority. Even the most liberal (in the proper sense) government has the prerogative of prosecuting those who engage in treason.

Separation of church and state is meant to safeguard liberty of conscience. It is not meant as a mask for revolution. One cannot plot the overthrow of one's government in the name of religious freedom. Even under Nero, the apostle Paul commanded deference to public officials (Rom. 13:1–7). Baptists have often confessed their determination to support the governments under which they found themselves, as long as those governments did not require them to violate Christ's commands. They do not countenance the preaching or practice of insurrection under the guise of religion.

Immoral Religion

As a general rule, governments must not interfere with the free exercise of religion. Nevertheless, religions must not be allowed to cross certain moral lines. For example, cults that practice human sacrifice ought to be prosecuted. The right to life is one that no religion should be permitted to transgress. Govern-ments have a duty to prosecute murder, even when murders are committed in the name of religion. The same would be true of cults that involve children in sex rites. For the government to interfere with such practices is no violation of the separation of church and state.

At one time, Mormons practiced polygamy as part of their religion. Some still do. Even if this practice were entirely free and consensual on the part of all who were involved, governments would be right to ban it. One need not hold a specifically Christian morality to understand how destructive the practice of polygamy is to both domestic and civil order. For states to outlaw polygamy is no infringement upon the free exercise of religion as Baptists have understood it.

In short, it is not necessary for a government to allow absolutely all practices under the rubric of religion. Separation of church and state does not commit the government to complete noninterference in matters of faith. When the practices of a religion transgress the boundaries of life, liberty, property, and decency, they move into the territory that God has committed to the authority of the state. Under these circumstances, governments are right to interfere.

The Evaporation of Consensus

From shortly after the Reformation, Baptists have been leading champions of the separation of church and state. They have pushed for both the disestablishment of churches and the free exercise of religion. When they first raised their voices, however, they were living and working in the environment of Christendom. The civilization around them had been molded by Christian categories that were largely imposed by established churches. For most of their history, Baptists have labored in societies that shared a consensus around more-or-less Christian perspectives and values.

Now all Christians find themselves facing a different situation. Christianity is rapidly becoming a minority voice in Western societies. The consensus that was established through centuries of Christendom has largely been replaced by the renewal of paganisms, the intrusion of militant Islam, the stranglehold of secularism, and the growth of postmodern relativism. Liberty of conscience worked well in an environment in which most consciences had been trained by Christian perspectives. Whether it will work equally well in an environment in which most consciences either remain untrained or are habituated to anti-Christian ideals remains to be seen.

One thing is clear. Christians in general, and Baptists in particular, are going to have to adjust their thinking and methods to the new situation. In the future, they will have less and less ability to appeal to the civil power for support of their moral perspectives. Instead, they are going to have to rely to a far greater degree upon the power of persuasion. This places upon them the obligations of thinking well and communicating effectively. They must adapt to being cultural outsiders who speak into their societies. Much of their cultural capital has already been spent.

With the shift in culture, a new possibility looms large. Christians argue for absolutes that are not popular with many people. For example, in Western cultures, sexual liberty has come to be seen as a fundamental right. By voicing absolutes in the area of sexual morality, Christians will be perceived as extreme and intolerant. Indeed, Christians are already experiencing pressure to attenuate their message on issues such as homosexual marriage. As the forces opposed to Christianity continue to flourish, it is possible that Christians who continue to voice their convictions will experience a hostile cultural backlash. At some point, they may lose the opportunity to practice their convictions, even within their own faith communities. Without becoming alarmist, Baptists should begin to think carefully about the appropriate responses that will become necessary as the cultural consensus continues to disintegrate.

Separation of church and state has been a key Baptist distinctive. This distinctive, however, was developed within an environment characterized by a largely Christian consensus. While Baptists remain firmly committed to the separation of church and state, their applications of this idea are being challenged by a new environment. They are likely to find that the separation of church and state will become more difficult to apply wisely in the face of new complications. Consequently, the coming generation of Baptists must devote itself to careful thinking about and sober implementation of this distinctive.

Part Two:

New Testament Order

7 Baptists and Organization

BAPTISTS IN AMERICA trace their roots directly to the first Baptist churches that emerged from English separatism during the middle third of the seventeenth century. From the earliest years, they have wrestled with the problem of finding an organizational pattern that would allow them to work together in cooperative enterprises. Three particular needs have made this problem acute.

First, they have felt the need for interchurch fellowship, encouragement, and accountability. This need arises because Baptist churches must answer several practical questions. Where will a church get its next pastor? How will a minister find his next church? Whose ordination should be recognized as acceptable? From what churches should a congregation accept members, and to which churches should it dismiss them? Whose discipline should a church recognize, and to what extent should the discipline of other churches be respected? To whom should Baptist churches turn when they need help and counsel? From whom should they expect to receive it?

Second, Baptists share a responsibility to train the next generation of pastors for their churches. They must ask themselves how they can produce pastors who combine a profound grasp of Scripture and doctrine with a mastery of the necessary skills for effective ministry. While one might glibly suggest that every church ought to prepare its own pastors, most churches today are not equipped to teach Greek, Hebrew, exegetical skills, systematic and historical theology, and ministry technique. What is true today has been true of most Baptist churches throughout their history. These deficiencies create a problem that Baptist churches must solve together.

Third, Baptist churches often find themselves facing undertakings that are too large or complicated for most individual congregations. Some of these activities (like Christian camping) are pursued because they are useful rather than because they are Biblically mandated. Some, however, are actually essential to the functioning of a New Testament congregation. For instance, a church cannot claim to follow the pattern of the New Testament if it is not engaged in the work of worldwide missions. Yet most churches by themselves are simply not able to send a trained church planter with a family (much less a team of church planters with families) to an unfamiliar country halfway around the world. Sending foreign missionaries is a huge undertaking, well beyond the capabilities of most individual congregations.

Principles of Cooperation

Baptist churches have always tried to respond to these challenges cooperatively. Tasks beyond the ability of the single congregation have typically been accomplished by churches or individuals working together. Baptists, however, do not believe that every form of extra-congregational organization is acceptable. For guidance in structuring their cooperative endeavors, Baptists have historically looked to three New Testament principles.

Congregational Autonomy
The first principle is the autonomy of the individual congregation. Baptists believe that each congregation is self-determining under Christ. They have consistently rejected all schemes that would subject local churches either to external hierarchies or to internal monarchies and oligarchies. Amongst Baptists, the *church* means the members, not the officers or the structure. It is the church itself, the organized members, that possesses decision-making authority under Christ. Biblically, the authority of the congregation is apparent in several ways.

Individual New Testament congregations exercised authority to choose their own servants and to call them into account (Acts 6:1–6; 2 Cor. 8:16–21; Acts 11:12, 18, 22; 14:25–27). The New Testament never depicts any individual imposing officers upon a church without the congregation's consent. Granted, in a couple of instances Paul and Barnabas (Acts 14:23) or Titus, acting under Paul's authority (Titus 1:5), ordained elders. Even in these instances, however, the congregation almost certainly participated in the decision. In New Testament churches, only congregations choose pastors and deacons.

In the New Testament, congregations also exercised authority to receive, exclude, and restore their own members. This authority is seen with special clarity in 1 Corinthians 5, where Paul addressed the problem of scandalous conduct among church members. As Paul wrote, the church was actually dealing with a specific instance of such conduct: a man was cohabiting with his father's wife. The striking thing about 1 Corinthians 5 is that, while Paul instructed the congregation in their duty to disfellowship the erring brother (1 Cor. 5:2–5, 7, 11–13), he himself did not remove the person from the congregation by apostolic fiat. Similarly, Paul did not simply declare a repentant member to be restored to the congregation, but he instructed the congregation in their duty to receive him (2 Cor. 2:4–11). The New Testament contains no examples of pastors receiving or dismissing members on their own initiative. Much less does it show outside officials interfering in matters pertaining to local church membership. This authority belongs to the congregation.

Choosing leaders and disciplining members are the most important decisions that a church can make. If the congregation is qualified to make these decisions, it is qualified to make any decision. By the same token, if no other authority has the right to impose these decisions upon a church, no other authority can rightfully impose any decision upon a church. The autonomy of the individual congregation needs to be nonnegotiable in any form of Baptist cooperation.

Cooperative Ministry

A second principle also guides Baptists in mutual efforts. It is the New Testament pattern of autonomous congregations cooperating with each other. For example, the book of Acts narrates an ongoing exchange between Jerusalem and Antioch, in which the so-called Jerusalem Council (really a local church's business meeting, Acts 15) is only one episode. The churches of Macedonia and Achaia also cooperated in a voluntary endeavor to raise funds for the poor saints at Jerusalem (2 Cor. 8—9).

Not only congregations, but also individual church members, appear to have cooperated for the advancement of New Testament Christianity. For example, members from several local churches participated in Paul's missionary teams. Some of the specific individuals included Barnabas, Silas, John Mark, Timothy, Demas, Secundus, Titus, Gaius, and Aristarchus. These individuals joined and left Paul's entourage at various intervals. Presumably each individual remained accountable to his sending congregation, but the group operated with de facto autonomy. Paul did not request permission from the elders at Antioch before he crossed the Bosphorus into Macedonia. On the contrary, Paul's circle displayed its own kind of organization and accountability. While it reported to churches, it operated independently of their direct oversight. In a sense, this missionary band could be seen as the first parachurch organization.

Voluntary cooperation between churches of like faith and order has good precedent in the New Testament. So does cooperation between members of those churches, even to the point of organizing outside the churches proper. In these episodes, Baptists have found a pattern for their own joint efforts.

Local Church Centrality

The third principle from which Baptists have taken direction in their cooperative work is the centrality of the local church in God's plan for this age. The apostle Paul declared the local church to be the "pillar and ground of the truth" (1 Tim. 3:15). God has not ordained any other institution for the completion of His plan during the present dispensation. Sooner or later, the responsibility for the advancement of the Lord's work must be shouldered by local churches. They must take leadership, and their prerogatives must be respected in any form of interchurch cooperation.

Original Sin

These are the three principles to which Baptists have appealed historically. A fourth principle also ought to be borne in mind, however. It is one that Baptists believe but that they have too often failed to reckon with. This principle is the enduring presence of original sin.

Various schools of theology describe this indwelling sin differently: the sin nature, the flesh, the old man, or idolatrous habits. While they differ over nomenclature, all Baptists recognize that every Christian is engaged in an ongoing war against a persistent tendency to exalt self at the expense of Christ and to gratify temporal appetites at the expense of eternal priorities. Original sin is certain to manifest itself in all human endeavors, and Christian endeavors are not exempt from this rule. Even in Christian organizations one should not be surprised to discover the centralization and abuse of power, the advancement of personal agendas through political machinations, and the attempt to control or manipulate others through indecorous means. In fact, all Christians should be constantly on guard against the temptation to resort to these sins themselves.

For Baptists, some form of mutual effort seems to be unavoidable. Coordinated effort without organization is impossible. Given that some organization is necessary, what form should it take? In answering this question, Baptists have experimented with several organizational structures. Six of the most important structures are described in the following sections.

The Associational Model

From the earliest days of their existence as an identifiable movement in England and America, Baptists have organized associations. The distinguishing characteristic of a Baptist association is that it is a fellowship of churches. In an association, churches choose to organize formally and to act in concert for the achievement of mutual goals.

Properly speaking, Baptist churches do not join an association. They enter into fellowship with it. Membership, as opposed to fellowship, would imply the surrender of some measure of congregational autonomy. In principle, an association can never exercise authority over a congregation.

Since churches cannot join associations, associations are not made up of churches. Instead, associations have their own separate existence and organization. When the association meets, each church that is in fellowship with it sends messengers. Messengers are not the same thing as delegates. A delegate exercises delegated authority to represent his or her church. This authority permits the delegate to speak in the church's name, and whatever agreements the delegate enters into become binding for the church.

This kind of delegated authority would constitute a significant infringement upon church autonomy. It would turn the association into a kind of congress of representatives, and every church would be obligated to obey the decisions of the congress. The result would be a representative form of church government in which each church exercised a voice through its appointed representatives. This is a pretty good description of Presbyterianism, but Baptists have historically rejected the notion of delegated authority as an infringement upon the autonomy of the local church.

Consequently, Baptist churches send messengers and not delegates to associational meetings. Messengers do not represent the churches. They speak only for themselves. Without delegated authority, the messengers cannot obligate the churches. The association can make only those decisions that affect its own business. It cannot exercise any legitimate binding authority over the churches that fellowship with it.

When the messengers report to their churches, each church must decide how far it cares to participate in the decisions of the association. To be sure, the association has the prerogative of establishing its own standards of fellowship. It may (and should) say, "To fellowship with us, you must meet these standards." Each church, however, has the choice to leave the association if a requirement is objectionable.

Associations are organized at several geographical levels. The most common is the local association. A local association usually exists to facilitate fellowship between churches in a single city, county, or similar area. If the scope of the association becomes larger than several counties (for instance, if it includes an entire state), it is often called a *general association* or a *convention*.

Several local associations may be nested within the geographical fellowship of a general association or convention. When this occurs, the local associations are often autonomous bodies rather than simply regions of the general association. The local associations may and probably will have a cordial and fraternal relationship with the general association and with each other, but no organic ties will connect them. A single church may fellowship with several levels of associations, or it may (in principle, though the practice is sometimes awkward) fellowship with more than one association at a given level. In other words, a single church may fellowship with two local associations and a general association, or it may fellowship with two general associations. For example, a church could fellowship with both the Minnesota Baptist Association and the Minnesota Association of Regular Baptist Churches, or it could fellowship with both the Wisconsin Association of Regular Baptist Churches and the Wisconsin Fellowship of Baptist Churches.

Baptist churches may organize associations for a variety of purposes. At minimum, associations can meet for simple fellowship. Usually, however, they organize to pursue some sort of cooperative efforts. Associations often create institutions such as schools or missionary sending agencies. They may also organize institutions for other purposes. These institutions are then held accountable by the association, either directly or through some sort of legal link. In some cases, the association acts as the governing board of the institution. In other cases, the governing board is elected directly by the messengers at the association meeting. In still other cases, the governing board is appointed by the elected officers of the association.

The associational model has been widely employed by Baptist churches. The entire Southern Baptist Convention is organized on the associational principle. The SBC owns and operates its own institutions, as does each of its state conventions. At every level, these conventions are theoretically controlled (at least indirectly) by the messengers from the churches.

The associational model is also clearly represented by the Minnesota Baptist Association, which is the old Minnesota Baptist Convention. During the controversy between modernists and fundamentalists, the state convention broke its ties with the Northern Baptist Convention, abandoning fellowship with the larger organization. The Minnesota Baptist Association operates its own church planting work and until recently owned and operated Pillsbury Baptist Bible College.

The General Association of Regular Baptist Churches and the New Testament Association of Independent Baptist Churches are also examples of the associational model, with one difference. While they are organized and operated as Baptist associations, they do not own or control their own agencies. The situation of the GARBC will be explored later in this chapter. For the moment it is sufficient to note that both the GARBC and the NTAIBC exist primarily to facilitate fellowship among churches.

The associational model offers several advantages for Baptist church cooperation. First, it creates a stable environment for whatever work is being done. The success of the work is not left to the whims of individual members or the prosperity of a single church. Success depends upon the cooperative efforts of local churches through their messengers, and that kind of cooperation enhances stability.

Second, accountability to an association tends to keep the work of the affiliated institutions focused and balanced. Institutions controlled by associations display less tendency to become derailed by individual pet projects. They are also less susceptible to the idiosyncrasies and peculiarities of individual leaders.

Third, in many cases the associational model can make financial support available instantly. This is especially advantageous for missionaries, who often receive support directly from the association or convention rather than having to spend the first years of their ministries raising money. This availability of funds is also helpful for the institutions. The association automatically provides its agencies with a primary base of support.

No one can doubt that these are significant advantages. Nevertheless, Baptists have rejected the associational model as often as they have embraced it. The reason is because associations also bring with them several disadvantages and dangers.

The first disadvantage is that the institutions may end up controlling the association, and the association may end up in de facto control of the churches. The tendency is for the association or its agencies to take over the responsibility of pastoral placement. Any time an agency serves as a gatekeeper between churches and ministers, it gains immense power over both.

A second problem with associations is that the churches often find themselves supporting associational programs and institutions rather than supporting individuals. This is a particular problem for missionaries, most of whom are as eager for the prayers of God's people as for their money. If the missionaries are getting their support directly from the association or convention (perhaps through its cooperative program), their contact with the churches will often be greatly reduced. The churches will find it proportionately more difficult to pray intelligently for, or be meaningfully involved in, the missionaries' work.

The third danger of associationalism is that the association can provide a matrix for transmitting infection from the institutions to the churches. If an institution tolerates political gamesmanship or false doctrine, the association becomes a medium through which the toxins eventually seep into the churches. More than one church fellowship has been led into error through its institutions.

Of course, in theory, a church can break fellowship with an association at any time. Indeed, this freedom to withdraw from an association is usually taken as the absolute guarantee of the church's autonomy. Formally, this liberty is recognized by virtually every Baptist association or convention. Reality, however, is more complicated. In practice, churches often find it difficult to sever their ties to associations and institutions. They become so emotionally (and financially) invested in the association or the agency that they cannot bring themselves to walk away.

A fourth concern with associationalism is that some local churches tend to abdicate duties to the institutions when they ought to be fulfilling those duties themselves. For their part, the institutions are often willing to accept the additional responsibility—after all, it adds to their prestige and makes them more indispensible. This situation can lead to a kind of role reversal in which institutions begin to take precedence over churches.

A final serious problem with associations is their tendency to centralize power. Because an association has its own existence and organization, it provides a power structure that the unscrupulous can use to promote themselves. It also furnishes a mechanism that these people can employ to exert pressure upon the churches. These political maneuvers may lead to informal but nevertheless very real interference with the autonomy of local congregations. The old Northern Baptist Convention was an excellent illustration of this kind of predatory association.

Thus, the associational model presents Baptists with both advantages and disadvantages. At times it has been used very effectively. At other times, it has created havoc among churches. To be fair, the weaknesses of the associational model are sometimes shared with other models of Baptist organization. No structure will ever be entirely safe as long as original sin is in play.

The Service Organization Model

Baptists in America have organized local associations from their earliest days. These associations have helped to facilitate ordinations, the transfer of members, and the mutual recognition of church discipline. Rather early on, however, the associations also showed a tendency to become intrusive. Consequently, when Baptists faced the challenge of organizing at the national level, they did not automatically choose the associational model.

National organization was precipitated by the conversion of Adoniram Judson to Baptist principles in 1812 while traveling to Burma as a Congregationalist missionary. His coworker Luther Rice, who had also converted, agreed to return to the United States to organize support for Judson. Rice envisioned a missionary organization that would be accountable to churches through an associational structure.

Rice, however, was not the only Baptist who had a vision for national organization. Francis Wayland was one of the most prominent Baptists in America. During his ministry he was pastor of the First Baptist Church in America (Providence, Rhode Island) and First Baptist Church of Boston. He was one of the founders of the Newton Theological Institution. For many years he was president of Brown University.

In contrast to Rice, Wayland believed that Baptist missionary work could be carried out best by an organization of individual Baptists. Individuals who were interested in supporting missions could become members of an independent sending agency. These members were, of course, responsible to their own churches, but the churches themselves exercised no direct control over the work of missions. In other words, the missionary organization would be an autonomous institution. Wayland's idea is called the "service organization model."

The debate between Wayland and Rice eventually led to the organization of two large regional bodies. The Southern Baptist Convention, organized on the associational principle, took responsibility for organizing the missionary work in the South. The American Baptist Missionary Union (as it came to be called) operated as a service organization to coordinate missionary work in the North.

Service organizations are autonomous agencies. They can be governed in several ways. Sometimes they are answerable directly to their members. More often they are governed by boards. In some service organizations the members elect the board. In many of these institutions, however, the board is self-perpetuating.

Baptists in the North eventually organized several autonomous agencies. In addition to the American Baptist Missionary Union, they created agencies for home missions, education, publication, youth work, and a variety of other purposes. These agencies all operated separately, though their memberships overlapped significantly. All of the agencies held their annual meetings at the same time and in the same location. These collective gatherings were called the Triennial Convention, or (later on) just the May Meetings.

When the Northern Baptist Convention was organized in 1907, it was promoted as an attempt to bring all of the agencies under a single roof. It also introduced the element of direct church involvement, leading to something that operated much more closely to the associational model. Unfortunately, the Northern Baptist Convention was under the influence of theological liberals from the day of its organization, and the liberals soon used the convention as a platform from which to attempt a takeover of the churches.

Though two centuries have passed since Judson's conversion to Baptist principles, service organizations are still common among Baptists, especially among those who think of themselves as independent. Many of the prominent mission agencies are organized on this model. Examples include the Association of Baptists for World Evangelism, Baptist Mid-Missions, Baptist Church Planters, Continental Baptist Missions, and the Baptist World Mission. Camps are often structured as service organizations. So are most educational institutions such as Clarks Summit University (Clarks Summit, Pennsylvania), Faith Baptist Bible College and Theological Seminary (Ankeny, Iowa), and Central Baptist Theological Seminary (Plymouth, Minnesota).

Occasionally the service organization model can be applied to an entire fellowship. An example is the Fundamental Baptist Fellowship International. This organization used to be called the Conservative Baptist Fellowship, and at that time it had an individual membership that elected officers. Later on, it was reorganized with a self-perpetuating board, but no membership at all (individuals could "identify with" but not join the FBF). Presently it offers membership, but the board is still self-perpetuating. The members do not elect the leadership.

The service organization model offers specific advantages over the associational model. The first is that no organic link exists between the agency and the local church. Consequently, if a local church detects a problem with a service organization, it is able to sever ties and withdraw support from the agency instantly.

Second, this model grants considerable flexibility to churches and individuals. Since service organizations are not supported automatically by an association, they must raise their support from individual congregations and church members. The churches have complete freedom to choose the agencies that they will support.

Third, even though service organizations have no organic accountability, they do respond to the promptings of the churches and individuals who support them. The accountability is informal, but it is real. An agency that displeases a sufficient number of its supporters had better be ready either to recruit a new constituency or to go out of operation.

Significant as these advantages are, the service organization model also presents certain disadvantages. The first is that, however useful the informal ties may be, institutions that are organized on this model have no direct accountability to the churches. The result is that, in their autonomy, these institutions can easily begin to behave as quasi-churches, taking over functions that rightly belong to the local church. Indeed, when churches cooperate with agencies, the lines of control can easily become blurred. One might ask, for example, when missionaries are accountable to the agencies that help them get to the field, and when are they accountable to their sending churches. Agencies and churches have collided more than once over this question.

Second, this model leads to considerable duplication of effort. The same constituency may be served by numerous mission agencies, seminaries, and other institutions. This proliferation of agencies leads to multiplied overhead and unintentional competition between institutions of similar conviction and purpose. Many believe that this multiplication constitutes an unfortunate waste of resources.

Third, under this model, missionaries are usually required to raise their own support, and they may be on the road for years doggedly asking for money in a protracted and exhausting deputation. Nevertheless, the funds must be promised before they can reach the field to which God has called them. Even with support in hand, the labor is not over. Every furlough, the missionary will have a long list of supporting churches, each of which requires a personal report.

Fourth, churches can develop such a sense of loyalty toward a particular institution that the safeguards of this model become illusory. Once this happens, any attempt to withdraw support from or sever ties with the institution will produce considerable trauma within the local congregation. In practice, therefore, whatever evils enter the institutions can end up infecting the churches.

Fifth, some local churches tend to relegate duties to the institutions when they ought to be fulfilling those duties themselves. When an agency has expertise in an area, churches may find it easy simply to let the agency manage that area. For their part, the institutions are often willing to accept the additional responsibility. This can create a kind of role reversal in which institutions take precedence over churches.

Finally, service organizations can provide a platform from which ecclesiastical politicians can seek to control churches. For a variety of reasons, institutional leaders often receive greater respect and deference than local pastors. Unscrupulous leaders can use this power to subvert churches when their pastors fail to support the institution's programs and agendas. One key tool that can be used to control churches is pulpit placement. Often, pulpit committees will look to the leaders of institutions for pastoral recommendations. This gives the executives a considerable say over who actually gets called to pastorates. Ministers who are not loyal to the institution never get mentioned.

Service organizations have a long tradition among Baptists in America. They have proven useful, but sometimes they have also behaved quite destructively. Some of the weaknesses of this model are shared with the associational model and with other models of organization. The next sections will examine several attempts to combine features of the associational and service organization models.

The Approval System

The year was 1934, and the fledgling General Association of Regular Baptist Churches was facing its first crisis. The elder statesman of the GARBC was Oliver W. Van Osdel from Grand Rapids. Since the 1870s he had been active in Northern Baptist circles, where he had become especially prominent in promoting the work of missions. In 1922 and '23, he had helped to create the Baptist Bible Union, an organization whose purpose was to oppose theological modernism. In 1927 the Baptist Bible Union took over control of Des Moines University and in 1929 was brought to the brink of collapse when a student riot closed the university. Now an old man, Van Osdel again stepped forward and led in reorganizing what was left of the Baptist Bible Union into the General Association of Regular Baptist Churches. More than anything, he wanted to see the new fellowship establish a mission board of its own, following the associational model.

Not everyone, however, was encouraged by the prospect of an associational institution. Robert T. Ketcham of Gary, Indiana, was a young leader who had been active in the Baptist Bible Union, and he was now an officer in the General Association of Regular Baptist Churches. Ketcham had been a member of the board when the Baptist Bible Union took over the operation of Des Moines University. He remembered keenly how events at the university had led to scandal, riot, and the collapse of both organizations. Ketcham was afraid that if the young GARBC operated its own institutions, the link between the agencies and the association would prove as poisonous as the tie between Des Moines University and the BBU.

The debate was impassioned. Van Osdel pleaded the cause of missions, insisting that the messengers had a duty to do something about this need. For his part, Ketcham argued against the dangers of agencies that were owned and operated by associations. Probably without realizing it, the two men were replaying the debate between Wayland and Rice over the associational model and the service organization model.

At the end of the debate, the association put Van Osdel and Ketcham in a room together and told them not to come out until they had a solution to the problem. When the two men emerged, they presented a plan that served the GARBC effectively for over sixty years. Their plan eventually came to be known as the "approval system."

By the 1930s, theological liberalism was firmly in control of the Northern Baptist Convention. Consequently, Baptists had started innumerable independent institutions to take over functions that had once been performed by convention agencies. Examples include the Council on Cooperating Baptist Missions (also known as the Mid-Africa Mission and, later, Baptist Mid-Missions), the Association of Baptists for the Evangelism of the Orient (later, the Association of Baptists for World Evangelism), the Sweet Baptist Mission to China, Leonardo Mercado's Mexican Gospel Mission, and the Interstate Evangelistic Association (headed by Harold Strathearn).

These independent organizations were available to the churches, but they were so new and often so small that the churches had little information about them. The churches were not able to judge which institutions merited their support. What Van Osdel and Ketcham suggested was that the GARBC executive committee (later, the Council of Eighteen) should offer to examine these agencies when they were seeking support. In particular the executive committee would evaluate the doctrinal position, organizational structure, and financial stability of each agency. The executive committee would then recommend the agencies that passed this examination.

In effect, the approval system was an attempt to combine the strengths of the associational model with those of the service organization model, while avoiding the weaknesses of both. To satisfy Van Osdel, it was meant to provide a way of making service organizations accountable to churches. To meet Ketcham's concern, it avoided the problem of a formal link between the association and the institutions, permitting the association to sever ties quickly if an institution became an embarrassment.

The approval system attempted to foster greater stability, balance, accountability, and focus than the service organization model. It also attempted to provide a structural guarantee of respect for the choices of individual congregations. After all, the association was not telling churches which organizations to support. The executive committee was merely recommending certain agencies that were worthy of help.

Like the service organization model, the approval system was meant to facilitate the rapid severing of ties if an institution went bad. Since approval was merely an executive recommendation, it could be withdrawn instantly and (it was thought) painlessly. In the early years, the GARBC actually did approve and quickly disapprove a variety of agencies. Furthermore, a variety of agencies sought approval only to drop it later on.

For decades it seemed as if the GARBC had hit upon the ideal compromise between the associational model and the service organization model. When Los Angeles Baptist Seminary strayed toward Pentecostalism, approval was withdrawn until the aberrant theology could be purged (which it was). When Wheaton College agreed to fund a chair of Regular Baptist Theology, it was approved—for one year—until the plan proved unworkable.

Over time, however, the approved agencies came to be regarded (at least popularly) as the property of the association. The Council of Eighteen became reluctant to withdraw endorsement from any institution. Loyalty shifted toward the agencies, and the result was a de facto return to the associational principle.

One reason for this shift was that the visibility of the agencies gave them a disproportionate amount of influence over the business of the association. Agency presidents and representatives became popular speakers who occupied many platforms in the course of a year. Given their exposure, they were well known to many of the messengers. Accordingly, they were easily elected to the Council of Eighteen, where they became the individuals who were approving their own institutions. By the year 2000 the approval system had become so problematic that it was dropped entirely.

The fact is, however, that every fellowship operates some form of approval system. Each group has to have some way of deciding who will be permitted to advertise at its meetings or who will be allowed to publish in its official paper. Whoever makes this decision constitutes an approving body, and whatever criteria are established constitute an approval system. It may be called by another name, but virtually every Baptist organization operates an approval system of some sort. In the GARBC, what once was called *approval* has been replaced by *partnership*, but the function and purpose is much the same.

The GARBC approval system was an attempt to combine the best features of the associational and service organization models. In a sense, it was a stroke of genius. It worked well for more than half a century. The problems that it faced were due, not so much to flaws within the system, as to the presence of original sin on the part of the people who made use of it. Original sin is a problem that no Christian or Christian organization ever escapes.

The Preachers' Fellowship

The approval system of the GARBC was one attempt to split the difference between the associational model and the service organization model. It was not the only such attempt, however. Another model of cooperation that has been widely employed among self-styled Independent Baptists is the so-called "preachers' fellowship."

The notion of a preachers' fellowship traces to a spat between J. Frank Norris and the GARBC. Norris had been one of the most public leaders in the old Baptist Bible Union, the parent organization of the GARBC. After the BBU was reorganized in 1932, Norris saw an opportunity to perpetuate his influence. For several years he attempted to insinuate himself into the leadership of the newly reorganized association.

Norris was not accustomed to asking for permission, and it seems to have escaped his notice that an association is a fellowship of churches. Aligning with an association requires church action, not merely a pastoral decision. Norris, however, showed up for the GARBC annual meeting with forged messenger credentials from Temple Baptist Church in Detroit. He had simply filled out the credentials on his own initiative, never asking the church for authorization. Whether a deliberate fraud or merely an oversight, when his action was exposed, Norris found himself discredited within the GARBC.

Norris's reaction was to found a new organization, the World Fundamental Baptist Missionary Fellowship. The name was later shortened to the World Baptist Fellowship, and it differed from the GARBC in its form of organization. While the GARBC was a fellowship of churches, the World Baptist Fellowship aimed to be a fellowship of pastors.

Eventually three great preachers' fellowships were formed. A 1950 split in the WBF resulted in the formation of the Baptist Bible Fellowship, headquartered in Springfield, Missouri. Shortly thereafter, the Southwide Baptist Fellowship was called into being. Of the three, the Southwide Baptist Fellowship had the loosest organization. It was never much more than an annual meeting. The WBF and the BBF tend to operate much like each other. Their voting membership consists of the pastors of churches that support the fellowship's missions and schools. Each church gets one vote at the fellowship meeting, and that vote is to be cast by the pastor or his appointee.

The WBF and the BBF both operate as their own mission agencies—indeed, the mission structure is integral with the structure of the fellowship itself. Preacher's fellowships may also own and operate their own schools. For example, Arlington Baptist College in Arlington, Texas, is owned and operated by the World Baptist Fellowship. Baptist Bible College in Springfield, Missouri, is owned and operated by the Baptist Bible Fellowship, as is Boston Baptist College in Boston, Massachusetts. The fellowship may also approve independent schools, much like the GARBC used to do. At any rate, each preacher's fellowship strongly identifies with specific educational institutions. The Southwide Baptist Fellowship looked historically to Tennessee Temple College as its most important training center, though other big churches have launched competing schools over the years.

In short, the preachers' fellowship effectively reduplicates the associational model with one important change. The churches do not make decisions. Only the pastors do. This change is in keeping with the philosophy of leadership that dominates those fellowships.

The preachers' fellowship offers certain advantages over the other models of organization. These organizations provide an effective and streamlined way of getting support from churches into the hands of missionaries and institutions. Because control is maintained by the pastors, decisions can usually be made relatively quickly. Since the few who control the organization are its most highly focused and committed constituents, the organization's distinctives are not as likely to become diluted over time.

Advocates of preachers' fellowships have typically argued that this structure best respects the autonomy and centrality of the local church. They believe that independent service organizations sacrifice the church's centrality, while associations can usurp the church's autonomy. One wonders, however, whether the preachers' fellowships do a better job of safeguarding these concerns. A college that is owned by the fellowship is still not under the control of the churches, even if it is under the control of the pastors. Furthermore, as the career of Norris himself illustrates, an unscrupulous pastor can find plenty of ways to coerce unwilling churches and preachers.

In fact, preachers' fellowships have fostered a perspective that confers celebrity status upon the most important leaders. While exceptions do exist, the tendency among the fellowship pastors is to see themselves as "the Lord's anointed" with special powers to govern the churches. These preachers sometimes develop a contemptuous attitude toward average church members, toward missionaries, toward teachers in colleges and seminaries, and even toward other pastors who are less visibly successful.

The preacher's fellowships also tend to fall prey to doctrinal and methodological instability. This is especially a problem when limited pastoral accountability is coupled with mediocre theological proficiency. Quirks that capture the imaginations of the preachers will quickly become the status quo of the organization—and may result in a purge of the institutions to rid them of dissidents.

Do these problems spring necessarily from the structure of the preachers' fellowship, or are they the consequence of other attitudes that fellowship pastors happen to hold? This is not an easy question to answer, but possibly the structure and the problems stem from the same source—an incorrect view of pastoral authority. At any rate, few, if any, problems are unique to this form of organization. Ultimately, the drawbacks found in the preacher's fellowships are much the same as those of the other organizational models.

The same liabilities seem to crop up in all of the previously mentioned forms of organization. This fact has led some Baptists to insist that no permanent structures should be established for ongoing cooperation between churches and believers. Instead, they have suggested two other patterns of organization. The next section will examine one of these: the ecclesiastical conglomerate.

The Ecclesiastical Conglomerate

Baptists have looked for ways to cooperate in performing certain tasks because most churches are not in a position to perform those tasks individually. Not many churches are capable of sponsoring their own camps, of coordinating their own missionaries on the field, or of providing full training for the next generation of leaders. What most individual churches cannot do alone, Baptists have attempted to accomplish through cooperative efforts.

In a few cases, however, large churches actually do have enough members, money, and competence to perform these tasks for themselves. Individual Baptist churches sometimes do own and operate their own agencies or institutions. Sometimes the church itself acts as the agency.

Usually, churches that perform one of these tasks will perform others as well. A single church that acts as a missionary sending agency will also operate a Christian school, a camp, a college, a publishing house, or a seminary. What emerges could be called the "single-church model" of church cooperation, except that it is not a usually a form of cooperation at all. In this model, one church simply performs the necessary tasks for itself. It becomes, so to speak, a self-sufficient, self-sustaining ecclesiastical conglomerate.

There are many examples of such Baptist conglomerates. Historically, the Weniger brothers built a conglomerate, including a seminary and conference center, around Hamilton Square Baptist Church in San Francisco. Lee Roberson's conglomerate, erected around Highland Park Baptist Church in Chattanooga, Tennessee, featured a college, a seminary, and a church-planting network that resulted in dozens of branch congregations around Chattanooga—all of which were governed from the home campus. Within certain circles, larger churches often move toward creating their own institutions.

A modification of conglomerate structure is to create institutions that are technically independent, but closely bound to a particular local church through moral commitment and financial dependence. This form of organization has also been pursued by contemporary Baptists. For example, Central Baptist Theological Seminary of Minneapolis is technically an independent service organization, but in reality the seminary could not exist without the hospitality of Fourth Baptist Church.

Any church that chooses to organize and sponsor its own work is well within its rights. In fact, of all Baptist models of organization, this is the one that is most centered upon the local church. This is the only model in which institutions have direct accountability to a particular local congregation. If the agency begins to deviate, the church can instantly call it into account.

Operating its own institutions brings definite benefits to the church. Institutional personnel become heavily involved in the ministry of their local congregation. Missionaries who come home on furlough may function as church staff members (what better way could anyone think of to promote missions?). College or seminary professors are able to exercise their gifts through visible, hands-on involvement in the ministry of the assembly. This model also provides a church with the most direct and personal interest in the lives and ministries of its personnel, and especially of its missionaries.

The ecclesiastical conglomerate also presents a number of disadvantages, however. The first and most obvious is that few churches are able to finance and staff such efforts by themselves. In almost every case, the sponsoring church ends up appealing to other churches for at least some help and support. This is most obvious in the case of missionaries. While many larger churches send their own missionaries to the field, almost none of them provide full support for the missionaries that they send. In almost every instance, the missionaries will be found asking other churches for financial assistance in getting to their field of service.

The same is true of educational institutions such as colleges and seminaries. Not many church-operated schools are prepared to fully fund their students, and not many of them admit only students who are members of the church. In almost every case, students receive some support from other churches, and they certainly come to the school from the memberships of other churches.

Of course, Baptists do not object to having one church support the personnel and activities of another church. Arguably, the New Testament provides a pattern for just such activity. The moment that a church recognizes that it cannot carry the whole burden by itself, however, it is back to cooperative effort. That, in turn, raises once again the whole question about the best way to organize for Baptist cooperation. The New Testament provides a clear pattern for one church to send support to another church, but it does not provide quite as clear a precedent for one church to accept support, students, and missionary candidates from other churches while refusing accountability to those churches.

In fact, smaller churches that look to ecclesiastical conglomerates for help are usually left with little or no real voice in their operations. Not unreasonably, the conglomerate may feel that it has been more than accommodating by simply making its services available to smaller congregations. Those who manage the conglomerate may wonder (sometimes with indignation) at the ingratitude of the little people who want a voice in how things are run.

The existence of the conglomerate may even hinder the development of cooperative endeavors. Without meaning to, a large and successful church may push aside the cooperative labors of other congregations. For example, missionaries who are looking for a sending agency may be attracted by the financial benefits of an ecclesiastical conglomerate, leading to the demise of cooperative missionary efforts among smaller congregations. The conglomerate may become a kind of "ministry magnet" that unintentionally suppresses other ministries.

When a conglomerate reaches this point, it is poised to become a danger. It is now in a position to ignore its sister congregations, or, even worse, to begin dictating to them. A successful conglomerate becomes a clearing house for pastorless churches and churchless pastors. Whoever controls pulpit placement can in reality control the policies of the churches.

The close tie between church and agency inherent in the conglomerate also creates internal problems for the church. Usually, the agency brings to the church a corps of highly trained, very capable employees. Exactly because they are capable, however, these leaders may be viewed as a threat to the balance of power within the congregation. Not surprisingly, the more politically driven conglomerates usually take measures to limit their influence, often by restricting their privileges as members of the church. Even worse for the church, if some theological or moral problem develops within the institution, the church cannot readily sever ties with the problem organization. Thus, agency problems almost always become church problems.

Many ecclesiastical conglomerates have attempted to deal with this dynamic by limiting the power of the agency and its employees within the church. Sometimes agency employees are forbidden from holding office in the church. They may not even be allowed to vote or to have a voice in the church's business. While one can sympathize with the rationale that leads to such measures, they constitute fairly clear violations of the soul liberty and priesthood of the believer as well as of congregational polity. They indicate a predatory tendency on the part of the conglomerate. A conglomerate that is willing to use its power to suppress its own people internally will usually become willing to use its power to push and shove other congregations externally.

Of course, not every conglomerate behaves in a predatory fashion, and predatory behaviors are certainly not unique to conglomerates. They can be found in any form of Baptist organization. Some ecclesiastical conglomerates have provided significant blessing for the Lord's people. We should not be naïve, however. As with every model of Baptist organization, the potential for abuse does exist.

The Ad Hoc Model

Baptists have worked together to accomplish a variety of goals. In order to work together, they have created different kinds of organizations and erected different sorts of institutions. Some Baptists, however, have questioned whether all of the institutionalism is necessary or even healthy. They have reasoned that most of the work can be left to individual people or congregations. They have suggested that where Baptists must cooperate on a scale larger than the local church, their cooperation should take the form of simple, ad hoc endeavors. Few or no permanent agencies or institutions should be created outside the local church.

Certainly Baptists do cooperate in ad hoc ways. Sometimes these occasional efforts are prompted by individuals. Other times they are prompted by churches. For example, a group of pastors may decide to pool the resources of their churches to put together a conference to address a particular theme. Or a particular church may appeal to sister congregations to help in meeting the urgent needs of a missionary. These forms of ad hoc cooperation occur regularly.

An instance of ad hoc cooperation occurred in 2005, when Hurricane Katrina devastated parts of the Gulf Coast. Members of a church in Illinois saw an opportunity for ministry to the victims of the disaster. The church, which was not large, made an appeal to other Christians and churches to help it while it helped the victims. Later on, the church requested assistance again as it attempted to minister to people who were affected by the mass shooting at the University of Northern Illinois. In both instances, other Baptists responded to the appeals for help. These were genuine examples of cooperative efforts. No permanent structures, agencies, or institutions were erected, however. When the job was done, no ongoing organization remained.

The ad hoc (informal, limited, impromptu) model offers distinct advantages as a form of Baptist cooperation. The first is that, under many circumstances, ad hoc cooperation can be evoked quickly and directed toward immediate, pressing concerns. No special policies and procedures have to be drafted, no boards have to be convinced, no meetings have to be called, and no votes have to be taken (except the meetings and votes of individual churches when they choose to participate). This makes for very flexible organization.

A second advantage of the ad hoc model is that only those who are interested in the immediate goal get involved. For that reason, the people who are directing the endeavor are likely to be very responsive to the wishes and suggestions of the cooperating churches and individuals. Everything is immediate and personal, and for that reason the ad hoc model tends to create a high degree of short-term investment and accountability.

Third, the ad hoc model creates no enduring organizations. Without organizations, there are no wheels to be turned, no strings to be pulled, and no ladders to be climbed. The possibilities for political struggles and power plays would seem to be minimized. This advantage may be the most important of them all.

Still, the ad hoc model also presents some disadvantages. Even some of the advantages turn out to be more ephemeral than they might seem. The reason is simple: no cooperation ever occurs without organization. The ad hoc model eliminates permanent institutions, but in the place of institutions it looks to entrepreneurial leadership. That is not necessarily bad, but it does result in two negative consequences for those who limit themselves to this form of organization.

First, entrepreneurial endeavors often lack the stability and stamina to accomplish large, long-term objectives. Almost by definition, sustained efforts require sustained organization. If the effort goes on long enough or grows large enough, what starts out as ad hoc organization will almost irresistibly transform itself into permanent institutionalism. If it does not, the effort will begin to falter.

Second, some individuals are better equipped to lead entrepreneurial efforts than others. People naturally begin to look to these individuals as the ones who consistently initiate and promote ad hoc efforts. Even if no permanent structures are created, power tends to gravitate toward the entrepreneurs. Even in ad hoc and informal relationships, a pecking order will develop. Ultimately, even the ad hoc model involves a system, however informal, that can be manipulated. Power can still be asserted and even abused. In other words, ad hoc organization is not a magic bullet against ecclesiastical politics.

In fact, precisely because no structure exists, restraining the abuse of power may become more difficult. When no permanent organization exists, neither do the mechanisms through which mistreated parties can pursue discipline or censure against abusive leadership. Where no offices exist, no one can be removed from office, no matter how flagrant the abuses.

The ad hoc model certainly has its place. It is one way of implementing the New Testament pattern that reveals Christians and churches working together.

It is certainly not the only way, however. And it is no warranty against ecclesiastical politics and power mongering.

Lessons on Organization

Baptists have experimented with several forms of organization. Churches and individuals have worked together in associations, in autonomous service organizations, under the approval system, through preachers' fellowships, in church-sponsored agencies, and on a simple ad hoc basis. They have had centuries of experience with these forms of organization. They ought to have learned certain lessons by now.

For example, they ought to have learned something about institutional loyalty. People love to attach their loyalty to bricks and mortar. Barring that, they will fasten their loyalty to an individual or an organizational structure. The actual nature of the structure does not seem to matter much. People can be as loyal to a service organization as they can to a convention. They can be as loyal to an entrepreneur as they can to the CEO of a conglomerate.

Assuming the best, any organization that Baptists create will be founded on sound principles. The loyalty of the founders will be to those principles. As the organization increases in age, size, wealth, and influence, however, it will begin to create a certain attraction to itself. People will begin to transfer their loyalty from the founding principles to the organizational structure itself.[1]

As this transfer takes place, the organizational structure can provide a shelter for doctrinal deviation or immoral conduct. Loyalty to the organization comes to be perceived as loyalty to truth. Leaders who promote the organization effectively are granted certain exemptions from accountability. That is one way in which ecclesiastical politicians maintain their power within Baptist organizations.

Carnally ambitious individuals are able to use any structure or any position to leverage themselves into power. The form of organization does not much matter. Any organization at all, even informal organization, provides a venue for climbers.

Once climbers have entrenched themselves in positions of power, abuse is almost inevitable. The leadership of the organization begins to perceive questions as challenges and challenges as opposition. Whether the power structures

---

1. This insight is borrowed from Dr. George Houghton of Faith Baptist Bible College and Seminary, who used to articulate it in his courses on church history.

are formal or informal, they can be used against the perceived opposition. Those whose loyalty is genuinely to the founding principles of the organization are faced with three wretched choices. First, they can simply walk away and start over again—but starting over is no guarantee that the same thing will not happen. Second, they can stay in the organization and quietly go about their business—the very thing that abusive leaders hope they will do, for quiet loyalists really make up the backbone of abusive power. Third, they can initiate action against the abusive leadership, which will inevitably precipitate an internecine war and transform the entire organization into a politically charged institution.

Given these risks, why bother with organization at all? Why not simply retreat into local churches and do the work of God? Could complete and actual independence be the answer? This alternative also presents problems.

First, complete independence will severely restrict what most churches are able to accomplish. How do they intend to sustain missionaries on the field? How do they intend to train their next pastor? Perhaps some churches will be able to accomplish these objectives, but many will not.

Second, creating an independent church is more difficult than it sounds. If any members join the church from outside, they will bring baggage with them. They will have attended this or that college. They will know this or that missionary, sent to the field through this or that agency. They will listen to recordings of this or that preacher. Even if the membership of the church is restricted to new converts, they are going to pick up books or hear religious broadcasts that introduce outside elements into the congregation.

Autonomy is not independence. While Baptists can and should have autonomous churches, none of these churches are truly independent. Given membership transfers, pastoral exchanges, shared challenges, and the influence of mass-produced Christianity, cross-pollination between churches is inevitable. Churches and parachurch institutions interact with one another continually. No church can avoid the intrusion of influences from outside the congregation (even the churches of the New Testament could not avoid these influences). Complete independence is an illusion. The only answer is to have a trained congregation that is mature and discerning enough to look out for itself.

Given the presence of original sin, Baptists can expect to meet with disappointments in all institutions, whatever organizational model they employ. Therefore, they should regard all institutions (whether associations, preachers' fellowships, conferences, conventions, missions agencies, seminaries or colleges) with a measure of suspicion. They should never drop their guard.

Regardless of which model Baptists follow, they should recognize that they are building institutions in the absence of much New Testament precedent. Consequently, Baptists should hold their organizations with trembling hands. They should be prepared to discard or destroy them quickly when necessary. Institutions are useful only as means to an end, not as a necessary implementation of New Testament polity. Baptists should never confuse their agencies with their churches.

The institutions that become politicized most quickly and most viciously are the ones that tie participation in decision making to financial support. When these institutions become doctrinally or morally aberrant, churches or individuals may withhold financial support. By withholding finances, these people or churches automatically lose their voice in setting the organization's policies. They are excluded from the opportunity to help correct the problem. Such institutions generally end up being run by the people with the least conscience.

The most important lesson is this. Original sin is at work in all human endeavors. For that reason, no structure will provide a permanent safeguard against the infections of doctrinal deviation or moral misconduct. The participation of people with integrity is the only bulwark against the deterioration of both agencies and churches.

Cooperative organizations are never entirely safe. If the right lessons have been learned, however, and if an attitude of vigilance is always present, they can be a source of significant blessing. Even the churches of the New Testament found them useful, as in the case of Paul's missionary entourage. Such agencies can provide the mechanism that is necessary for Baptists to work together in accomplishing more than any single church could accomplish alone.

8 Church Councils

SOME BAPTIST CHURCHES like to call themselves independent, but no congregation is ever completely independent. The decisions and actions of one church may affect many others. Each congregation will be influenced, not only by other churches, but by associations, fellowships, itinerant preachers, mission agencies, publishing houses, colleges, seminaries, religious broadcasters, and other organizations to which its members are exposed. Avoiding all of these connections is neither possible nor desirable.

The New Testament ideal is not for churches to be independent, but to be autonomous. Under Christ, each church is governed by its own congregation. No external hierarchy or organization has the right to set policy for a Baptist church, and each church must determine its own degree of involvement with leaders and organizations outside its own membership.

The combination of autonomy and interdependence creates certain weaknesses for Baptist churches. Working together can seem cumbersome in comparison to the streamlined and tightly managed structures of some other denominations. Decisions that affect multiple churches can be complicated to make and impossible to enforce. Nevertheless, Baptists have found that the combination of interdependence and autonomy also brings certain strengths as they work together. One is that individual churches and their members tend to feel a greater degree of ownership and interest in their overall ministry. Another is that churches, while acting autonomously, are nevertheless able to call upon one another for assistance and counsel.

Occasionally, churches will face challenges that exceed the wisdom of the individual congregation. Also, they may be called upon to make decisions that they wish to be recognized by sister congregations. Under such circumstances,

Baptist churches commonly call upon one another for advice. The normal mechanism that churches use for seeking and offering advice is to call a council of messengers from churches of like faith and order. The following discussion will offer a description of how a Baptist church council works. It will also survey the occasions upon which Baptist churches most frequently call for councils.

Organization of Church Councils

A Baptist church calls a council only when it wants advice. When a council has been called, its only function is to offer advice. Councils have no legislative powers. They do not possess the authority to enforce their decisions. The only power that a council can exercise is the power to recommend. Once it has offered its recommendations, the church that called the council may either accept the council's advice or reject it.

Church councils are not standing bodies. They are called only to address specific situations. They come into existence, hear the situation, and offer their advice. As soon as they have made their recommendations, church councils are dissolved. Among Baptist churches, the same council can never meet twice.

Normally only a church can call a council. As in other aspects of Baptist polity, councils are assembled by action of the church that wishes to receive advice. The congregation will agree to call for a council to meet at a particular place, date, and time. When it issues the call, the church will specify the situation that the council will be asked to address. The clerk of the host church will then contact other churches of like faith and order, to notify them of the council.

Usually each church is invited to send its pastor or pastors, plus a stated number of members. Typically the number invited from each church is small (perhaps two members plus the pastor) so that the council does not become unwieldy. Those who respond to the invitation are called *messengers* of their churches. They should not be labeled *delegates*, because they carry no delegated authority.

The host church must plan sufficient time for the council to hear and discuss the business for which it has been called. Ordinarily, a council meets for at least half a day. Since many of the messengers may travel a considerable distance, the host church should plan to serve at least one meal (lunch for a morning council or supper for an afternoon council). Otherwise, the council members pay their own expenses to attend.

After the messengers arrive at the host church, they must form themselves into a council before they can proceed to hear the business for which they were called. A standard format exists for organizing a council, and (with some variation) it follows several steps. Usually the senior pastor of the host church will greet the messengers and introduce this process. In the absence of a pastor, the chairman of the deacons or some other church leader can provide the initial coordination.

First, the clerk of the host church will read the record of the church's action in calling for the council. The clerk will then call the roll of those churches that were invited to send pastors and members to the council. These messengers become the deliberative body during all subsequent steps.

Next the messengers will nominate and elect a temporary moderator for the council. Once elected, the temporary moderator assumes the chair and then receives nominations and presides over the election of a temporary clerk. This temporary clerk immediately begins to maintain the written record of the council.

Third, the temporary moderator receives nominations for the permanent moderator and then the permanent clerk. Not uncommonly, the temporary moderator and clerk are asked to continue in these tasks. Once these officers have been chosen, they assume their roles for the duration of the council. The council then votes to seat itself, after which it is in session. Sometimes guests are also present at the request of the host church. The council may choose to seat some or all of these as messengers in the council, provided they are members in churches of like faith and order.

Occasionally a host church will seek to appoint its own moderator for the council. This is almost always a mistake. The council is a temporary body, but it is an autonomous body. It is called by the host church, but it must be able to make its own decisions if its advice is to be of the best quality. Any pressure from the host church, or any attempt to sway the outcome of the council, is likely to be ill received by the council. If the church has already determined what it wishes to do, it has no reason to call the council.

Another issue that some councils face is the presence of individuals who are not members in churches of like faith and order. Sometimes pressure is applied to seat these people as messengers, often for sentimental reasons. Councils should resist this pressure. To advise a Baptist church, one must understand the principles and values that govern Baptists. A person who does not share baptistic convictions or understand Baptist polity is in a poor position to offer counsel. Furthermore, the advice that councils offer to churches is a crucial mechanism for maintaining the continuity of New Testament order as Baptists understand it. People who are not committed to upholding that order cannot help to fulfill the responsibilities of the council.

Once the messengers have been seated, the council may proceed with its business. Different kinds of business require rather different formats, but the council's responsibility is always to learn enough to be able to offer sound advice to the host church. Normally the council will begin with a time during which it examines the matter for which it was called. Often guests and members from the host church will be present during this time. When the messengers believe that they have adequate information, they will vote to go into executive session. Guests and church members will be dismissed from the room, and the messengers will deliberate the matter under consideration. The council will draft its advice in the form of recommendations that will be communicated to the church. Once its recommendations are complete, it will end the executive session and invite the guests and church members back into the room.

The council's clerk has the job of reading the recommendations to the church. Naturally, the recommendations are also supplied to the church as part of the written record of the council. In the case of ordination and recognition councils, one recommendation is usually that the host church publish the results of the council (at least if the results are favorable).

When it has completed its recommendations, the council votes to dissolve. Once this vote passes, the council ceases to exist. It cannot be called back into session. If the church needs further advice, it must call for the formation of another council.

Types of Church Councils

Historically, Baptist church councils have been called for three sorts of occasions. Each occasion results in a particular kind of council. Only one kind of council is common today. Another is infrequently called. The third is called very rarely. In addition to these three ordinary councils, Baptists have sometimes been known to employ a fourth type of council, though its legitimacy is suspect. A survey of these four types of councils follows.

Ordination Councils

By far the most common occasion for calling a church council has been for the ordination of a minister. Today, ordination councils are the only type of council that most Baptist churches ever call. Though most councils have gone out of use, ordination councils are still held regularly among virtually every variety of Baptist churches.

In spite of its name, an ordination council cannot actually ordain a minister. Among Baptists, only local churches possess the authority to ordain. The council can do nothing to add to the church's power, nor can it lessen the church's authority. Unless a candidate is ordained by a particular congregation, he cannot function as a Baptist minister.

If a Baptist church has the authority to ordain, why should it call a council? The primary answer to this question can be summed up in one word: *advice*. Before a man is set apart by ordination to the gospel ministry, the church must be sure of his Christian experience, his character and qualifications, his call to ministry, his giftedness, and his doctrine. The church will gain a good overall impression of these matters in its experience with the candidate, but to be sure of his qualifications, it usually wishes to subject him to a specific examination. A council of pastors and brothers in Christ from churches of like faith and order can provide valuable assistance and advice in conducting this examination.

A second reason for calling an ordination council has to do with the portability of ordination. In this respect, ordination differs from licensing. A church may license a man as a minister to improve his gifts, but the license is temporary, and it is tied to his membership in that particular congregation. If he moves his membership to another church, he loses his license. Ordination, however, does not expire, and it is not tied to membership in the ordaining church. When an ordained minister moves between churches, he does not need to be reordained. The new church simply accepts his ordination. It can feel comfortable receiving a minister from another church because a Baptist minister is almost always examined, not simply by the particular congregation that ordains him, but also by an entire council of pastors and Christian brothers from churches of like faith and order. The recommendation of the council is what makes lifelong ordination possible among autonomous Baptist churches.

During the council, the messengers will first examine the candidate for his Christian experience and his call to ministry. They will want to hear his testimony of salvation and baptism. They will want to know why he wishes to be a minister. They will often ask what he plans to do if the council does not recommend him or if the church does not ordain him. While Baptists differ over what they mean by a call to ministry, all agree that, to be ordained, a minister should experience some sense of specific vocation.

If the candidate is married, the messengers will also want to hear from his wife. They will not ask her detailed doctrinal questions, but they will want to listen to her testimony of salvation and baptism. They will also want to know whether she supports her husband's desire for and sense of call to the ministry.

Once the council has questioned the candidate concerning his Christian experience and his call to the ministry, it will turn its attention to his doctrine. Customarily, the candidate prepares a written doctrinal statement for the council. Due to time constraints this statement cannot go into great detail, but it should be comprehensive. Copies should be available for each member of the council. Sometimes the church will mail copies of the statement to the participating churches before the council so that messengers can read it ahead of time. More frequently, the candidate will be asked to read his statement aloud, section by section. In some cases, the candidate will prepare a detailed statement but also include a shorter summary for each section. He will read only the summary, but the messengers will skim the rest of the section.

Typically, the sections of the statement will follow the ten traditional divisions of systematic theology, namely, the doctrines of Scripture, God, Christ, the Holy Spirit, angels, humanity, sin, salvation, the church, and last things. After the candidate presents each section, the messengers are free to ask any relevant question over that area of doctrine. Their job is to find out what the candidate knows and believes. They also will try to find out what he does not know.

The purpose of the council is not to instruct the candidate. The council is not an occasion for the messengers to argue with the candidate or with each other (though both are common enough at ordination councils). The purpose of the council is to find out what the candidate believes so that it can make an appropriate recommendation to the church. The moderator of the council has the responsibility of not allowing the council to get bogged down in controversy or unnecessary detail. He also has the responsibility to protect the candidate from irascible messengers.

The moderator's task is sometimes harder to perform than it sounds. Part of what the council does is to ensure the doctrinal integrity of the candidate and, consequently, of the churches to which the candidate will minister in the future. To do this, the messengers have to be able to ask hard questions. Every Baptist fellowship has its own areas of controversy, and these areas are bound to surface in ordination councils. The messengers have a right to know that the candidate has thought about the issues. They also have a right to know where he stands. Whether positive or negative, their recommendation to the church will be based partly upon his answers. When they have found out what the candidate knows and believes, however, the council needs to move on with its business.

As they are examining the candidate's doctrine, the messengers will also examine his practice. They will ask what he would do in a wide variety of situations. Some of these questions do not fit neatly under any of the doctrinal categories, so the moderator usually opens the floor for general questions after all ten doctrinal areas have been covered.

After the candidate has been examined, he and his family will be dismissed temporarily from the meeting so that the council can examine the candidate's character and giftedness. This examination is usually conducted by hearing the testimonies of people who have known the candidate, either in his present ministry or in previous situations. In the case of younger candidates, one or more teachers who helped to train him will often say something about his theological acumen. Deacons or other members of the church may testify as to his effectiveness in ministry. Through these testimonies the messengers will gain understanding of the candidate's strengths and weaknesses.

Once the messengers have heard testimony about the candidate's character and giftedness, the council will go into executive session. All guests and church members will be dismissed so that the messengers can discuss their findings in privacy and make a decision about what to recommend to the church (the decisions of the counsel are normally made by majority vote after deliberation). A variety of recommendations is possible. If serious flaws are found, the council may simply recommend that the church not ordain the candidate. If the candidate seems promising but is ill prepared, then the council may recommend a delay in ordination until the candidate has made up certain deficiencies. If the candidate is somewhat better prepared but still deficient, the council may recommend that the church proceed with the ordination as long as the candidate seeks further instruction in certain areas. Of course, if the candidate is both qualified and prepared, the council may straightforwardly recommend that the church proceed with the ordination.

The council can also express its opinions on subsidiary matters. For example, when candidates are especially well prepared, the messengers may commend them on their knowledge of Scripture and the system of faith. If the council recommends that the church proceed with the ordination, it may also recommend that the church publish its action through local news venues (occasionally the council takes this responsibility upon itself). The council may recommend that an offering be received to assist the new minister in purchasing his library. Very frequently the council will move to express its appreciation for the calling church, recognizing that councils are not obligatory and that serving as a messenger in a council is a privilege as well as a duty.

After the council has completed its deliberations and drafted its recommendations, it invites the candidate, the church members, and the guests to return. The clerk of the council will then read the council's recommendations one by one. Once all of the recommendations have been submitted to the church and any lingering questions have been addressed, the council votes to adjourn. At that point it ceases to exist.

Because many messengers have to travel long distances to attend the council, it has been common in the past for the ordination service to follow the council immediately. Unfortunately, this juxtaposition sometimes puts pressure on the council to recommend an ordination, even though some messengers might be hesitant. More recently, as transportation has become easier and cheaper, churches have begun to schedule the ordination service separately from the council—sometimes by weeks or even months. This system has some drawbacks, but it is generally to the benefit of the messengers, the candidate, and the ordaining church.

The church should prepare an ordination certificate for the council. If the ordination is held at a separate time, many of the messengers may not be able to return for the service. Every messenger, however, should place his signature on the ordination certificate. At the ordination service, any ministers who participate should also sign the certificate, as should the officers of the ordaining church. Not surprisingly, most of the space on a Baptist ordination certificate is taken up with signatures. These signatures are part of the process that makes lifelong ordination possible among Baptists.

Recognition Councils

Recognition councils have never been as common as ordination councils, but in recent years their frequency has diminished sharply. Their decreasing regularity is due mainly to the diminishing influence of associationalism among some Baptists. Where organized fellowships of churches exist, some form of recognition council is still extremely valuable.

Recognition councils are typically called by new churches that wish to seek fellowship with congregations of like faith and order. A new church often encounters two impediments to fellowship with other churches. Externally, the order of the church is probably unknown to many of the churches with which it might wish to fellowship. The established churches need a mechanism for assuring themselves that the new congregation really does share their faith and practice. Internally, the new church may experience some deficiencies in organization and even in doctrine. The congregation may not have foreseen the situations that it might encounter, and it may not have adopted mechanisms for responding to them. Advice from sister congregations can do much to help the new church correct any deficiencies.

The recognition council was designed to address both of these problems. The point of a recognition council is that it gives messengers from other churches the opportunity to examine the faith and order of the new congregation. In the recognition council, the host church makes its organizing documents available for inspection by the messengers. Typically, the messengers will also have opportunity to question the pastor and other leaders of the new church. The council will want to know why the new congregation was organized, what its purpose is, and how it identifies itself. They will want to know what doctrine the church believes, how its organizational structure works, and how it plans to address common situations in church life. The questions will vary from council to council because churches encounter different challenges in different times and places.

The council will certainly want to examine the new church's covenant; for next to the Bible, the covenant is the most important document that any church possesses. The covenant is what makes it a church rather than simply a gathering of believers. In the church covenant, the members of the congregation make a solemn promise to one another. Entering the covenant is the equivalent of swearing an oath. In this promise, they agree to perform certain responsibilities toward one another, and these responsibilities disclose what the members understand the nature and mission of their church to be. For many years, church covenants followed a predictable pattern, but lately churches are displaying an increasing tendency to depart from older terminology and ideas. Recognition councils should not thoughtlessly endorse the church's covenant, but should ask seriously how it might be strengthened, recommending improvements as necessary.

Next in importance to the covenant is the church's confession or statement of faith. Indeed, the confession should be considered a part of the covenant. It is where the church articulates the doctrines that it agrees should characterize its ministry. The recognition council will wish to examine the doctrinal statement in considerable detail. Different groups of Baptists exhibit varying degrees of doctrinal latitude and different doctrinal directions. Some are more inclined toward dispensationalism and premillennialism, while others are more inclined toward covenant theology and greater latitude on eschatology. Some do not tolerate Calvinism, while others may be decidedly Calvinistic in their soteriology. One of the concerns of the messengers will be for the doctrinal fit between the new church and the congregations with which it wishes to fellowship.

A church confession ought to articulate clearly the church's commitment to the fundamentals of the faith. It should position the church doctrinally and practically as a Baptist congregation. It should also respond to some of the hotly debated issues within contemporary Christianity. It ought to define the church's position on open theism, on the reality of Hell, on the meaning of justification, on charismatic gifts, and on women's roles. Some of these issues are addressed (at least implicitly) by traditional statements such as the New Hampshire Confession (1833), and many churches simply adopt one of these statements and then revise it to fit the church's needs.

Some churches write their constitution so that their statement of faith can never be revised or amended, thus hoping to guarantee the doctrinal fidelity of future generations. While their goal is commendable, this stipulation is not really useful. On the one hand, if future generations do deviate, they are likely to ignore the doctrinal statement. On the other hand, new doctrinal issues arise on a regular basis, and a church needs the flexibility to address these in its confession. Revising the statement of faith should not be easy, but neither should it be impossible.

Other documents that the recognition council will wish to review include the church's articles of incorporation, the constitution, and the bylaws. In many churches these may all be combined into one document (typically the constitution). Other churches may function with only two of the three.

One of the concerns of the recognition council should be to ensure that the new church has made the effort to meet its state's legal requirements for organization. Most states require all corporations to adopt articles of incorporation when filing with the state. Of course, not all churches are legally incorporated, and if they are not, they will have no articles of incorporation. Incorporation is a legal standing controlled by the state. If a church seeks incorporation, it must comply with the state's requirements. Those requirements will vary from one jurisdiction to another, and churches should seek professional legal assistance in meeting them. Most recognition councils lack the legal expertise to ensure that the church has done this correctly, but the messengers can at least ascertain whether the church has sought incorporation and what steps it has taken to secure it. The articles of incorporation will typically state the name, location, and purpose of the church, identifying it as a specifically religious organization. Depending upon the jurisdiction, they may also name the original officers or trustees. Articles of incorporation should be kept as general as possible. Once they are filed with the state, they become difficult or impossible to modify. In some cases, the articles of incorporation will be indistinguishable from the church's constitution.

The council may also advise the church regarding tax exemption. While the council cannot offer legal advice, it can ascertain whether the church has thought carefully about whether it should file for tax exemption. It can also make sure that the church's constitution contains a dissolution clause that will permit tax exemption by guaranteeing that all of the church's assets will be distributed to other tax-exempt entities.

In the discussion of such organizational matters, it should be noted that the difference between church constitutions and bylaws is a matter of debate. Broadly speaking, the constitution articulates such matters as the name, purpose, and general structure of the church, while the bylaws define the procedures for conducting business. The constitution defines what the church is, while the bylaws describe how it works. In many churches, however, this distinction is not maintained, and all of this information is simply put into the church constitution.

The distinction between articles of incorporation, constitution, and bylaws is not as important as their content. Between them, these documents need to address specific questions. The work of the recognition council is to ensure that all of the questions are answered. These include the following:

1. What is the church's name?
2. What is the church's purpose or mission, and what specific expressions (sometimes called objects) does that mission or purpose entail?
3. What are the qualifications for membership, and how are members received, dismissed, and disciplined?
4. What are the offices (both spiritual and legal), what are the qualifications for officers, and how are officers chosen and dismissed? Specifically, how is a pastor called and how can he be dismissed?
5. Will the church have any standing committees, and if so, what is their nature and how are their members chosen?
6. What are the duties of members, officers, and committees?
7. What are the powers of members, officers, and committees?
8. What is the procedure for resignations, for vacating an office, and for filling a vacant office?
9. What voting procedures will the church employ under both normal and exceptional circumstances?
10. How will the church address conflicts of interest on the part of officers and members?
11. When will the church hold business meetings, and when is the annual meeting?

12. What is the procedure for calling special business meetings?

13. What is the procedure for amending the church's governing documents?

14. How can the church be dissolved, and, in the event of its dissolution, who will receive the church's assets?

The constitution and bylaws are governing documents. The church may also adopt administrative documents in the form of policies and procedures. It may further adopt planning documents in the form of strategic, operational, and assessment plans. In contrast to the governing documents, both administrative and planning documents are more informal in nature and will change regularly. A recognition council may be interested to know that such documents exist, but the messengers will probably lack the time to examine them in much detail.

The council will examine the church's central documents section by section. For each section, questions will be directed to the church's pastor or other leaders. When the messengers have completed their examination, they will continue to interview the pastor and other church officers. The council will want to hear these individuals describe why the church was formed, what its commitments are, how its ethos is characterized, and what it intends to accomplish. The messengers may ask specific questions about how the church plans to address certain issues or to handle certain problems.

As with ordination councils, the moderator of a recognition council bears the responsibility to keep the business moving. Some messengers may wish to use the council as an occasion to advance some personal bias. Others may use it as on opportunity to debate some controversial topic. The moderator should head off these distractions and keep the council focused upon its examination of the church's documents and officers.

Once the examination is complete, the council will go into executive session. Members of the host church will be dismissed so that the messengers can discuss their examination frankly. At this point, the council will draft its recommendations to the church. As with all church councils, a recognition council possesses no legislative authority over the church and no judicial authority to enforce its recommendations. All that the council can do is to advise.

If the council finds that the church is well organized, it may recommend that sister congregations recognize it as a church of like faith and order. If it finds weaknesses in the church's organization, it can recommend ways to address them. If the church is out of order, the council may recommend that sister congregations not recognize it as a church of like faith and order. If the church is seeking fellowship with an association, then a positive recommendation from the council may be required. In any case, the council's recommendations are only advice. The host church and the sister churches are all free to take the council's advice or to ignore it as they wish.

Organizing a church is a complicated affair. Even experienced church planters will encounter new obstacles in each new church that they establish. Every church faces different circumstances, and it should adapt its organization to its particular situation. For this reason, recognition councils will usually present new churches with a long list of recommendations, most of which will simply be items to consider. The host church should take these recommendations as helpful advice and not as criticisms.

When the council has made its recommendations, it votes to adjourn. At that point, the council ceases to exist. Once a council has formally dissolved, it cannot be called back into session. If the church requires further advice, it must call a separate council.

When a council recommends recognition of the host church, its voice should carry a great deal of weight. If the council has done its job well, it should have examined the new congregation in considerable detail. Its recommendation should provide assurance to sister churches that the new assembly is indeed a church of like faith and order. This should have the effect of opening doors of fellowship and cooperation with other mutually recognized churches. Traditionally, churches that mutually recognize one another may also transfer members through letters of dismission rather than through more complicated means.

Advisory Councils

The least frequent type of church council is the advisory council. Of course, all church councils are broadly advisory in nature. In the case of recognition councils and ordination councils, the advice is directed toward a specific and common situation. Sometimes, however, a church encounters a difficulty that falls outside the normal categories of ordinations and recognitions. It may wish to seek counsel from sister churches concerning a particular issue. Any Baptist church has the prerogative of calling a council when such occasions arise.

For example, a church may be facing external pressures. Perhaps it has encountered a problem in its community. Perhaps it has come into conflict with a sister congregation. Perhaps it has encountered some difficulty over a governmental requirement. All of these are legitimate reasons for seeking advice from other churches.

Alternatively, the church may be enduring some internal dispute and cannot see its way to a clear solution. Sometimes pastors and congregations fall out with one another. Sometimes factions develop within a congregation. Under these circumstances, the calm and deliberate advice of messengers from other churches may show a church a solution that it would not otherwise notice.

An advisory council is not a church court. It does not conduct a trial or render a verdict. It does not arbitrate disputes. It only offers advice, and its advice can be either accepted or ignored as the host church chooses.

The format of an advisory council is similar to that of an ordination council or a recognition council. The host church takes the same steps to call the council. The messengers organize the council in the same way. The main difference is in the subject matter. An advisory council does not review a doctrinal statement as in an ordination council. It does not review governing documents as in a recognition council. Rather, it will hear the matter with which the church is confronted.

When a council is called because of internal disputes, the church should be very careful to ensure that the council hears representatives from all sides of the dispute. These representatives will probably be chosen by the church, though the council may ask to hear others. The messengers may ask questions to be sure that they fully understand all perspectives. They will want to understand the history of the dispute, the core issues that are at stake, and subsidiary issues that may have accrued to the original problem.

If the council is called because of external challenges, it is likely to hear only the church's story. While in principle it can request the presence of outsiders, it has no power to compel their presence if either they or the host church should refuse. Nevertheless, the council should do its best to gain a thorough understanding of the situation so that it can offer competent advice.

As with other kinds of councils, an advisory council will declare an executive session after it has examined the situation for which it was called. The messengers will have the opportunity to discuss the situation frankly, and out of their discussion they will draft recommendations to the church.

No church is ever required to call an advisory council, no matter what challenges it may face. In fact, advisory councils are seldom used any more. This is unfortunate. By calling a council, a church may hear valuable advice that will help it in its difficulties. Also, if a church wants its decisions to be honored and supported by other churches, then having their advice ahead of time is a wise move. When one church's decision affects other churches, it has some responsibility to take their counsel into account.

Since advisory councils are designed to help churches with internal disputes, perhaps this is the point at which to say something about whether churches should recognize one another's discipline. Ideally, church members who have been disfellowshipped for good reason should not be received as members by other churches. One of the main points of church discipline is to restore the disciplined members to full fellowship with the Lord and with their congregations. Removing members from fellowship is the last step in discipline, taken only in the most extreme cases. In this step, a congregation delivers a disobedient member to Satan for the destruction of the flesh. No other congregation should ever want to subvert this disciplinary process.

This is not to suggest that churches should publish lists of members whom they have placed under discipline. On the contrary, such information is normally the privilege only of the disciplining congregation itself. Before they receive new members, however, churches should always ask whether the prospective members are presently under church discipline or whether they are moving their membership to avoid church discipline. Among churches that have recognized one another, a letter of dismission certifies that a given individual is a member in good and regular standing. At the very least, the pastor of the church receiving the member should communicate with the pastor of the church from which the member has come. A brief conversation may provide enough information to disclose whether any difficulty exists with the individual's membership.

Churches should not normally receive members who have been disfellowshipped for good reason. The problem is trying to agree upon what constitutes "good reason." The various denominations have historically held divergent standards of discipline in important areas. Today even Baptist churches differ widely in the offenses that they consider to be worthy of discipline. Frankly, some churches and pastors are simply abusive, disciplining any member who does not submit to their domineering control. Others, of course, are exceptionally lax, but that presents a different kind of problem.

Among churches that have recognized one another, a good case can be made for mutually respecting each other's discipline. When churches have recognized one another through the mechanism of church councils, they can be reasonably confident that they share common values and perspectives. Even if they do not know the details of disciplinary cases, they will know the kind of consideration that went into discipline.

Churches that have not recognized one another, however, do not necessarily share this community of commitments and values. Baptists have gradually divided into many different branches and traditions, and they can be amazingly diverse. Doctrines and conduct that might seem laudable in one group are deemed offensive to another. Under these circumstances, churches cannot simply suppose that disciplined members were disfellowshipped over legitimate accusations or credible evidence. The receiving church will have to conduct its own inquiry to ascertain whether the prospective members should be received into its fellowship. If this inquiry is obfuscated by the disciplining church, it really has no right to complain if its disfellowshipped members are received by another church.

Baptist churches are autonomous. Each church exercises discipline over its own members. No outside authority (including another church) has the right to stop a Baptist church from disfellowshipping a member that it considers recalcitrant. On the other hand, no outside authority (including the disciplining church) has the right to stop another Baptist church from receiving that disfellowshipped member into its own congregation. In other words, no church has the right to demand that another church recognize its discipline. That kind of recognition is a privilege that must be earned through respectful communication and mutual accountability between the churches.

Ex Parte Councils

The main types of church councils are called for ordinations, recognitions, and advice in other situations. Very rarely, churches will be invited to send messengers to an ex parte council. An ex parte council is essentially an advisory council, but rather than being called by a church, it is called by a faction. It is almost always the result of internal conflict within a church. One party to the conflict may wish to gain the advice (or, more often, the support) of sister churches. That party will be the one to call for a council.

Usually, ex parte councils are a bad idea. Little can be learned by listening to one side of a dispute. Indeed, offering advice without hearing a matter is something that Proverbs denounces as folly (Prov. 18:13). For this reason, Baptist churches have usually been reluctant to send messengers to ex parte councils. Councils called by one side in a dispute are generally taken to be evidence of bad faith.

Sometimes, however, no bad faith is involved. On occasion, churches can and do experience principled disagreements over important issues. Sometimes the issues are important enough, and the convictions are deeply enough held, that the two sides seem irreconcilable. No ill will may be involved; indeed, all of the principals may care deeply about one another and genuinely respect each other. Nevertheless, one group decides that it cannot live with what the other group determines to do. Such disagreements are akin to those between different denominations, though on a smaller scale.

Under these circumstances, a minority party may experience genuine perplexity and may sincerely wish to obtain advice from sister churches. If so, a council may be the best way of obtaining the needed advice. Even so, the minority party might better appeal to the majority so that the entire church could call a council to advise it in its disagreement. Nevertheless, churches may choose to send messengers to advise a minority within a church under these circumstances. The council may help the minority to reframe their perspective, or it may help them decide upon the proper course of action to pursue. If the difference really cannot be resolved, the council may even advise the minority to seek a peaceable dismissal from the majority in order to begin a new church that upholds their principles.

These kinds of disagreements, however, are extremely rare. Almost always, an ex parte council represents some form of political jockeying on the part of one faction within a church. Unless the concerns are clearly legitimate, Baptist churches generally do well to steer clear of ex parte councils.

Summary

Among Baptist churches, councils are never obligatory. When they are called, councils can never exercise authority over local churches. Their only function is to offer advice. When they have completed this task, they go out of existence.

Nevertheless, most Baptists have found councils to be indispensible. They are particularly valuable in the case of ordinations. They also provide a mechanism through which churches can recognize one another as sister congregations. Furthermore, they may be able to help churches by rendering advice during times of challenge or division.

Church councils are an important channel through which the principles and values of Baptist churches are transmitted. When Baptist churches are invited to send messengers to a council, they should always do their best to comply. Pastors in particular should make a priority of attending councils. These meetings are one of the principal ways in which healthy fellowship between churches can be maintained.

9 Landmarkism

THE LANDMARK BAPTIST movement began in the American South during the mid-nineteenth century. It was initially led by James Robinson Graves, James Madison Pendleton, and Amos Cooper Dayton. Later, James Milton Carroll emerged as a significant voice through the publication of his booklet *The Trail of Blood*. Landmarkism has never been a majority view among Baptists, but its advocates have been vigorous and sometimes contentious. It has resulted in the formation of at least two fellowships: the Baptist Missionary Association and the American Baptist Association. It is quite influential in some circles of the Southern Baptist Convention. Among Baptist fundamentalists who think of themselves as Independent (with a capital *I*), Landmark views are widespread. American missionaries have also spread Landmark ideas to other parts of the world, especially Southeast Asia.

Wherever Landmarkism emerges, it poses problems for regular (historic) Baptists. It adds several ideas to the definition of the word *Baptist*, leading its advocates to bring caustic rebukes against those who hold more mainstream views. Because of its contentious nature and its determination to redefine Baptist principles, Landmarkism merits discussion in a treatment of Baptist distinctives and polity.

A complete critique of Landmarkism would require a separate volume. Consequently, our present discussion will be somewhat cursory. First, it will survey the distinctive teachings of Landmarkism. Then it will examine some of the more pivotal teachings individually and test them against both Scripture and mainstream Baptist thought.

To those who have never been exposed to Landmark Baptists, some of these teachings may seem to border on the bizarre. This strangeness may lead one to think of Landmarkism as a cult. That, however, would not be a fair assessment. While some of their ideas may seem peculiar, Landmark Baptists nevertheless teach and preach the gospel with great clarity. They are certainly evangelical Christians and members of the Body of Christ.

Landmark Baptist Theology

Landmark Baptists differ from other Baptists mainly in their ecclesiology, that is, their doctrine of the church. Their thinking about the church revolves around a network of concepts. To understand Landmarkism, it is necessary to see more than just the individual concepts. One must appreciate the connection between them.

Landmarkism begins by insisting that the word *church*, when it is used in its technical sense in the New Testament, refers only to local congregations. In other words, Landmarkism denies the existence of any universal or invisible church. It differs from Roman Catholicism, which teaches that the true church is universal and visible. It also differs from evangelical Protestants, most of whom have taught that the true church is universal and invisible. Historically, most Baptists have agreed with Protestants in affirming a universal, invisible church. Landmarkism, however, insists that the only true churches are both visible and local. Landmarkers may sometimes speak of "the church" in a collective sense, but when they do, they mean either the sum total of all true local churches or else the church program in God's economy. Landmark theology has room only for the local church.

When did God's program for churches begin? Landmarkers agree with dispensationalists that the church was not present in the Old Testament. But dispensationalists begin the church with the Day of Pentecost, while Landmarkers believe that it began with the ministry of John the Baptist. John's preaching announced the imminence of the kingdom of God, and Landmarkers identify the kingdom with the church program. Local churches comprise the kingdom, and they have done so since the days of John.

As we have noted, Landmarkers believe that the church exists only in the form of visible local churches. Nevertheless, not every organization that claims to be a church really is. That being the case, Landmarkers need some test to distinguish true churches from false or pretend churches. That test is baptism. A baptized membership is essential to the existence of a true church. Since (as Landmarkers see it) Catholics, Eastern Orthodox, and all Protestants have neglected true baptism, none of their churches are really churches. Furthermore, none of their ministers are really ministers. Landmarkers infer that Baptists should never allow a minister from one of these non-churches (e.g., a Presbyterian or Methodist minister) into their pulpits, even if he believes and preaches the gospel.

Landmarkism defines true churches by baptism, but that definition opens another question. What constitutes valid baptism? Landmarkers answer this question by insisting that valid baptism must meet four criteria: a proper mode, meaning, subject, and administrator. The mode must be complete immersion in water. The meaning must be the death, burial, and resurrection of Jesus. The subject must be a professing believer. The administrator must be someone who has received valid baptism under the authority of a true (i.e., Baptist) church. Historic Baptists agree with Landmarkers on the necessity of proper mode, meaning, and subject. They do not agree with the necessity of a proper administrator.

The Landmark theory requires an unbroken chain of baptisms from the days of John the Baptist down to the present day. Valid baptism requires a proper administrator. A proper administrator must be one who has received valid baptism—from a proper administrator, who in turn must have received valid baptism from a proper administrator. The perpetuity of valid baptisms is one of the most obvious features of Landmark thought.

Not only does the insistence upon a proper administrator lead to a perpetuity of baptisms, it also leads to a perpetuity of churches. Since valid baptism is always administered under the authority of a local church, the existence of valid baptisms requires the existence of true churches (and vice versa). Accordingly, Landmarkers believe that true Baptist churches (i.e., churches characterized by valid baptism) have existed in every era of church history, perpetuating their baptisms generation by generation from John to the present. This theory is sometimes called Baptist successionism.

Combining these ideas produces some strange results. Landmarkers do not believe in the existence of a universal church, but only of local churches. Since the church is called the Bride of Christ, they apply this label to each true local church. The only true churches, however, are Baptist churches; that is, churches that have perpetuated valid baptisms. Therefore, the Bride of Christ consists only of Baptists. Other Christians will make it to Heaven, but only Baptists will enjoy the status of being the Bride of Christ. Because of this feature of their teaching, Landmarkers are sometimes called Baptist Briders.

According to the Landmark understanding, believers who have not been baptized by a proper administrator have not really been baptized at all. This includes people who have been immersed as believers in non-Baptist churches. Landmarkers refer to these baptisms as alien immersion, and they do not accept it as valid baptism. Christians who have been baptized in non-Baptist churches will be required to submit to rebaptism before they can be received into the membership of a Landmark church.

Landmark Baptists attempt to argue for their theory in several ways. First, they try to establish an unbroken succession of Baptist churches on historical grounds (J. M. Carroll's *The Trail of Blood* is the most famous example of this attempt). Second, they challenge those Biblical texts used to prove the existence of a universal church, attempting to show that these passages actually refer somehow to the local assembly. Third, they try to leapfrog history by appealing directly to theological evidence for the perpetuity of true churches. The favorite proof text for this teaching is Matthew 16:18. A discussion of Landmarkism must take account of these arguments.

Baptist Successionism

The Landmark theory both requires and depends upon a historic succession of Baptist churches from the time of John to the present day. Landmarkers insist that true (Baptist) churches have existed in every period of church history. These churches were often a persecuted minority within Christendom, and thus constitute a "trail of blood." Many Landmark Baptists claim to be able to trace this trail of blood through groups like Montanists, Novatians, Donatists, Cathari, Albigenses, Paulicians, Arnoldists, Petrubrusians, Henricians, and Waldenses. Landmarkers claim that all of these were Anabaptists (rebaptizers), which they see as an older name for Baptists.

The best that can be said of Landmark history is that it is a highly speculative piece of historical revision. Some of these supposed Anabaptist groups seem to have preached the gospel, but others were likely heretical. Landmarkers sometimes counter that the charges of heresy came from enemies attempting to blacken the reputations of these groups. Nevertheless, the positive evidence for their orthodoxy—let alone their Baptist principles—is sometimes scant. Thus, few non-Landmark historians are willing to accept the "trail of blood" as historically verifiable. The evidence simply does not exist.

Then why are Landmarkers so tenacious about their version of Baptist history? The answer is simple. They assume their history before they ever approach the evidence. They believe that valid baptism is required to have a true church, and they believe that an unbroken chain of true churches is necessary for valid baptism. Thus, their theology forces them to embrace Baptist successionism whether or not any historical evidence supports it. Given this theological deduction, they are willing to give any historical sect the most favorable reading that they possibly (and sometimes impossibly) can, to make it a link in the chain. For Landmark Baptists, a trail of blood is a theological necessity. Without it, their whole system evaporates.

Most Baptist historians believe it is impossible to trace any trail of blood. Even if it were possible, individual Landmarkers could not know whether they were standing in it. Establishing the general contours of the trail is one thing. Establishing the particular links that enable one to trace one's own baptism back to John the Baptist is quite another. At the end of the day, individual Landmarkers can have no historical confidence that their baptism actually qualifies as valid baptism or that their particular church qualifies as a true church.

The majority of Baptists have not accepted the Landmark reconstruction of Baptist history. In fact, the majority of Baptists simply do not care whether a trail of blood can be proven. If it could, it would be an interesting curiosity, but it would make no great difference. Most Baptists do not trace their lineage through a chain of baptisms to John. They trace themselves through direct study into the pages of the New Testament. Mainstream Baptists believe that the validity of baptism and the legitimacy of a local church do not depend in any sense upon proper baptismal administrators understood in terms of successionism. If somehow a group of natives on a remote island came into possession of a New Testament, believed on Christ, began to immerse one another in the name of the Father, the Son, and the Holy Spirit, and organized themselves into congregations after the pattern of the New Testament, they would have legitimate claim to be true Baptist churches. The lack of baptismal succession would make no difference at all.

The Gates of Hell

In the absence of historical evidence, Landmarkers typically skip directly to theological reasons for holding Baptist successionism. If they cannot point to an actual historical trail of blood, they attempt to articulate Biblical reasons for believing that such a succession must exist. The classic proof text for the Landmark position is Matthew 16:18, "And I say also unto thee, That thou art

Peter, and upon this rock I will build my church; and the gates of hell shall not prevail against it."

This verse contains both a positive and a negative promise. The positive promise is that Jesus will build His church. The negative promise is that the gates of Hell will not prevail against it. The negative promise is most important to Landmarkers. They take it as assurance from the Lord that satanic opposition or demonic forces will never be able to triumph against the church, and they understand *church* to mean true local churches that practice valid baptism. For Landmarkers, this translates into a promise that true Baptist churches must exist in every era of church history. For true churches to be blotted out at any point would mean that the gates of Hell must have prevailed.

One does not need to hold Landmark theology to believe that God has never left Himself without a witness. Whatever is essential to the faith has indeed been preserved in the face of persecution. Though it may have been suppressed or even annihilated at one time or place, it came to flourish in another. Believing that the gospel was kept alive in the midst of opposition and persecution is responsible and defensible. It is not sufficient, however, for Landmark theology. Landmarkers are not content that the gospel should have been preserved and maintained. They insist that the continuity of the church depends upon an unbroken chain of valid baptisms, and consequently this succession of baptisms is the thing against which the gates of Hell must not prevail.

Does Matthew 16:18 require an unbroken chain of valid baptisms? How one answers that question will depend upon the answers to two other questions. The first is whether a proper administrator (understood in terms of baptismal succession) is essential to valid baptism. The second is what Jesus meant by the "gates of hell" not prevailing.

The majority of Baptists have never thought a proper administrator was essential to valid baptism, especially if *proper administrator* is defined in terms of baptismal succession. The modern Baptist and Anabaptist movements began when individuals became convinced that their infant baptism was not true Christian baptism. Without an alternative, they simply began baptizing one another. With a few exceptions (e.g., John Smyth), they were not particularly bothered by the lack of baptismal succession. Baptists historically have not believed that the validity of baptism depends on the administrator's qualifications. If baptism is administered with the proper meaning, mode, and subjects, Baptists have accepted it. Baptismal succession is not essential to valid baptism.

If baptismal succession is not essential to valid baptism, then it is not essential to the definition of a true church. If it is not essential to the definition of a true church, it cannot be part of Jesus' promise in Matthew 16:18. Even if Jesus were promising some sort of unbroken chain of true churches, baptismal succession would not be part of that chain. For this reason, most Baptists have rejected the Landmark application of this verse.

The greater problem, however, consists in determining what Jesus actually was promising. What is the meaning of "the gates of hell," and how will they not prevail against the church? In answering this question, modern Christians may be too easily misled by popular mythology, which depicts Satan as the ruler of Hell. In reality, he never rules in Hell, and there is no Biblical indication that Hell is a stronghold for him or his underlings.

The Biblical teaching about Hell is actually rather complicated. The New Testament contains three words that are translated as *hell* in English versions of the Bible. The least common word is *Tartarus*, which occurs only in 2 Peter 2:4. Peter said that God cast some of the sinning angels into Tartarus, where they are kept in chains of darkness awaiting judgment. These angels, confined as they are, offer no threat to the church.

The second word that can be translated *hell* is the word *Gehenna*. Originally a reference to the Hinnom Valley outside Jerusalem, *Gehenna* came to symbolize God's judgment and wrath upon sin. Jesus referred to Gehenna as a place where the wicked would be judged (Matt. 23:33). Gehenna is most likely equivalent to the Lake of Fire in Revelation 21.

However, the word Jesus chose in Matthew 16:18 is the word *Hades*. This is the word that the New Testament writers used to translate the Hebrew word *Sheol*. Both terms appear to function as labels generally for the realm of the dead. Both saved and lost people enter Sheol/Hades. Of course, the treatment that these groups receive in Hades is quite different, with the blessed experiencing paradise and the lost experiencing torments (Luke 16:19–31).

When Jesus spoke about the "gates of Hades," He was not inventing new terminology. This exact phrase occurs in the Greek (Septuagint) translation of Isaiah 38:10, "I said in the cutting off of my days, I shall go to the gates of the grave: I am deprived of the residue of my years." Here the phrase "gates of the grave" translates the Hebrew "gates of Sheol." God had told Hezekiah that he was about to die: his days were going to be cut off, and he would be deprived of the years of life he had expected. He was about to enter the "gates of Sheol." Clearly, to enter the gates of Sheol (*Hades* in Greek) means to die. "Gates of Hades" functions as a metaphor for physical death.

The Old Testament also uses the expression "gates of death" in a similar fashion. In Psalm 9:13, David referred to God as the one who lifted him from the gates of death. He meant that God is the person who saved his life. In Job 38:17, God asked Job whether the gates of death had been opened to him. The point of the question is to ask whether Job could see beyond death into the afterlife. The expression "gates of Sheol" (in Greek, "gates of Hades") is very similar. It is simply a metaphor for death itself. Anyone who dies passes the gates of Hades.

What did Jesus mean when He said that the gates of Hades will not overpower the church? After all, church saints do die. They do pass through the gates of Hades. Nevertheless, Jesus' promise means that death will not have the last word. Death cannot contain those who have believed on Jesus, any more than it could contain their Lord. For the one who has been united to Christ and is part of the church, death has no sting and the grave poses no victory (1 Cor. 15:54–55). Every church saint will rise again to rejoice with the Lord Jesus Christ.

Thus framed by a correct understanding of the idiom "gates of Hades," Jesus' promise that these gates would not prevail against His church must be understood as a metaphorical promise of a triumphant bodily resurrection. That promise also contains implications for understanding the word *church*. No promise of resurrection applies universally to all members of all local churches. Some members of some churches make false professions of faith and will ultimately be condemned. The only way that Jesus' promise can apply universally to the whole church is if the church to which He referred is composed only of truly saved individuals. That means that the church of Matthew 16:18 must be the church universal, the invisible Body of Christ.

Of course, Landmarkers cannot admit this, because they deny the existence of any universal, invisible church. They insist that the word *church* can properly apply only to local congregations. Their theology dictates their interpretation of Matthew 16:18. As we have seen, however, Matthew 16:18 ought to be understood as a reference to the universal church.

The problem for Landmarkers is that they begin by denying the existence of any universal church. Once they have eliminated that category, any Scripture that seems to refer to a universal church must be reinterpreted to apply to the local congregation. Consequently, if we wish to respond to Landmarkism, we must deal with the Landmark rejection of the universal church.

The One Body

Rather than dealing with all of the arguments for and against the existence of a universal church, we shall examine only one key text, 1 Corinthians 12:13, which states, "For by one Spirit are we all baptized into one body, whether we be Jews or Gentiles, whether we be bond or free; and have been all made to drink into one Spirit." A right interpretation of this verse forces us to answer several questions. What spirit is in view? The Holy Spirit, or some sort of attitude such as a hypothetical "spirit of unity"? When Paul referred to baptism, was he talking about water baptism or something else? What is the one body, and how do people get into it? Who is included in the "we" to whom Paul referred?

Before dealing with these questions, we should say a word about the labels *universal church* and *invisible church*. People who use these words together mean that the church is universal because it includes either all believers from all times or all believers within a particular time frame. For example, covenant theologians typically put Old Testament saints in the church, while dispensationalists traditionally include only those who are saved between Pentecost and the Rapture. The temporal boundaries of the universal church are not the issue in this discussion. The question is whether some spiritual body exists that includes all saints (whether from all times or from a particular time), therefore transcending the local congregation, and whether that universal body can rightly be called *church*.

This universal church is sometimes called the *invisible* church. Its invisibility is obviously not absolute. The invisible church includes visible Christians who are still living in the world. This church is called *invisible* because the vital elements that constitute its being are invisible. These elements are usually taken to be, first, genuine faith in the gospel, and, second, the baptizing work of the Holy Spirit. No one can observe empirically whether another person possesses genuine faith or has experienced Spirit baptism. Since these constituting elements are invisible, the universal church is also called *invisible*.

The question is whether such a universal, invisible church exists. The majority of Baptists have believed that it does. Landmark Baptists believe that it does not. While several passages of Scripture are debated in this dispute, the key text is 1 Corinthians 12:13. Landmarkers understand this verse as a reference to water baptism. They suggest that, in the face of divisions in the church at Corinth, Paul was reminding the church's members that they were united in purpose when they were baptized and entered the church's fellowship. To paraphrase the verse, Paul told the Corinthians that, "we were all water-baptized in a spirit of unity into the membership of the local church, which is the body of Christ." According to the Landmark view, the "one spirit" is an attitude of solidarity, the baptism is water baptism, and the one body is the local congregation, of which the Corinthians became members by their water baptism.

This interpretation can be challenged at several points. The first is the identity of the one spirit or Spirit (*pneuma* in Greek). The context is replete with uses of the term *pneuma*. The noun can be found in verses 3 (twice), 4, 7, 8 (twice), 9 (twice), 10 (as a plural), and 11. The plural use in verse 10 refers to the gift of the discerning of spirits. Otherwise, all of the singular uses refer to the Holy Spirit. No uses of *pneuma* in the immediate context refer to an attitude or disposition. Taken together, the usage of *pneuma* in the immediate context make the odds extremely high—indeed, astronomical—that Paul was referring to the Holy Spirit in 1 Corinthians 12:13.

According to Paul, "we" are all baptized in or by one Spirit into one body. The one Spirit must be the Holy Spirit. Who, then, is included in this baptism? Who is *we*?

The pronoun *we* must include both Paul and his readers, the members of the church at Corinth. That much is immediately obvious. A glance at the epistle's greeting (1 Cor. 1:1–2) reveals further information. Paul was not the only writer of the epistle. He was joined by Sosthenes. Nor were the Corinthians the only recipients. Paul meant the epistle to go beyond the church at Corinth, to all those everywhere who call upon the name of the Lord Jesus Christ. In other words, Paul meant this epistle to be truly universal in scope, addressing it to all believers everywhere. Accordingly, the "we" of 1 Corinthians 12:13 must include Paul, Sosthenes, the Corinthian believers, and probably all believers everywhere.

That being the case, what is the "one body" to which Paul was referring? Is it the local congregation at Corinth, or is it something bigger? The question here is not whether a local church can be called the body of Christ. It can. The question is whether a single local church can account for the language that Paul used in this verse.

If "we all" includes Paul (let alone all believers everywhere), the one body cannot possibly refer to the church in Corinth. The New Testament never indicates that Paul was ever a member of the church at Corinth. Even if he had been, he could not have entered the church by baptism, for he was baptized by Ananias at Damascus (Acts 22:16). Because he included himself in the one body, Paul forced his readers to understand that the body transcends the individual church at Corinth. If (as seems likely) he also meant to include all those everywhere who call upon the Lord Jesus Christ, the one body must be as wide in scope as the individuals who were included in the address of the epistle. It must be universal.

Then what about the baptism? By now, the answer to that question should be clear. If the word *pneuma* refers to the Holy Spirit, and if the one body transcends the local church, the baptism cannot possibly be water baptism. It is baptism in or by the Holy Spirit, and it is of such a nature that it places individuals into a single body that includes believers from multiple local churches. This is exactly what is meant by the expression *Spirit baptism.*

Paul's teaching in 1 Corinthians 12:13 definitely indicates, first, that a universal Body of Christ exists; second, that this body includes all believers and not just the members of a particular congregation; and third, that this body is constituted by baptism in or by the Holy Spirit. Can the word *church* rightly be applied to this body? This is the only question that cannot be answered from the immediate context.

It can be answered from Ephesians 1:22–23, however. In the context of Ephesians 1, the apostle Paul was discussing the infinite height to which the Lord Jesus has been exalted. Christ has been raised from the dead and seated in the heavenly places (v. 20). He occupies a position that is far above every other kind of authority (v. 21). Indeed, He will exercise this authority into eternity (v. 21). All things have been placed under Christ's feet (v. 22), and He has been given as head to the church which is His body (v. 23). In the context of the cosmic lordship and universal headship of Christ, the Body of Christ that is in view here is very likely the universal Body that includes all believers and transcends local assemblies. If we see a universal body in 1 Corinthians 12:13, we cannot avoid seeing the same body in Ephesians 1:22–23. Furthermore, Paul clearly labeled this body as "the church, which is his body." In other words, the universal Body of Christ can rightly be called the church.

To reiterate, the Body is universal because it comprises all believers (whether absolutely or during a particular age). It is invisible because the two elements that constitute it (faith in the gospel and Spirit baptism) are invisible. It is, however, a real entity, created by the Spirit, living under the headship of Christ, and beloved of God. It is the *church* in the truest sense of that term.

The Bride of Christ

Once we recognize the existence of a universal church, no reason exists for restricting the Bride of Christ to local congregations. The clearest text that develops the image of the Bride of Christ is Ephesians 5:22–33, where the apostle Paul used the relationship between husbands and wives as an analogy for the relationship between Christ and the church. Paul stated that Christ loved the church and gave Himself up for her (v. 25). He did this to make her holy by cleansing her with the water of the Word (v. 26). His goal was to present her to Himself as a glorious church without spot or wrinkle. Rather, she is to be holy and flawless (v. 27). Participation in this church makes individual believers into members of Christ's Body (vv. 29–30), which He nourishes and cherishes.

The language of this passage is far more applicable to the universal church than it is to local congregations. Individual churches sometimes include members who have professed faith falsely. They are unsaved people concerning whom some of these things cannot be said. They are not being nourished and cherished by Christ. They are not being made holy by cleansing with the water of the Word. It is not Christ's intention to present them to Himself. Indeed, they are still children of wrath (Eph. 2:3). Only the universal, invisible Body of Christ is known to comprise only believers. If we already believe that the universal Body of Christ can be called the church, we will almost inescapably see the universal, invisible church in Ephesians 5:22–33.

If our understanding is correct, the Bride of Christ consists of all true believers (at least during the present age). It is not restricted to local churches, and it is certainly not limited to Baptist churches. The notion of a Baptist Bride evaporates in favor of a Bride consisting of all genuine believers, all of whom are loved deeply by their Lord.

Alien Immersion and Rebaptism

Landmark Baptists insist that a proper administrator is essential for valid baptism. A proper administrator is someone who baptizes under proper authority, and a proper authority is a Baptist church. In other words, for baptism to be valid, it must stand in the succession of baptisms that reach back to John the Baptist.

All Baptists agree that invalid baptism is not genuine baptism at all. Since Landmarkers insist upon a proper administrator for valid baptism, and since a proper administrator has to baptize under proper (i.e., Baptist) authority, they believe that baptism performed in non-Baptist churches is invalid. In other words, non-Baptist baptism is not baptism at all, even if it is performed by immersion and in the name of the Trinity. Landmarkers refer to immersion in non-Baptist churches as alien immersion.

Since Landmarkers consider alien immersion to be invalid (not genuine baptism), they do not accept church members who have received it. Instead, they insist that a candidate for membership must be baptized in a genuinely Baptist church. A candidate who was baptized in a non-Baptist church will be required to submit to rebaptism to become a member. This includes not only candidates who were baptized in the traditional Protestant churches (such as Lutheran, Presbyterian, or Methodist), but also those who were baptized in community churches or Bible churches.

The majority of Baptists reject the Landmark approach to rebaptism. They have three reasons. The first is the difficulty of verifying baptismal succession. However strongly one might believe that Baptist successionism is true, no one is actually able to trace all of the necessary baptismal links to the time of John. Most people can remember who baptized them, but they have no idea who baptized that person. Even Landmarkers are unable to trace their baptism administrator by administrator or even church by church. Therefore, even they possess no real assurance that their baptism is not alien immersion. Faced with this predicament, the Landmark refusal to accept alien immersion makes no sense.

The second reason that most Baptists reject the Landmark approach is because nothing in Scripture indicates that the validity of baptism hinges upon the qualifications of the administrator. The notion of a proper administrator is an inference from other elements in Landmark ecclesiology. If the rest of the system is false, the restriction of valid baptism to proper administrators falls by the way.

Baptists do generally believe that the local church is the proper authority for baptism. Most Baptists, however, distinguish irregular baptism from invalid baptism. Baptism that is not performed under proper authority is always irregular, but unless other factors interfere (such as improper meaning, mode, or subjects), it is nevertheless valid. Mainstream Baptists object to irregular baptism, but they still receive it as actual baptism as long as it preserves the proper meaning, mode, and subjects.

The third reason that most Baptists object to the Landmark approach is because rebaptism corrupts the meaning of the ordinance. Baptism is a picture of the gospel. It is a symbolic depiction of the death, burial, and resurrection of the Lord Jesus Christ. Baptism can no more be repeated than these events can be repeated. To submit to a second baptism is as much as to say that Jesus had to die, to be buried, and to rise again a second time. This symbolic confession is heretical and sinful. No Bible believer should be willing to risk even a symbolic subversion of the gospel. By requiring the rebaptism of those who have experienced "alien immersion," Landmarkism forces Christians to sin against the gospel itself.

Most Baptists simply do not concern themselves with the question of alien immersion. If an individual has been immersed in the name of the Trinity upon profession of faith in the gospel, and if the meaning of the ordinance is not damaged by some other factor (such as the implication of baptismal regeneration), historic Baptist churches will receive the baptism as genuine and valid. Baptist churches have admitted members who have been baptized in a wide variety of evangelical Protestant churches. They have also admitted members who have been baptized irregularly. They may frown upon the irregularity, but their disagreement is reserved for the administrator (who should know better) and not for the baptismal candidate (who probably would not).

Baptists and Other Denominations

Much of the original energy behind Landmarkism was stirred up by Baptist pastors who would invite ministers from other evangelical denominations into their pulpits. According to the Landmark view, the churches in these other denominations were not real churches, and their ministers were not real ministers. To host a Presbyterian or Methodist minister in a Baptist pulpit was akin to ecclesiastical fraud.

This Landmark position forces us to ask how Baptists should view other denominations. Can their churches be seen in any sense as true churches? Should their ministers ever be welcomed into Baptist pulpits? Is religious involvement with non-Baptists permissible at any level?

These questions are rather intricate, and the debate over them can become complicated. Even non-Landmark Baptists have disagreed at times in their answers. Nevertheless, a tentative position can be sketched.

Much of the debate revolves around the marks of a true church. Anyone can claim to be a Christian. Anyone can start an organization and call it a church. Not surprisingly, organizations claiming to be churches profess all sorts of aberrant and even heretical teachings. Simply because an organization or group of people claims to be a church does not mean that it is one. To distinguish true (real) churches from false ones, one needs a kind of checklist of properties that apply to true churches. These properties are called the marks of a true church.

True churches are not necessarily healthy churches. The marks of a true church do not guarantee a healthy church. If one wants to find a healthy church, one needs to look not only for marks of the church's being (*esse*) but of its well-being (*bene esse*). The present discussion is not concerned with the marks of a healthy church, but simply with the marks of a true church. These are the marks that distinguish churches from non-churches.

One preliminary mark is so obvious that it usually goes unmentioned. An essential element to being a church is the intention to be a church. Not every gathering of Christians is a church. A theological seminary is not a church. A missions agency is not a church. A workplace Bible study is not a church. A Christian camp is not a church. These bodies do not intend to be churches, and if a group of people (including Christian people) does not mean to be a church, it is not a church.

Gospel believing theologians have wrestled to articulate the marks of a true church ever since the Reformation. Assuming the intention to be a church, they have consistently named two and sometimes three other marks. The first is the pure preaching of the Word. The second is the correct administration of the ordinances (many will say "sacraments"). The third, not always articulated, is church discipline.

The pure preaching of the Word does not mean that every verse of the Bible has to be articulated with precision. Nor does it imply that a single doctrinal error invalidates the existence of the church. The pure preaching of the Word is about the gospel—to be a true church, a religious organization must proclaim the gospel without contradiction. The preaching of a false gospel means that a particular assembly is not a church but an assembly of heretics. The unadulterated gospel is an essential mark of any true church.

Much the same may be said concerning the administration of the ordinances. This mark does not require absolute agreement over the implementation of baptism and the Lord's Table. It is meant to exclude those ways of observing the ordinances that imply a denial of the gospel. For example, Roman Catholicism teaches that the Mass involves the transubstantiation of bread and wine into the material body and blood of Jesus, which is then re-presented sacrificially to God by a priest who possesses special powers as mediator. This way of administering the Lord's Table directly contradicts the gospel message of Christ's once-for-all sacrifice for sins. Because of its denial of the gospel, the Roman Catholic Church must not be recognized as a true church of Jesus Christ.

Not all gospel-believing theologians have emphasized church discipline as a mark of a true church. Among those who have, the gospel again seems to be the center of focus. The gospel can be denied overtly in the teaching of the church. It can be denied symbolically in the administration of the ordinances. It can also be denied practically in the way that church members live. Some have suggested that a true church must not permit its members to live in ways that deny the gospel, but must call them into account so that they either reform or are expelled from fellowship.

Baptist Definitions of the Church

These are the tests that most Protestant theologians would articulate as marks of a true church. For their part, Baptists have been rather more specific. Their definitions of a local church reflect their specificity.

One of the earliest Baptist confessions of faith was the London Confession (1644), commonly known as the First London Confession. In article 33, it defines a church as "a company of visible saints, called and separated from the world, by the word and Spirit of God, to the visible profession of faith of the Gospel, being baptized into that faith, and joined to the Lord, and each other, by mutual agreement in the practical enjoyment of the Ordinances commanded by Christ their head and King." This definition stipulates both salvation and baptism as essential aspects of a church.

The New Hampshire Confession (1833) has been widely used among Baptists in America. While it was drafted nearly two centuries later than the First London Confession, its definition of a church (article 13) is very similar.

> We believe that a visible Church of Christ is a congregation of baptized believers, associated by covenant in the faith and fellowship of the Gospel; observing the ordinances of Christ; governed by his laws, and exercising the gifts, rights, and privileges invested in them by his word; that its only proper officers are Bishops, or Pastors, and Deacons, whose qualifications, claims, and duties are defined in the Epistles to Timothy and Titus.

Here, too, salvation, baptism, and the observance of the ordinances are included in the definition, but church officers are also mentioned.

J. E. Hopper was a Canadian Baptist who wrote at the end of the nineteenth century. He defined a local church as a "company of believers in a given place united together by covenant to maintain the worship, doctrines, ordinances and discipline of the gospel."[1] In some ways this definition is very close to the standard Protestant definition, but it includes regenerate membership and may imply more by "ordinances and discipline" than some Protestants would prefer.

From a Southern Baptist perspective, theologian John L. Dagg wrote, "A Christian Church is an assembly of believers in Christ, organized into a body,

---

1. J. E. Hopper, *Manual for Baptist Churches* (Saint John, NB: George W. Day, 1894), 5.

according to the Holy Scriptures, for the worship and service of God." This definition also specifies regenerate church membership. The rest of the definition seems a bit vague, but it gets fleshed out in Dagg's subsequent discussion. For example, he is quite clear that unbaptized persons must not be received into church membership, though he recognizes that unimmersed (Protestant) believers should be received "into our affections."[2]

Also writing from a Southern Baptist context, Ervin F. Lyon offered the following definition: "A gospel church may be defined as a company of saved persons, voluntarily banded together in accord with the laws of Christ to the end that His kingdom may be fully established on earth."[3] Lyon again repeats the qualification of regenerate membership. It is not clear what details he would include under, "in accord with the laws of Christ," though he immediately mentions the observance of baptism and the Lord's Supper as well as the maintenance of discipline.[4]

One of the best-known northern Baptist treatments of Baptist polity is Edward Hiscox's *New Directory for Baptist Churches*. Though this work has been revised many times, its original edition has often been reprinted and continues to be something of a standard. Hiscox actually offered two definitions of a church. In one place, he stated that "[Baptists] hold that a Church is a company of disciples, baptized on a profession of their faith in Christ, united in covenant to maintain the ordinances of the Gospel, and the public worship of God; to live godly lives, and to spread abroad the knowledge of Christ as the Saviour of men."[5] Later on, he offered a more detailed definition.

> A Christian Church is a company of regenerate persons, baptized on a profession of faith in Christ; united in covenant for worship, instruction, the observance of Christian ordinances, and for such service as the gospel requires; recognizing and accepting Christ as their supreme Lord and Lawgiver, and taking His Word as their only and sufficient rule of faith and practice in all matters of conscience and religion.[6]

Henry G. Weston was a contemporary of Hiscox. In his discussion of the constitution of the New Testament church, he defined a church as "a body of

2. John L. Dagg, *Manual of Theology, Second Part: A Treatise on Church Order* (Charleston, SC: Southern Baptist Publication Society, 1859), 74, 96.

3. Ervin F. Lyon, *Baptist Fundamentals* (Dallas: Baptist Standard, 1923), 42

4. Ibid.

5. Edward T. Hiscox, *The New Directory for Baptist Churches* (Philadelphia: American Baptist Publication Society, 1894), 15.

6. Ibid., 20.

professed believers in Christ, baptized on a credible confession of faith in him, associated for worship, work, and discipline."[7] For Weston, both regenerate church membership and baptized church membership were essential to the definition.

The above statements come from diverse Baptist sources. Some are from confessions that represent entire groups of churches, while others are from pastors, theologians, and professors. They span a period from the seventeenth century to the twentieth century. Some are English, some Canadian, and some American. Of the American statements, some are southern and some are northern. For all their differences, however, they articulate remarkably similar definitions. Virtually all of these definitions draw attention to the covenantal nature of a local church, which is another way of pointing out its intentional or voluntary character. Beyond that, almost without exception Baptists have insisted that regenerate church membership is part of the definition of the church. Usually they have included believer immersion. Sometimes other elements have been added as well.

Given these definitions, it would appear that Baptists would be forced to deny that the assemblies of other denominations could be called churches. That is exactly the conclusion to which many Baptists have come. Landmarkers especially have refused to recognize assemblies from the Protestant denominations as churches, but they are far from alone.

Nevertheless, other Baptists have been eager to qualify or soften this perspective. Baptist polity has a mechanism that permits at least some qualification. That mechanism is the distinction between a church per se, and a fully or completely organized church. For example, the Philadelphia Confession states that "a particular church, gathered and completely organized according to the mind of Christ, consists of officers and members" (27.8). By speaking of a church that is "completely organized," the Philadelphia Confession implies that a church can be a church without being fully ordered.

This distinction shows up in some discussions of the relationship between Baptists and other denominations. For example, Augustus H. Strong dealt with this question in his magisterial tome on systematic theology.

> The principles mentioned above are the essential principles of Baptist churches, although other bodies of Christians have come to recognize a portion of them. Bodies of other Christians which

---

7. Henry G. Weston, *Constitution and Polity of the New Testament Church* (Philadelphia: American Baptist Publication Society, 1895), 22.

> refuse to accept these principles we may, in a somewhat loose and modified sense, call churches; but we cannot regard them as churches organized in all respects according to Christ's laws, or as completely answering to the New Testament model of church organization. We follow common usage when we address a Lieutenant Colonel as "Colonel," and a Lieutenant Governor as "Governor." It is only courtesy to speak of pedobaptist organizations as "churches," although we do not regard these churches as organized in full accordance with Christ's laws as they are indicated to us in the New Testament. To refuse thus to recognize them would be a discourtesy like that of the British Commander in Chief, when he addressed General Washington as "Mr. Washington."[8]

Strong went on to say that Baptists ought to "refuse to call any other Body of Christians a regular church, that is not organized according to Christ's laws."[9] Here, however, the qualifying word *regular* is important. Strong was not denying that the churches of other denominations are churches in some respect. He was denying that they are regular, that is, fully ordered.

Complicating the question is the fact that both the English word *church* and the Greek word *ekklesia* have a range of uses. For Southern Baptist theologian John L. Dagg, this imprecision made room for some flexibility in nomenclature. He began by stating the problem very precisely. "If baptism is a prerequisite to church-membership, societies of unbaptized persons cannot be called churches; and the doctrine, therefore, unchurches all Pedobaptist denominations [those that baptize infants]."[10] How did Dagg deal with this issue? He wrote:

> Church is an English word; and the meaning of it, as such must be determined by the usage of standard English writers. Our inquiry has been, not what this English word means, or how it may be used. We have sought to know how Christ designed his churches to be organized. This is a question very different from a strife about words to no profit. In philological inquiries, we are willing to make usage of the law of language; and we claim no right, in speaking or writing English, to annul this law. . . . Even the Greek word *ecclesia* was applied to assemblies of various kinds; and we are bound to admit the application of it to an assembly of unbaptized persons, solemnly united in the worship of God.[11]

---

8. Augustus H. Strong, *Systematic Theology* (Philadelphia: Judson Press, 1907), 891.
9. Ibid.
10. Dagg, *Manual of Theology*, 97.
11. Ibid.

Edward Hiscox may be the most accommodating of all. His work on Baptist polity includes a discussion of the so-called signs of the church: unity, holiness, apostolicity, catholicity, and perpetuity. His discussion was aimed at articulating the sense in which each of these signs is genuinely applicable. Hiscox insisted that they are ultimately applicable only to the universal, invisible church, but he also attempted to apply them to local congregations. In a surprising concession, he said, "If catholicity may be interpreted to mean a recognition of the essential spiritual unity of the faith in all of Christ's redeemed people, and a willingness to accord sainthood to all of every name and nation who bear the image and have the spirit of their Lord, then every congregation of evangelical disciples is a Catholic Church."[12]

Voices like those of Strong, Dagg, and Hiscox represent a fairly concessive attitude toward other denominations. The perspective of these theologians raises an interesting question. How far can a church depart from the proper definition before it can no longer be called a church?

An analogy may be helpful. A dog by definition is (among other things) a quadruped. If it loses a leg, does it cease to be a dog, or is it simply a damaged dog? How many appendages can it lose before it can no longer be called a dog? Eventually, if one lops off enough parts, the dog dies. The same principle applies to churches. How many characteristics can be lost before a church can no longer be called a church? Baptists do not have a single, straightforward answer to this question.

Most Baptists agree with two assertions about who should and should not be recognized as a church. On the one hand, they admit that if a fully baptistic church chooses to call itself a Bible church, it should nevertheless be recognized as a true church. In fact, it should even be recognized as a completely organized church. In the present discussion, the name of the assembly is not the issue.

On the other hand, virtually all historic Baptists (together with other gospel-believing Protestants) agree that a congregation is not a true church if it denies the gospel. Even if it calls itself *Baptist*, any organization that denies the gospel cannot be a true church of Jesus Christ. If it is called a church at all, it should be called an apostate church.

In between these two poles lies a whole range of possible departures from Baptist convictions. What if the church is governed by elders? What if it observes feet washing as an ordinance? What if it practices trine immersion? What if it accepts members who have received sprinkling or pouring upon profession

---

12. Hiscox, *New Directory*, 33.

of faith? What if it accepts members who were immersed as infants? Baptists reject all of these practices as unscriptural. The question is whether each of these errors damages an essential mark of the existence of a church, or whether it simply negates an aspect of full organization.

The simple truth is that different Baptists draw their lines in different places. The Landmark approach—refusing to accept baptism from anything other than a Baptist church—is surely mistaken. Short of the Landmark position, however, the application of Scripture and baptistic principles has not been entirely unified.

Involvement with Non-Baptists

In their attitude toward churches of other denominations, Baptists agree at some points but disagree at others. The same can be said of their willingness to become involved with Christians of other denominations. This difference was a source of brittleness during some of the conflicts over early Landmarkism. Many Baptists had been in the habit of exchanging pulpits with ministers of other denominations. Landmarkers and some others, however, insisted that the congregations of those denominations were not churches and their clergy were not ministers.

Given this disagreement, perhaps the best place to start would be to articulate the points at which most Baptists agree. On the one hand, Baptists agree that they owe a duty to their Lord to obey His directions for church order as they understand them. Accordingly, they should not receive any unbaptized person as a member of a Baptist church, even if that person is clearly a brother or sister in Christ. This includes people who have received sprinkling or pouring, whether as infants or as adults. However warmly Baptists may feel toward such individuals, and however ready to recognize them as brethren, the New Testament grants no authority for a church to receive an unbaptized member. In his discussion of this problem, John Dagg admitted that such people might be classified as weak brothers because they do not understand the teachings of Scripture. Nevertheless, he argued that Baptist churches should not receive them into membership.

> We admit the obligation to receive such a brother, but not in any sense that requires an abandonment or neglect of our own duty. . . . We owe nothing to a weak brother which can render it necessary for us to disobey God. If a weak brother feels himself reproved when we yield our personal obedience to the Lord's command, we are not at liberty to neglect the command, for the sake of keeping

the unity of the Spirit in the bond of peace. . . . Every church owes
its first obligation to Christ, and is bound to regulate its organization and discipline in obedience to Christ's command. If, by strict
adherence to the divine rule, we cannot secure the co-operation of
a weak brother, we must do our duty, and leave the result to God.
. . . [I]f a church be required, for the accommodation of a weak
brother, to give up the principles of organization learned from
Christ, and adopt others, she owes it to Christ, and to the weak
brother himself, firmly to refuse.[13]

On the other hand, Baptists also owe a duty to the Lord concerning genuine believers in other denominations. The first part of that duty is to recognize
these brothers and sisters as members of the invisible, universal church, the
Body of Christ. Even Landmarkers, who reject the notion of a universal, invisible church, often recognize the existence of some greater entity (perhaps the
"family of God") that unifies all those who have trusted Christ as Savior. Within
this greater unity exists a duty to receive and love one another. Brothers can
welcome, encourage, support, sympathize with, and pray for one another even
when they do not agree on all matters of church order.

Also, Baptists owe it to Christians in other denominations to assume the
best motives on their part. Significant differences do exist, and these differences must not be minimized. Nevertheless, it is terribly unjust to assume that
a brother's point of view arises because of mere stupidity or stubbornness. An
attitude of arrogance or condescension is always out of place.

Baptists also have a duty to represent their fellow Christians fairly, even
(perhaps especially) during disagreements. Too often Baptists are guilty of slan-
derous misrepresentation in their depiction of other denominations. To cite
only one example, the practice of infant baptism is not the same thing as a belief
in baptismal regeneration. Many Baptists, however, seem unable or unwilling
to distinguish the two, and the result is grievous to many pedobaptists. Such
misunderstandings are perhaps to be expected on the part of ordinary church
members who may not know better, but pastors and other Christian leaders
must go out of their way to represent their brothers fairly.

These are the areas over which Baptists should be able to agree. Some
Baptists are willing to go further. Some have been willing to cooperate with
Christians of other denominations through interdenominational service organizations. During the second quarter of the twentieth century, theological
liberals held firm control of the machinery of the Northern Baptist Convention.

---

13. Dagg, *Manual of Theology*, 96–97.

Baptists in that part of America virtually had to turn to interdenominational agencies to send missionaries or educate their young people. While the older agencies of the convention have now been replaced by many fine Baptist organizations of a more conservative stripe, many Baptists still make use of interdenominational organizations.

Many Baptists have also been willing to get behind multidenominational "snowplow" organizations. These organizations exist to represent many Christian denominations before secular establishments. For example, during the third quarter of the twentieth century, the American Council of Christian Churches spoke for over two million Christians. It defended their interests before powerful commercial and governmental bodies, achieving some noteworthy successes. The ACCC included a wide variety of denominations, some of the most influential of which were Baptist. For many years the General Association of Regular Baptist Churches was the largest member of the ACCC. The World Baptist Fellowship was another influential constituent. Part of the attraction of the ACCC was its willingness to avoid any collaborative activity (including joint evangelistic campaigns) that would require any of its constituent churches to compromise its distinctives.

Of course, both interdenominational agencies and multidenominational organizations bring leaders from different denominations onto the same platforms. Under such circumstances, a gentleman's agreement is always in force: one does not use the platform to preach one's own distinctives. Many Baptists have been willing to extend these same relationships—and the same gentleman's agreement—to the pulpit of the local church. In some circles, Baptist congregations are not at all surprised to hear a Presbyterian or a Methodist preach from their pulpit. They are not offended if their pastor chooses to preach for one of those denominations.

In making such decisions, no single norm exists among Baptists. Many feel uncomfortable with some of these relationships, while others relish them. No clear Biblical rule seems to govern them all, however. Each church and each minister has to come to its own conclusions regarding its level of involvement with non-Baptist denominations.

10 Baptismal Regeneration

BAPTISTS RECOGNIZE two ordinances: baptism and the Lord's Supper. Most other professing Christians also recognize these ordinances, though some may add additional rites. Most non-Baptists refer to these ordinances as *sacraments*. Baptists and others have debated exactly what these ordinances do. Baptists believe that both ordinances are symbols or pictures of the gospel. Communion (the Lord's Supper) depicts symbolically the sufferings of Jesus for our sins. Baptism is a symbolic reenactment of the death, burial, and resurrection of Jesus.

As we saw in the chapter on believer immersion (chap. 2), many people who claim to be Christians have understood baptism to be a saving ordinance. In some cases, these people have thought that baptism actually wiped out one's guilt for both original sin and personal sins. For these people, baptism is seen as a sufficient condition of salvation, at least until one commits another serious sin. They believe that a person who is baptized is actually saved—at least for the moment—with no other qualification. Roman Catholicism teaches something like this.

Others deny that baptism is a sufficient condition of salvation, but they believe that it is still a necessary condition. In other words, they acknowledge that baptism by itself cannot save, but they still believe that it is an essential step in the process of gaining eternal life. According to their view, people still need to believe on Jesus and perhaps even confess Him, but they are not actually saved until they have been baptized. This is the doctrine of the Stone-Campbell movement, sometimes called restorationism. This movement has given rise to denominations such as the Churches of Christ (noninstrumental) and the so-called Christian Churches and Churches of Christ.

While the Catholic position and the Stone-Campbell position are not identical, both can rightly be called *baptismal regeneration*. The idea behind baptismal regeneration is that baptism is somehow necessary for the application of forgiveness and the reception of eternal life. Whether baptism is viewed as a sufficient condition or a merely necessary condition of salvation, those who believe in baptismal regeneration agree that unbaptized individuals are not saved, even if they have believed on Christ (a rare exception is sometimes allowed for a "baptism of desire," in which a person wishes to be baptized but is physically prevented from receiving baptism).

In the chapter on believer immersion, we interacted briefly with the teaching of baptismal regeneration, but delayed a full discussion. The arguments for and against baptismal regeneration are sufficiently involved that the subject deserves a separate treatment of its own. This chapter will explore baptismal regeneration in greater detail.

Baptists believe that baptism is important, but they reject all versions of baptismal regeneration as a contradiction of the gospel. The Bible teaches that the reception of salvation depends entirely upon faith in Jesus Christ. Baptists insist that those who teach baptism as either a necessary or a sufficient condition of salvation are not genuinely Christian at all. We see a difference between the evangelical denominations (such as historic Presbyterians and Methodists, for example) that believe the gospel even though they disagree over polity, and groups that deny the gospel (such as Roman Catholics or the Churches of Christ). The former are to be recognized as Christian, while the latter are not.

Those who teach baptismal regeneration claim to have Biblical evidence for their position. Often they cite Scripture in the attempt to prove that the Bible teaches baptism as a prerequisite for salvation. Too often, Baptist pastors have failed to prepare church members to confront these uses of Scripture; as a result, some Church of Christ ministers have been able to claim that most of their converts are former Baptists.

In this chapter we will attempt to accomplish four tasks. First, we will provide some linguistic background with a study of the idiomatic expression *baptize into* (*baptizein eis*). This linguistic background is necessary for understanding the proof texts that are used for baptismal regeneration. Second, we will examine the Biblical texts that are most frequently used to prove baptismal regeneration. We will interpret them contextually and demonstrate that none of them clearly requires persons to be baptized in order to be saved. Third, we will investigate the example of the thief on the cross. Baptists sometimes attempt to use this pericope as a proof against baptismal regeneration, and many advocates of baptismal regeneration are prepared with a response. We will consider both the passage and the response. Finally, we will offer clear evidence that baptism is not a prerequisite of salvation, but that salvation occurs when an individual simply believes the gospel and trusts the Lord Jesus Christ.

The Use of "Baptize Into"

Several of the proof texts for baptismal regeneration use a combination of words that is common in Greek but less usual in English. They combine some form of the word *baptize* (in Greek, *baptizein*) with the Greek preposition *eis*. This preposition is very flexible in Greek: it usually means *into* or *unto*, but it is sometimes translated as *in*, *for*, or in other ways. To interpret the Biblical text correctly, we must understand the ways in which this combination (*baptizein eis*) is used in Scripture. For the sake of comparison, this combination will consistently be translated *baptize into* in the following discussion.

The best method for understanding the use of any construction is to look for passages in which its meaning is unambiguous rather than passages in which its meaning is doubtful. The doubtful passages should then be read in light of the unambiguous uses. Some of the passages that use *baptizein eis* can be examined rather quickly.

Matthew 3:11 contains the first occurrence of the idiom *baptizein eis*. The text states that John baptizes in water into (*eis*) repentance. This claim is especially useful for two reasons. First, it stands parallel to texts in which John's baptism is said to be a baptism *of* (rather than *into*) repentance (Mark 1:4; Luke 3:3). These other texts suggest that John's baptism was a baptism either *pertaining to* or *coming from* repentance. Those who submitted themselves for baptism were already repenting, and they signaled their repentance by baptism. Consequently, when John said that he baptized in water into repentance, the idiom *baptizein eis* meant that their baptism identified these people as repenters. Theirs was a baptism of identification with repentance.

Second, John's claim is important because it is one of very few texts that speak of baptism into (*baptizein eis*) an abstraction. In this case, the abstraction is repentance. John's wording gives us an important clue as to what it means to be baptized into (*baptizein eis*) an abstract thing. In this case, being baptized into the abstraction (repentance) indicates that those who were baptized were being identified as people who already possessed that abstraction. John baptized them because they were already repenting. Repentance was character-istic of them before they were baptized.

Another important use of *baptizein eis* occurs in Matthew 28:19–20. These verses are sometimes called the Great Commission, and most Christians be-lieve that these verses are an important description of what Jesus expects of His followers. In these verses, Jesus commanded His followers to make disciples, in part by baptizing them into (*eis*) the name of the Father, the Son, and the Holy Spirit. In this text, people are being baptized into a name—here, the name of the Trinity. Being baptized into a name is a fairly common use of *baptizein eis* in the New Testament. To be baptized into a person or into a person's name means to be identified with that person through baptism. In this instance, Jesus' follow-ers were to make disciples by identifying those believers with ("baptizing them into") the name of the Father, the Son, and the Holy Spirit.

Two passages that are less clear are Mark 1:4 and Luke 3:3. Both of these passages say that John's baptism was a baptism of repentance unto (*eis*) the forgiveness of sins. What is not clear in the text is whether the forgiveness of sins is being connected with baptism or with repentance. In other words, are the subjects being baptized into the forgiveness of sins, or do they experience repentance into the forgiveness of sins? If the first alternative is true—if the prepositional phrase is being connected with baptism—it would mean that baptism identifies the subjects as those whose sins have been forgiven. Since the passage is ambiguous, one should not try to prove too much from it.

Another clear use of *baptizein eis* is found in Acts 8:16, in which Samaritan believers are said to be baptized into (*eis*) the name of Jesus. As mentioned above, to be baptized into a person or into a person's name means that the baptism identifies the recipient with that person. By submitting to baptism in Jesus' name, the Samaritan believers were identifying visibly with the Lord Jesus Christ.

A similar use of *baptizein eis* occurs in Acts 19:3. In this passage, the apostle Paul encountered disciples who evidenced some form of spiritual deficiency. He asked them whether they had received the Holy Spirit when they believed, to which they replied that they had never even heard of the Holy Spirit. Then Paul asked them into (*eis*) what they were baptized, and they replied, "Unto [*eis*] John's baptism" (Acts 19:3). Paul wanted to know just who these disciples were, and one way of finding out was to ask about their baptism. Their bap-tism would identify them with somebody or some program, and Paul wanted to know who or what it was. When he asked, "Unto what were you baptized?" (Acts 19:3) he was asking what they had identified with. Their reply indicated that they had identified with John and his baptism, which was not Christian baptism. Paul went on to correct the deficiency. The point is that *baptizein eis* is all about identification.

In 1 Corinthians 1:13–15, Paul chided the believers in Corinth for their partisan spirit. The church, which was split by bitter factions, had chosen spiritual mascots to try to cover their carnality. Some church members identified themselves with Paul, some with Apollos, some with Peter, and some (probably in an attitude of spiritual smugness) with Christ. Paul was not flattered by the group that chose to use his name. With considerable irony he asked them, "Was Paul crucified for you? Were you baptized into [*eis*] the name of Paul?" (1 Cor. 1:13). He was reminding these ecclesiastical politicians that their baptism did *not* identify them with Paul and his program, but with something else. He then expressed gratitude that he had personally baptized only a handful of the Corinthian converts. That fact alone (he opined) should keep people from saying that he had baptized into (*eis*) his own name. In other words, Paul did not want the Corinthian believers identified with him. He wanted them identified with Christ, who had been crucified for them. Their baptism into Christ's name accomplished exactly that kind of identification.

One of the most revealing uses of *baptizein eis* can be found in 1 Corinthians 10:2. This verse states that, during the Exodus, the children of Israel were baptized into (*eis*) Moses in the cloud and in the sea. Paul was trading on the idea that when they crossed through the Red Sea under the cloud, the Israelites were (in a manner of speaking) immersed. His point is that this immersion in the cloud and sea identified the nation of Israel with Moses. After they crossed the sea, no doubt could exist about whom the Israelites were following. They were now bound to Moses by their identification with (baptism into) him. Once again, in this text *baptizein eis* denotes identification—here, identification with Moses.

According to 1 Corinthians 12:13, all Christians are baptized either *by* or *in* one Spirit into (*eis*) one body. This body is identified in the context as the Body of Christ. Whether our baptism is in or by the Spirit is beside the point for the moment (either is grammatically possible). What matters is that our relationship to the Spirit identifies us with the Body of Christ. Indeed, in this instance, *identification* may be too mild a word. Probably Spirit baptism actually unites believers to the Body of Christ. In verse 27, Paul stated that Christians *are* the Body of Christ. This appears to involve more than abstract identification. It appears to involve spiritual union with the Body and with each other.

Similarly, Galatians 3:27 insists that those who have been baptized into (*eis*) Christ have put on Christ. Most likely this verse is again talking about the baptism in or by the Spirit (1 Cor. 12:13) rather than about water baptism. The result of this baptism is an identification or union with Christ that pertains to all Christians, regardless of ethnicity, social standing, or gender (Gal. 3:28). In Galatians 3:27, *baptizein eis* once again denotes (at minimum) identification with Christ.

This survey of passages that employ the expression *baptizein eis* is revealing. While the expression can be used literally (Jesus was baptized into the Jordan River), it is often used idiomatically. The idiom regularly denotes the idea of identification. To be baptized into a person or a person's name is to be identified with that person through baptism. To be baptized into an abstract quality is to be identified as someone who is characterized by that quality. When people were baptized by John into repentance, they were identified as those who had repented. When the Ephesian disciples were baptized into John's baptism, they were identified with John and his program of repentance. Spirit baptism identifies and even unites people with the Body of Christ or with Christ Himself. The ideas of identification and union are uppermost in the idiomatic use of *baptizein eis*. This use needs to be borne in mind when approaching the verses that are used to prove baptismal regeneration.

Proof Texts for Baptismal Regeneration

Advocates of baptismal regeneration do advance Biblical arguments for their position. Typically, they will present from six to ten key texts to try to prove that the Bible teaches their doctrine. Not all of these texts are of equal weight. Some of them simply duplicate the points made in other texts. The following discussion will examine the most important texts to determine whether they require belief in baptismal regeneration or whether some other interpretation is equally (or more) plausible.

> *Mark 16:16*
> *He that believeth and is baptized shall be saved; but he that believeth not shall be damned.*

Those who believe in baptismal regeneration point out that this verse specifies two conditions of salvation: belief and baptism. They argue that both conditions must be met before someone is actually saved. However, this understanding of the verse confuses a condition with a circumstance. Clearly the verse does specify one condition of salvation—belief. But whether it specifies a second condition is unclear. If one wished, one could add yet further circumstances to the list without altering its force. Instead of simply saying that he who believes and is baptized will be saved, the verse might predicate salvation of he who believes and is baptized and lives in Chicago. It could predicate salvation of he who believes, is baptized, lives in Chicago, and is a Bears fan. Or he who believes, is baptized, lives in Chicago, is a Bears fan, and drives a Chevrolet.

The listing of additional circumstances does nothing to alter the basic promise of the verse. These circumstances are not necessary conditions of salvation, but merely situations in which people might find themselves when they believe. Whether someone is in Chicago, Des Moines, or Mumbai, believing is the condition of salvation. Whether one is a fan of the Bears, the Broncos, or the Lions, believing is the condition of salvation. Whether one drives a Chevrolet or an ox cart, believing is the condition of salvation. Whether one is baptized or not, believing is the condition of salvation.

How do we know that believing (and not baptism) is the only condition of salvation specified in this verse? Because the verse does not say that whoever is not baptized will be damned. It says that whoever does not believe will be damned. The verse teaches that someone who does not believe will be condemned forever. It does not teach that someone who has not been baptized will be condemned. Mark 16:16 holds no terrors for the person who happens to drop dead between the place of belief and the baptismal tank.

Why, then, does the verse mention baptism at all? Out of all the possible circumstances that may attend the act of believing, why does it single this one out? Probably because in the accounts recorded in the New Testament, baptism is normally administered immediately after someone professes faith. In fact, in a very real sense, baptism *is* the visible and external profession of faith. Baptism is how people declare that they believe. The notion of an unbaptized believer is entirely foreign to the New Testament. Biblically, belief and baptism go together so inevitably that they should almost be uttered in the same breath. In other words, baptism is very important as a profession of faith and a first step of obedience after salvation. It is not, however, a part of how one receives salvation.

Acts 2:38
Then Peter said unto them, Repent, and be baptized every one of you in the name of Jesus Christ for the remission of sins, and ye shall receive the gift of the Holy Ghost.

The context of this verse is Peter's sermon on the Day of Pentecost. Those who were gathered in the Upper Room had received the promise of the Spirit, attracting considerable attention from the crowds that were gathered in Jerusalem. These were largely the same crowds that had been present at the crucifixion of Jesus. Probably more than a few of Peter's hearers were among those who had cried out, "Crucify him!" (Luke 23:21). Just a few weeks later Peter demonstrated Scripturally that Jesus is the Messiah and that the crowd was guilty of murdering Him (Acts 2:14–36). Peter's words went straight to the hearts of his listeners, who asked, "What shall we do?" (Acts 2:37).

Acts 2:38 is Peter's answer to the question. The question, however, involves more than a single problem. At one level, Israel as a nation rejected the Messiah and delivered Him to be crucified. The nation, *as a nation,* stood to receive collective judgment instead of the promised kingdom of God. At another level, even if the kingdom were to be given to the nation, the people in this crowd were personally responsible for rejecting Jesus' authority as Messiah. Unless something could be done about their rejection and its consequences, a national kingdom would do them no good. In fact, the arrival of the kingdom would be their judgment. Consequently, Peter's response had to deal with both the national rejection and the personal rejection.

Peter was addressing two problems. Naturally, his reply contained two parts, one of which was embedded within the other. The first part of the reply used plural verbs and was addressed to the nation as a whole, represented by the crowd. The second part used a singular verb and was addressed to the individuals within the crowd.

To the crowd as a whole, Peter commanded repentance. The crowd—and the nation—had to change their minds about Jesus and recognize Him as the Messiah. If they would repent, said Peter, they would receive the gift of the Holy Spirit. The crowd had just witnessed manifestations of this gift, and Peter had tied the gift to the kind of activities prophesied in Joel 2. If the crowd (and nation) would repent, they could expect the promised eschatological outpouring of the Spirit. Since this gift would be given only to saved people, Peter was essentially promising salvation to Israelites on the condition of repentance.

Between saying "repent" and "ye shall receive," Peter inserted another command. This command was phrased in the singular and was addressed to the individuals in the crowd. In fact, Peter made it clear that his command applied to "every one of you." It was the command to be baptized in the name of Jesus.

The preposition here is not the same one that Jesus used when He commanded His followers to baptize people into (*eis*) the name of the Father, the

Son, and the Holy Spirit (Matt. 28:19–20). It is not the same preposition that Paul used when he asked whether the Corinthians had been baptized into (*eis*) the name of Paul (1 Cor. 1:13). Rather, Peter commanded people to be baptized upon (*epi*) the name of Jesus. To be baptized upon the name of Jesus meant to be baptized upon Jesus' authority. In other words, Peter was saying that, for the individuals in this crowd, baptism constituted a confession that they had individually repented and recognized the authority of Jesus as the Messiah.

Peter also stated that their baptism would be into (*eis*) the remission of sins. As we saw above, the expression *baptizein eis* (to baptize into) functions idiomatically to indicate identification. For example, John's baptism identified the subjects as those who had repented (Matt. 3:11). When John baptized people into (*eis*) repentance, he was not baptizing them so that they might repent, but because they were already repenting. Similarly, when Peter commanded the individuals in the crowd to be baptized into (*eis*) the forgiveness of sins, He was not suggesting they be baptized so that their sins might be forgiven. Rather, he wanted them to be identified as those whose sins had already been forgiven. Baptism functions as a badge of (or identification with) the forgiveness of sins.

If *baptizein eis* is rightly understood as an idiom expressing identification, then there is not a whiff of baptismal regeneration in Acts 2:38. Peter did not promise forgiveness on condition of baptism. Rather, he commanded baptism because of forgiveness. To be baptized is not a step toward getting saved, but the token or mark of being saved.

Acts 22:16

And now why tarriest thou? arise, and be baptized, and wash away thy sins, calling on the name of the Lord.

At first glance, Acts 22:16 certainly seems to imply baptismal regeneration. In the context, Saul of Tarsus had been struck blind on the road to Damascus. He was waiting in Damascus for God to send someone who would tell him what to do. When Ananias arrived, he healed Saul's blindness and spoke the words of this verse. Virtually all of the English versions translate this verse so that it sounds as if Ananias was issuing a series of connected commands that would lead to Saul's salvation.

The grammar of the passage is not so simple. The verse actually contains two imperatives or commands, each of which is modified by a participle. The two commands are connected by the Greek word *kai*, which means "and" or "also." The first command with its participle could be translated, "When you have arisen, get yourself baptized." The second command with its participle could be translated, "Get your sins washed away by calling on the name of the Lord." The question is how these two commands are related to each other. Is the second command somehow dependent upon the first, or are they distinct?

If someone says, "Go to the bank and deposit the check," the act of depositing the check seems to depend upon going to the bank. The two are really a single command. On the other hand, if someone says, "Go to the gas station and stop at the cleaners," the two commands are clearly distinct. Stopping at the cleaners is a separate act from going to the gas station. If, however, someone were to say, "Go to the hardware store and buy some ice cream," the connection between the two commands is unclear. One would not typically purchase ice cream at a hardware store, but some hardware stores might conceivably have a cooler full of frozen treats. One would have to know more about the situation to tell whether the second command depended upon the first.

Ananias's words in Acts 22:16 are like the last example above. The semantics of the passage could work either way. Ananias might have been telling Paul to get himself baptized so he could get his sins washed away. Or he might have been delivering two separate commands, that is, to get himself baptized *and also* to get his sins washed away. Without knowing more of the details of the situation, an interpreter cannot make a confident decision. In other words, Acts 22:16 is genuinely ambiguous concerning the relationship between baptism and the washing away of sins.

If Acts 22:16 does depict baptism as washing sins away, it is the only verse in the New Testament to do so. Baptism is regularly treated as a profession of faith, a badge of identification, and a symbolic picture of the death and resurrection of Christ. It is not treated as a picture of sins being washed away—at least, not unless that is what Acts 22:16 is doing.

The other interpretation of this verse is equally possible, however. Ananias may have been issuing two separate commands, each with its own modifier. If that is what was happening, the semantics of the verse could be translated: "And now why are you waiting? When you have got up, get yourself baptized. Also, get your sins washed away by having called upon the name of the Lord." In this case, baptism is not being treated as a washing, for the washing away of sins and the baptism in water are distinct acts.

In terms of the connection between the commands, Acts 22:16 is an ambiguous or obscure passage. In making the theological decision about baptismal regeneration, neither side should rely very heavily upon this verse. If other, clearer verses are available, they should be allowed to decide the question.

However one reads the relationship between the commands, Acts 22:16 is crystal clear about one thing. Washing away sins is an effect of calling upon the name of the Lord. Scripture repeatedly affirms that those who call upon the name of the Lord will be saved (Joel 2:32; Acts 2:21; Rom. 10:13). Ananias may have mentioned baptism simply because it is the external mark or badge of a Christian. Paul, who had been persecuting the church, certainly needed to wear that badge. In both testaments, however, calling upon the name of the Lord is what secures salvation.

Romans 6:3
Know ye not, that so many of us as were baptized into Jesus Christ were baptized into his death?

Galatians 3:27
For as many of you as have been baptized into Christ have put on Christ.

These two passages are generally treated similarly to one another by people who argue for baptismal regeneration, so we will discuss them together here. The argument for baptismal regeneration begins by noting that the benefits of salvation are extended to people who are "in Christ." The question is how one gets to be in Christ. On the basis of these two passages, advocates of baptismal regeneration argue that one is placed in Christ by water baptism. In other words, one is baptized into Christ, thus receiving the spiritual standing of being "in Christ," which conveys the benefits of salvation.

Unfortunately for this argument, the connection between being "in Christ" and being baptized "into Christ" is rather weak. The Greek text of the New Testament uses "into Christ" language for several different acts. For example, in the idiom of the Greek New Testament, one "believes into" (*eis*) the Lord Jesus Christ (John 3:16; Phil. 1:29). The apostle Paul also wanted Christians to grow up into (*eis*) Christ (Eph. 4:15). So does one get to be "in Christ" by believing into Christ, by being baptized into Christ, or by growing up into Christ? Clearly the use of the phrase *into Christ* provides little help in answering this question.

In fact, neither Galatians 3:27 nor Romans 6:3 makes any specific connection between water baptism and the Christian's standing in Christ. In Galatians, the preceding context (vv. 24–26) emphasizes faith alone as the sufficient condition of salvation. This is the point of the whole comparison with Abraham. The subsequent context (v. 28) is part of an argument for the unity of all church saints in Christ Jesus. The language is strikingly similar to the language in 1 Corinthians 12:13, a passage that emphasizes the unity of the Body of Christ as the result of baptism in or by the Holy Spirit. While Paul did not repeat the word *body* in Galatians 3, the concept appears to be identical. In other words, the baptism that Paul was thinking of in Galatians 3:27 is almost certainly the same baptism that he referenced in 1 Corinthians 12:13. That being the case, the baptism of Galatians 3:27 is not water baptism at all, but baptism that involves the activity of the Holy Spirit.

Many have guessed that Romans 6:3 is also talking about Spirit baptism rather than water baptism. While this interpretation is certainly possible, it seems less likely. The context of Romans 6 does not connect the meaning of baptism with the unity of Christ or of His Body. Instead, it connects baptism with the death, burial, and resurrection of Jesus. This connection means that the baptism in Romans 6 is probably water baptism, just as it is in 1 Peter 3:20–21, which also connects baptism with the resurrection and (implied) death of Jesus.

Even so, Romans 6:3 does not teach that water baptism positions an individual in Christ Jesus. We have already seen that the idiomatic use of *baptize into* (Greek, *baptizein eis*) has the idea of identification. Consequently, Romans 6:3 is probably teaching that by symbolically identifying believers with Jesus Christ, water baptism necessarily identifies them with His death. By being baptized, Christians are (so to speak) pinning on the badge that marks them as followers of Jesus who have trusted in His finished work.

A Special Problem: Ephesians 4:5
One Lord, one faith, one baptism.

The discussion in this chapter has distinguished water baptism from baptism in or by the Holy Spirit. While this distinction is widely accepted, objections are sometimes registered. One objection is that Ephesians 4:5 teaches that there is only one baptism. According to some, the presence of both water baptism and Spirit baptism would make two baptisms, which (as they see it) would be a violation of this verse. They insist that the church can have water baptism or Spirit baptism, but it cannot have both.

The people who employ this argument do not agree among themselves as to whether the "one baptism" is Spirit baptism or water baptism. Hyperdispensationalists recognize only Spirit baptism, while Landmarkers acknowledge only water baptism. People who believe in baptismal regeneration naturally favor the view that the "one baptism" of Ephesians 4:5 is water baptism.

Whichever conclusion one draws, the argument is nonsense. It simply ignores the fact that Paul's remarks (as all communications) must be placed within a frame of reference. By refusing to recognize an utterance's proper frame of reference, or by repositioning it within a different frame of reference, one can make an utterance mean almost its opposite.

By way of illustration, suppose someone raises the question of whether we will be permitted to play musical instruments after the resurrection. Someone else responds that we may be permitted to play some instruments, but we shall be forbidden to play the trumpet. For evidence, this person appeals to 1 Corinthians 15:51–52, which teaches that the resurrection occurs at the "last trump." Since the resurrection trumpet is the last one (so the argument might go), no one will ever be permitted to play the trumpet again, not even in eternity future.

This argument completely neglects to ask, "Last with reference to what?" The trumpet may be the last one within a particular frame of reference, but outside that frame of reference, plenty of other trumpets might be blown. Would not eternity seem a bit poorer if its inhabitants were never permitted to perform Bach's second Brandenburg concerto?

Ephesians 4:5 posits one baptism, but that one baptism exists within a specific frame of reference. The context discloses what that frame of reference is. From the beginning of the chapter, the apostle Paul began to beg his readers to walk worthy of their calling (v. 1). This walk was to involve humility, gentleness, and patience of the sort that would lead Christians to put up with one another in love (v. 2). Because of these attitudes, they would be earnestly endeavoring to preserve the unity of the Spirit in the bond of peace (v. 3). Believers do not create unity, but they can preserve the unity that the Spirit creates. Paul then named seven great commonalities that unite all Christians everywhere: one Spirit, one body, one hope, one Lord, one faith, one baptism, one God and Father (vv. 4–6). The one body (v. 4) is clearly the Body of Christ, which Paul had already referenced in 1:22 and 23 and in 2:16. This is the same Body that Paul said is constituted by the baptism in or by the Holy Spirit (1 Cor. 12:13).

The frame of reference for the "one baptism" is the unity of believers that involves one Spirit and one Body. Consequently, the one baptism of Ephesians 4:5 is almost certainly a reference to the baptism in or by the Holy Spirit. It is the baptism that constitutes believers as members of the Body of Christ. The existence of Spirit baptism does not prohibit us from administering water baptism, but water baptism is not part of the discussion in Ephesians 4:1–6. Water baptism does not unify believers by uniting them to the Body of Christ. A discussion of water baptism would require a different frame of reference—one dealing with the death and resurrection of Christ. Water baptism simply is not germane to Paul's discussion in Ephesians 4:1–6.

Good reasons exist for recognizing both water baptism and Spirit baptism. A later discussion in this chapter will point out one of the most persuasive reasons. Of the two, however, only Spirit baptism unites believers in the Body of Christ, so only Spirit baptism fits within the frame of reference in Ephesians 4:1–6. When Paul insisted upon one baptism, he was not referring to every kind or occurrence of baptism. Paul himself baptized Crispus, Gaius, and at least two members of the household of Stephanas (1 Cor. 1:14–16), totaling at least four baptisms. What Paul meant is that within the frame of reference of those things that unite the church, only one baptism matters. Consequently, appealing to Ephesians 4:5 to exclude either water baptism or Spirit baptism is a significant theological mistake.

1 Peter 3:21
The like figure whereunto even baptism doth also now save us (not the putting away of the filth of the flesh, but the answer of a good conscience toward God,) by the resurrection of Jesus Christ:

Seemingly, the most straightforward proof text for baptismal regeneration is 1 Peter 3:21. The verse states in so many words that baptism now saves us. Do these words not constitute a clear and definite affirmation of baptismal regeneration?

Of course, Baptists do not think that the affirmation is either clear or definite, but they do acknowledge that this verse is a difficult one to understand. It involves a number of interpretive complexities that pose significant challenges even to those most skilled in the Scriptures. Several matters are genuinely obscure in both the text and its context. Nevertheless, the things that are not clear should not be allowed to cloud the things that are.

Some Baptists believe that the verse is simply trading on the fact that baptism is the public profession of faith in Christ Jesus and that no New Testament Christian ever neglected baptism. Viewed in this way, baptism becomes a metonymy for salvation (a metonymy is a figure of speech in which someone refers to a thing by naming something else that is closely related to it). Baptism could then function much as the wedding ring does in the modern wedding service.

The turning point of the wedding service occurs when the couple swear the marriage oath. Traditionally, each vows to take the other as spouse, to have and to hold from this day forward, for better or worse, for richer or poorer, in sickness and in health, to love and to cherish, until death parts them. With the swearing of this oath, the couple is married in the eyes of God. If the service were interrupted after this point, they would be husband and wife.

Often, however, the partners will next be asked what token they have brought as a pledge of the sincerity of their vows. At that point, each partner will produce a ring to give to the other. Along with the ring, each partner will swear another oath, saying, among other things, "With this ring I thee wed." The actual marriage already occurred before the exchange of rings. The new declaration does not make the couple any more married than they already are. What it does, however, is emphasize the gravity of the vows and the sincerity of the participants. The ring becomes a visible token of the marriage, worn on the finger as an emblem of the oath that was sworn. While not quite precise, it would nevertheless be correct for either partner in later years to say, "I married you when I gave you this ring."

Something like this happens when a sinner prays for salvation. God gives salvation as a gift in answer to the faith that exists in the repentant heart. The prayer is an expression of that faith, but it is not the instrument through which the sinner is saved. It is the occasion of salvation, but not a condition. Nevertheless, Christians may well say that God saved them when they prayed, even though they were believing before they uttered the prayer. The prayer was not the instrument of receiving salvation, but it was a token of the faith being exercised—which was the instrument.

As the ring is to marriage, and as the sinner's prayer is to repentant faith, so baptism is to salvation. It is the external expression of the inward exercise of faith. It is the visible badge or token that identifies one as a believer in Jesus Christ. In that sense, Christians can speak of baptism saving them. While this is correct in a sense, it is also imprecise; for, like the sinner's prayer, baptism occurs only after the fact of salvation. Nevertheless, the faith that saves is confessed both through the prayer and through the visible act of baptism. It is possible that Peter meant no more than this.

Contextually, however, a different understanding of 1 Peter 3:21 may be preferable. Peter began this problematic passage by noting that Christ, by means of the Spirit, went and preached to the spirits in prison (v. 19). Exactly how and when Christ did this preaching is one of the debated features of this passage. At least some of the spirits are identified as people who disobeyed at the time when Noah was preparing the ark (v. 20). In the ark, however, Noah and his family were saved through the water. This is a key part of the argument: they were not saved *by* water but *through* water. The people who were in the water were not saved. They died. Only the people who were in the ark were brought alive through the water.

When Peter declared that the eight souls were saved through water, the salvation was clearly physical. The people who were in the water drowned. The people who were in the ark escaped death. This observation alerts us to the fact that when Peter spoke about salvation, sometimes he meant physical deliverance.

Another example of this use of "salvation" occurs in 1 Peter 4:16–19, where Peter was discussing Christians who are persecuted for their faith (v. 16). This persecution, which constitutes physical suffering, is an aspect of judgment that begins at the household of God but ultimately affects those who do not obey the gospel (v. 17). Consequently, when Christians suffer within God's will, they should commit the safekeeping of their souls to Him (v. 19). Unbelievers are in a different situation: if Christians can scarcely be saved (physically delivered) from such afflictions, what must become of the ungodly? Here Peter was definitely thinking in terms of salvation as physical deliverance from suffering.

Noah's family, sheltered in the ark, was saved (brought safely) through the water of the flood. Where others received death, they received life. This image of life from death carries over into 1 Peter 3:21. Somehow the experience of being delivered physically—of life out of death—corresponds to Christian experience today, and in that sense baptism now delivers Christians.

Peter specified how baptism does not work. It does not remove the filth of the flesh. Some versions and interpreters take this to mean that baptism does not work by removing dirt from the body, but who ever supposed that it did? The word for *filth* does not denote soil or dirt, but rather some sort of uncleanness or pollution. The term *flesh* is one Peter used elsewhere in an ethical sense rather than as a reference to the physical body. For example, in 1 Peter 2:11 he mentioned the lusts or strong desires of the flesh that wage war against the soul. In this instance, he clearly was not equating *flesh* with *body*, and there is no reason to think that he meant to equate them in 1 Peter 3:21 either. If both *filth* and *flesh* are taken in an ethical sense, Peter was declaring that baptism does not wash away sins or the sin nature. If this reading is correct, Peter was actually denying baptismal regeneration.

Given that baptism does not take away sins or the sin nature, what does it do? Peter said that it is an answer or pledge (*eperotema*) that either proceeds from or seeks for a good conscience before God. Since baptism is commanded by Jesus Christ as part of the Great Commission, refusing baptism would constitute a gross contradiction for any professing believer. To refuse baptism would be a clear step of disobedience at the very beginning of the Christian life. It would consequently open a believer to the kinds of chastening that accompany severe disobedience (Heb. 12:5–8; 1 Cor. 11:29–32). By being baptized in accordance with Christ's command, the believer commences the Christian life with a step of obedience which, if maintained, will avoid the chastening that comes from waywardness.

In view of these considerations, the "salvation" of 1 Peter 3:21 is most likely physical deliverance from chastening. God permits some physical affliction in the life of every believer, but disobedient believers may experience chastening as an aspect of correction. Baptism stands at the head of the list for a life of obedience. That kind of life will deliver (save) believers from corrective chastening. Specifically, baptism and the obedience that it promises will accomplish this deliverance through the resurrection (and implied death) of Jesus Christ, Whose finished work is the ground of all blessing for Christians.

To summarize, 1 Peter 3:21 is probably not about eternal salvation. It is probably about temporal, physical deliverance from corrective chastening. Peter clearly used the word *saved* to mean physical deliverance in verse 20. Since the point of verse 21 is that the Christian life somehow corresponds to the deliverance in verse 20, the word *save* should reasonably be taken to mean physical deliverance there, as well. A life of obedience (of which water baptism is the beginning) represents the best way of avoiding those afflictions that God permits in order to correct His children when they disobey.

Summary

The passages that we have examined are the principal texts used to try to prove baptismal regeneration. In this discussion, *baptismal regeneration* stands for the belief that baptism is either a necessary or a sufficient condition of salvation. An investigation of these texts has shown that none clearly requires baptism for someone to be saved, and none clearly promises salvation in exchange for baptism (except in the sense of physical deliverance from chastening). Some of these texts are ambiguous. They could fit adequately with baptismal regeneration if it were true, but they do not prove it on their own. Since these are the main texts used in support of baptismal regeneration, and since none of them clearly teaches that doctrine, the most appropriate conclusion is that the New Testament does not require baptism as a condition of gaining salvation.

The Thief on the Cross

Baptismal regeneration cannot be proven from the text of Scripture. Can it be disproven? One of the most frequent approaches to refuting baptismal regeneration is to appeal to the example of the thief on the cross (Matt. 27:38–44; Luke 23:39–43). The thief was promised salvation without baptism. The inference that is typically drawn is that this thief provides a pattern for salvation throughout the Church Age.

Advocates of baptismal regeneration reject this argument. They are fond of pointing out that the episode with the thief occurred before Jesus died and rose again. They reason that the thief stood on Old Testament ground, whereas baptism is a New Testament ordinance administered for church saints. Since baptism was not prescribed in the Old Testament, there was no reason to expect the thief to be baptized. Today, however, baptism is commanded for all Christians.

Superficially, this objection seems convincing. Even people who believe that Israel is the Old Testament church acknowledge that a change occurred with the death and resurrection of Christ. The form of order in the New Testament church is certainly not the same as the form of order in Old Testament Israel. Since baptism belongs to the New Testament, the fact that the thief on the cross was not baptized should come as no surprise.

Baptismal regenerationists emphasize that baptism is instituted only after the death and resurrection of Christ. One might be tempted to reply by pointing to John's baptism, for John did indeed baptize people before the death and resurrection of Christ. Appealing to John's baptism, however, will not convince many people. Aside from Landmarkers, very few professing Christians have thought that John's baptism was the same as Christian baptism. This includes most of those who advocate baptismal regeneration. For example, the Roman Catholic Council of Trent pronounced a condemnation upon anyone who equates John's baptism with Christian baptism (Session VII, Canon I). The Churches of Christ believe that John ministered under the Old Testament law, which was in effect until Jesus died. Those of his time lived under a different covenant and received salvation in a different way. These two groups probably account for the majority of people who argue for baptismal regeneration, and neither of them will be persuaded that John's baptism was necessary for the thief on the cross.

Advocates of baptismal regeneration believe that the thief on the cross is not relevant to the question of whether baptism is necessary for salvation.

Their argument, however, misses the main point. Granted, the story does not directly address the subject of baptism, but baptism is not the point. What the story does address is the subject of faith. Even if baptism was not part of the economy under which the thief was saved, his example of saving faith is still instructive.

When he was put on the cross, the thief was still an unbeliever. In fact, the gospel record indicates that initially both thieves mocked Jesus (Matt 27:44). During the hours on the cross, however, the thief experienced a change of mind (in other words, he repented). He became convinced that Jesus was the Messiah and would come into His kingdom. He trusted Jesus to remember Him in the kingdom, and Jesus assured him of a place in Paradise. The thief died a saved man. On the cross, however, he could do nothing—nothing at all—to merit salvation or to contribute to it in any way. All that he could do was to turn to Jesus in faith and to trust Him for salvation. The thief on the cross is a prime exhibit of salvation through faith alone.

How is the example of the thief relevant to baptismal regeneration? In order to answer that question we must first understand what occurred at Calvary. Granted, the thief was saved before the death of Christ, perhaps as the last person to be converted under the Old Testament administration. Within a very short time after the thief's conversion, Jesus died, to be raised again on the third day. In His death and resurrection, Jesus offered Himself as a once-for-all sacrifice for sins. The Old Testament law was rendered inoperative, and a new era was ushered in. The characteristic of the new era is that salvation has now been completely provided.

Here is where the example of the thief becomes relevant. Clearly the thief received salvation through faith alone. Yet if baptismal regeneration is true, people on our side of the cross cannot receive salvation through faith alone, but must also submit to the rite of water baptism. What could be stranger than to suppose that the death and resurrection of Jesus made salvation more difficult than it had been under the Old Testament law? Yet this supposition is exactly the consequence of insisting upon baptism in order to gain salvation. Faith, which was sufficient for the thief on the cross, is no longer sufficient. Some ritual is now necessary. In other words, by dying and rising again, Jesus has made salvation harder for people to achieve.

This supposition is not only strange, it is rare nonsense. It flies in the face of everything that Scripture teaches about the cross work of Christ. It also ignores Paul's repeated appeal to Abraham as an example of one who believed God, and it was counted to him for righteousness (Rom. 4:3; Gal. 3:6). This appeal to Abraham forms the basis of Paul's argument for justification through faith apart from works of the law (Rom. 4:1–25; Gal. 3:1–29). Abraham is the Biblical model for justification through faith, and the thief on the cross fits this model. To suppose that people after the death and resurrection of Christ must follow a more difficult pattern is simply preposterous.

A Test Case for Baptismal Regeneration

While the thief on the cross does offer a valuable lesson about the impossibility of baptismal regeneration, this point would be more convincing if a similar example could be found that took place after the death and resurrection of Christ. Such an example could, of course, either prove or disprove baptismal regeneration. To prove baptismal regeneration, we would have to find a case that involves someone who genuinely believed on Jesus for salvation, but whom Scripture treats as lost because of the failure to be baptized. If anyone has ever suggested such a case, I have never heard about it.

To disprove baptismal regeneration, the case would have to be just the opposite. It would have to involve a person who believed the gospel and who was definitely saved, even though that person was not yet baptized. In fact, such a case does exist. It is found in the conversion of Cornelius the Gentile.

The story of Cornelius is told twice. Acts 10 tells how God sent the apostle Peter to evangelize Cornelius and his household. After the event, Peter returned to Jerusalem, where members of the Jerusalem church challenged him for having gone to Gentiles. In response, he repeated the entire story. Peter's narrative appears in Acts 11. Collating these two accounts gives a clear picture of Cornelius's conversion.

According to Peter, he was sent to tell Cornelius how to be saved (Acts 11:13–14). In other words, Cornelius was an unsaved man when Peter arrived at his home. Though he is called a devout and God-fearing man (Acts 10:2), this probably means simply that he was attracted to the monotheism of Israel and trying to learn more. Having prepared Cornelius's heart for the message, God sent Peter to tell him how to be saved.

Peter's message to Cornelius is recorded in Acts 10:34–43. Peter announced that God's work had come to focus upon Jesus Christ, who is Lord of all. Peter briefly summarized Jesus' ministry, death, and resurrection. He stated that God had appointed Jesus as the judge of the living and dead, then he positively declared that everyone who believes on Jesus receives forgiveness of sins through

His name. Peter certainly had more to say, as he himself intimated in Acts 11:15. Nevertheless, in his introductory remarks, Peter had already preached the gospel. He had declared the crucifixion and resurrection of Jesus. Implicit in this declaration was a call for Cornelius and his household to trust Jesus for the forgiveness of sins.

Peter was still speaking when he was interrupted (Acts 10:44–46). To the amazement of Peter and his companions, the Holy Spirit fell on those who heard the word. Peter recognized this as the very same activity of the Spirit that had occurred on the Day of Pentecost (Acts 11:15–17). Peter also connected this activity with the promise of Jesus that His disciples would be baptized in or by the Spirit (Acts 1:5). This was the "gift of the Holy Ghost" given on Pentecost (Acts 10:45).

This baptizing of the Spirit is the same activity that Paul discussed in 1 Corinthians 12:13. There he says that "we all" have been baptized into one body in or by one Spirit. The "we all" includes not only Paul and the Corinthian believers, but also Sosthenes (his coauthor) and all those everywhere who call upon the name of the Lord Jesus Christ (1 Cor. 1:2). For all such people, says Paul, Jesus Christ is Lord. In other words, during the present age, this baptizing in or by the Spirit unites all believers everywhere into the one Body of Christ. It is clearly a gift that applies only to saved people.

Since Cornelius and his household received the gift of the Spirit, understood by Peter to include the baptizing work of the Spirit, then Cornelius and his household must have been saved. Yet this outpouring of the Spirit occurred before Peter had asked for any external action from his listeners. By his own account, Peter was just beginning his message. The text clearly states that he was interrupted while speaking. His remarks had included no invitation to raise a hand, walk an aisle, speak a word, pray a prayer, or submit to baptism. Cornelius had done none of these things. The only thing that happened was that Peter preached the gospel, including the promise that whoever would believe on Jesus would receive forgiveness of sins in His name.

At the time that they received the gift of the Spirit, neither Cornelius nor the members of his household had made any external response whatever. Outwardly, they were still listening intently to Peter's message, and Peter fully planned to continue preaching. Peter had already preached the gospel. Cornelius had heard everything that was necessary to be saved. When Peter communicated the promise of forgiveness to those who would believe in Jesus, Cornelius and his household must have believed. This inward conversion—this change of mind about Jesus—this repentance and faith—was all that was necessary for salvation. Cornelius and his household were saved and received the gift of the Spirit through faith alone, apart from any external act or response.

Cornelius provides the pattern for saving faith. What God requires for salvation is simple trust in Jesus as Savior. When people begin to trust Jesus Christ inwardly, God forgives their sins. While the gift of the Spirit is not always accompanied by the external phenomena (such as speaking in tongues) that Cornelius experienced, God still gives His Spirit to everyone who believes on Christ. Each believer is spiritually baptized into the Body of Christ. All of this occurs upon belief in Jesus, not upon outward confession or prayer or baptism.

Only after Cornelius was clearly saved did Peter command him to be baptized in water (Acts 10:46–48). Water baptism *is* commanded, but it is commanded only for those who have already believed and who are already saved. Baptism does not lead to salvation. Salvation leads to baptism. This pattern is unmistakable in the example of Cornelius and his household.

Conclusion

Many people who profess to be Christians teach that baptism is necessary for salvation. They appeal to several texts of Scripture to establish their theology of baptismal regeneration. In this chapter, we have examined the principal proof texts. We have seen that these texts do not require baptism for salvation. We have also examined the case of Cornelius and his household. In this instance, salvation and the baptizing in or by the Spirit definitely occurred separately from, and prior to, baptism in water. Cornelius and his household were saved without any external action, solely on the basis of inward trust in Jesus Christ. This is the pattern for salvation in the New Testament. Water baptism is commanded for those who believe, but in no way is it instrumental in securing salvation.

11 Organizing a Baptist Church

BAPTISTS BELIEVE in planting churches. They plant new churches in communities where no Biblically ordered church exists. They plant churches when established congregations depart from the faith. They plant churches to multiply ministry. Of course, some also plant churches for less worthy reasons, but in any case, Baptists are strongly committed to planting churches after the pattern of the New Testament.

Every Baptist should be prepared to participate in the ministry of church planting. In most church covenants, Baptists promise that when they leave their church, they will join another church of like faith and order as soon as possible. If they find themselves in a community without a church of like faith and order, they should be prepared to participate in an effort to estabilsh one.

Finding a good church is becoming more difficult. Theological disparity among people professing to be Baptists is rapidly increasing. The old differences between liberals and fundamentalists are simple by comparison. New doctrinal differences have arisen, and these are being compounded by practical and methodological disputes. Many churches look very different today than they did as recently as twenty or thirty years ago. Depending upon their convictions, some Baptists may have a very difficult time finding a church with which they can covenant. Their alternative is to help start a church.

Many communities have no gospel-preaching church, let alone a Baptist church. Organizations such as Continental Baptist Missions and Baptist Church Planters are regularly sending teams into these communities to do the work of Biblical evangelism, and Biblical evangelism involves planting churches. These teams include not only vocational church planters, but also associate church planters, retirees, and tent makers (bivocational church planters who can support themselves while contributing their insight, labor, and maturity to the church-planting effort). Many ordinary church members could participate in such a team.

What is involved in organizing a Baptist church? The process is not as complicated as some might think. This chapter will sketch the general procedure. While more detailed help can be gained from organizations that specialize in church planting, the following discussion will outline the steps that are necessary to guide a group through the process of starting and organizing a church.

Preliminary Activities

Not every community needs another church. Not every community can support another church. Before beginning to gather a congregation, a church-planting team should assess both the needs and the possibilities within the community that they are considering.

Church-planting organizations can provide valuable help in this assessment. They know how to find demographic information for the community, including its patterns of growth or shrinkage, its employment picture (especially important if the team includes tent makers), and its religious influences. They can also help in locating nearby congregations that might take an interest in assisting a church plant.

The team will need to assess its own resources. It needs to know the abilities and experience of each team member, and it has to judge whether those abilities are a match for the situation. It also needs to have a reasonable estimate of the number of individuals in the community who have a potential interest in a new church. It needs to evaluate the level of financial support that it is able to rely on. If a church planter can count on a starting congregation of ten families, and if each of those families tithes, then a church can be brought to self-support status much more quickly than if the church-planting team goes in with no leads.

The team will often be wise to seek an established church to mother the new congregation. Even if the mother church cannot contribute much by way of finances, its prayers, counsel, and encouragement can make a huge difference for the church plant. Also, under the authority of the mother church, the new plant can observe the ordinances, which it should not do if it is merely an independent Bible study or fellowship.

If, after assessment, the decision is made to proceed with the church plant, the team will need to relocate to the community. Members of the team who are tent makers will have to find work. The team will begin a survey of the community to locate individuals who show interest in a Baptist church. Evangelistic outreach, including personal and group Bible studies, will form an important aspect of the team's activity.

Organizing a Fellowship

Most church plants do not begin by organizing a church. In fact, the team should not even consider organizing a church until a sufficient number of individuals have been reached and discipled so that the church can at least have qualified deacons. During the interim, the work will experience a certain amount of flux. Some of the people who seemed interested will drop away from the group, but others will come in. More flux will arise from the fact that church plants tend to attract a certain number of people who hold some eccentric theological position and who hope to find an opportunity for themselves in the new congregation. For these reasons, the team should wait for the effort to stabilize before organizing an actual church.

The Temporary Fellowship

As an interim step, the church-planting team should organize a temporary association of individuals that can be called a fellowship or a congregation. The fellowship will have its own membership, and as the church plant begins to progress, more of the decisions should be made by these members. Since the fellowship is not a church, members of the church-planting team can maintain membership in their own churches during this step while also holding membership in the fellowship. The fellowship is not a covenanted body, but the church-planting team should supply an initial organizational plan (a constitution) and a doctrinal basis. The distinctives of the future church should be emphasized clearly from the outset so that everyone who joins the fellowship understands exactly the direction that the work is going. Every person who becomes a member of the fellowship should know and agree with the ethos and the doctrinal basis of the organization. Even at this stage, no one should be received into the fellowship who would not be qualified to be a member of a Baptist church.

Officers

As the fellowship begins to coalesce, it will have to choose officers. The members will need to elect a moderator, a secretary or clerk, and a treasurer.

The moderator should normally be the leader of the church-planting team. The secretary or clerk will begin keeping careful records of the membership roll and of all business transacted in the meetings. The treasurer will, of course, keep financial records. Needless to say, a bank account should be opened as soon as possible, and giving should commence within the fellowship. This stage of development is not too early to begin to seek legal advice about incorporation and tax exemption. A fellowship can be incorporated on its own, but often it can shelter under the incorporation and tax exemption of the mother church.

Besides these individual offices, the church should also appoint a service committee consisting of at least two men. This committee will function alongside the leader of the church-planting team, much as deacons function alongside a pastor. One streamlined form of organization is for all of the fellowship's offices (i.e., moderator, clerk, treasurer) to be filled by members of the service committee, but this is not absolutely necessary.

When the fellowship organizes as a church, all of these offices will be terminated. One of the first duties of the new church will be to elect officers under its own constitution. The individuals who serve in the church offices may be the same ones who served the fellowship, but a new election will be required.

Meeting Space

While the initial church plant may be able to meet in someone's living room for a few weeks, it will need to find another meeting place quickly. Sometimes schools will allow churches to use their facilities. Public libraries may have meeting space. Most funeral homes have a chapel, and many will allow a church to use it on Sundays. Occasionally a business such as a bank will have a meeting room that it will allow a church to use. These are possible temporary locations.

The ministry of the fellowship will be greatly enhanced if it can locate a facility where it can leave its seating and equipment in place. This location would be better still if it included at least a small space for a church office. Even a commercial space in a small strip mall can be furnished and arranged to create a reasonably church-like atmosphere.

Preparation for Organization

Assuming that the fellowship is attracting a sufficient number of individuals to organize a church, a good bit of preparatory work needs to be done. Much of this work will focus on the governing documents of the new church. These documents will include a covenant, perhaps articles of incorporation (depending on the jurisdiction and whether the church chooses to incorporate), a constitution (which may include bylaws), a charter, and a constituting act.

For many years, Baptist churches have used a standardized church covenant. Now, however, many churches are revisiting and updating their covenants. Since the covenant is essentially a vow, it is a document that merits attention. It expresses the solemn obligations that the members take upon themselves toward one another. It should express all of the obligations and only the obligations to which the members intend to commit themselves as members of the church. As a rule, it is better to adopt a traditional covenant than to have new believers trying to make up a covenant ad hoc.

If the church will require articles of incorporation, the fellowship should seek legal counsel. These articles are for the use of the government and should be kept as minimal as possible. The church's actual plan of operation will be spelled out in its constitution.

For their doctrinal statements, many Baptist churches use a revision of the New Hampshire Confession (1833). This confession is rather brief, but it can be easily tailored to the doctrinal emphases of the group. Often the fellowship will be best served to adopt the confession of the mother church. Alternatively, the church planter can supply a model confession that the church can adopt as it statement of faith.

Actually, the church might consider adopting more than one confession of faith. The core of the Christian faith is summarized in the great creeds of antiquity—the Apostle's Creed, the Nicene Creed, and the Athanasian Creed. If they are rightly understood, not a word of these documents contradicts anything that Baptists believe or that the Bible teaches. They also have the advantage of spelling out certain doctrines with great precision and care. If a church adopts these great creeds along with its own statement of faith, it is acknowledging that it stands in a long heritage of Biblical teaching. The richness, precision, and continuity of these creeds are all good things.

Constitutions can be complicated affairs, and no one constitution will meet the needs of every church. The church-planting team should be able to supply the congregation with several sample constitutions as models. Legal advice is valuable in making sure that any governmental concerns are met, but acceptance by the congregation is far more important.

When a church plant includes many mature believers, the fellowship may appoint committees to work on both the statement of faith and the constitution. In some cases, these committees will present the church with completed documents, but this procedure leaves the congregation with a large mass of information to digest in a short period of time. A better procedure is for these committees to present a bit of their work every week so the congregation can understand it and offer advice on it. These sessions also become teaching occasions for the church planter to explain why Baptist churches do things one way rather than another. Then when the completed documents are presented, everyone will already know what they say and everyone will already have had an opportunity to voice any concerns.

When a church plant includes mainly new Christians, the members may not be prepared to work through all the details of a constitution and confession. Under these circumstances, the documents of the mother church can be adopted by the fellowship. Alternatively, the church-planting team can supply documents for the fellowship to adopt. As the membership matures, later revision is always possible.

The constituting act is a short resolution by which the fellowship transforms itself into a church. Many churches have used something like the following wording.

> *Resolved*, that, guided by the Holy Spirit, and relying upon His continued guidance and the blessing of the Triune God, we do, here and now, by this act constitute ourselves a New Testament Baptist Church to administer His ordinances, advance His worship, encourage Christian fellowship, and to be governed by His will as revealed in the New Testament.

When the assembled members of the fellowship adopt this resolution, they immediately cease to be a mere fellowship of individuals and are constituted as a New Testament Baptist church.

While a charter is not legally or spiritually necessary, it does represent a milestone for the congregation. The charter is a founding document of the church to which all of the original members affix their signatures. Typically, the charter is kept open for several months beyond the actual organization of the church. Within that period, any new members are allowed to sign the charter and to become charter members. The charter should always begin with the name of the church, followed by the date upon which it was adopted. As with the constituting act, the wording of the charter is fairly standard.

> We the undersigned, guided as we believe by the Holy Spirit, and relying upon His continued guidance and the blessing of the Triune God, have by the adoption of a proper resolution constituted ourselves a New Testament Baptist church to administer

the ordinances, advance the worship of God, encourage Christian fellowship, and to be governed by the will of Christ as revealed in the New Testament, and to that end we affix our signatures to this charter.

Church Name

One other question that needs to be answered during the preparatory stage is what the church will be called. Since the name reflects upon the church's message, the church-planting team will usually be very involved in its selection. Alternatively, the mother church will sometimes select the name of the new church. Trendy church names tend to sound odd when styles change, so they should be avoided. The church does need to ensure that it is not duplicating the name of a church that already exists within the community. After the church's name has been chosen, the service committee should ensure that it is properly registered to prevent infringement.

Organizing the Church

Much more work goes into preparation for a church than into actually organizing it. If all of the preliminary work has been done well, the organization can be completed in a relatively brief meeting. This meeting should be scheduled ahead of time by congregational vote. It should be well publicized so that all members of the fellowship are aware of the place and time. At the preliminary meeting when this vote is taken, the congregation should also be given the opportunity to do a final review of the church's documents. The fewer surprises at the actual organizational meeting, the better.

The organizational meeting will be called to order by the moderator of the fellowship. This meeting will be the final meeting of the fellowship. By voting the church into existence, the congregation will vote the fellowship out of existence. Once the meeting has been called to order, the following agenda should be followed.

1. Opening prayer by the moderator or his designee.
2. Presentation and adoption of the constituting act.
3. Presentation and adoption of the constitution and statement(s) of faith.
4. Election of regular church officers, including deacons, according to the constitution.

5. Issuing of a call to a pastor if one has been determined beforehand. Usually, this will be the leader of the church-planting team.
6. If desired, a motion to call a recognition council of messengers from churches of like faith and order.
7. Adjournment.
8. Celebration of the Lord's Supper, administered by the new pastor and deacons.
9. Signing of the charter by all members.

From this point onward, the interim fellowship ceases to exist and the church begins to function as a church. It may now baptize and observe the Lord's Table under its own authority. It is now a covenanted body with the duty to hold its members accountable and to discipline them if necessary.

Going Forward

Although the congregation is now an autonomous New Testament church, the organizational process is not yet complete. Several other issues will need to be addressed. These include the following.

Permanent Facilities and Pastor

At this point, the church is probably still meeting in temporary facilities. It also has a pastor who, up to this point, has been a church planter. He may be drawing all or most of his support from outside the church.

Now is the time for the church to file for incorporation if it intends to do so. It is also the time to file for recognition as a tax-exempt organization—again, if it intends to do so. Legal counsel is usually necessary for both of these matters.

Before long, the pastor and the church need to have a frank conversation about the pastor's future. Does he plan to pastor the church for a while, or does he plan to move to another church plant when the church can support itself? Is he supported by other churches? If so, how long will they continue his support? Does he have to work at an outside job? The church needs to know the answers to these questions so that it can plan effectively for the future. If the pastor has to work an outside job, the church's priority should be to support him sufficiently to free him for full-time ministry.

The church also needs to concern itself with a permanent meeting place. Few congregations can thrive in the long term in rented facilities, though exceptions to this rule do exist. If possible, the church needs to begin saving and strategizing to purchase property and to erect a building. If the pastor has to work an outside job, however, raising his salary should become the church's financial priority. A building is not essential to a fully ordered church, but a pastor is.

One other matter that the church will want to consider is its larger circle of fellowship. Chapter 7, on Baptists and organization, sketches several kinds of cooperative relationships that the church might consider. Any of them is an option, but a new church with a small congregation will benefit greatly from the help and cooperation of other churches. It should seriously consider involvement in local, state, and national associations or other fellowships of likeminded Baptists. It should also consider how it wishes to define its relationship to them. The answers to these questions will depend largely upon the individual congregation's values and priorities.

Planting a Baptist church does not require genius, but it does take dedication and hard work. The labors of planting a church are far more difficult than pastoring an established church. The rewards, however, are significant. New church plants are characterized by a spirit of excitement. Every step is a first step as the members realize that they are shaping a work that may endure for generations. The level of commitment is usually high, especially if the initial team includes more than a single family. When Baptists find themselves in a community that needs a New Testament church, they should embrace the opportunity to plant one, for God may have put them there for just that purpose.

Sources for Further Study

Often a book such as this one will conclude with a bibliography. Simply listing references, however, gives no sense of the value of the sources or how they might be used. Instead of simply reproducing bibliography, this appendix aims to provide some direction for readers who want to pursue further study of the Baptist distinctives and Baptist polity.

One of the best ways to gain an understanding of how Baptist thought has developed over time is to study their creeds and confessions. Many historic Baptist doctrinal statements are now available on the Internet, but one is always cautious about editing (intentional or otherwise) that may have taken place. A reliable print source does exist for these statements, however.

Lumpkin, William L., ed. *Baptist Confessions of Faith*. Valley Forge, PA: Judson Press, 1969.

Lumpkin's anthology includes all of the most important confessions and many of the minor ones. It either reproduces the text critically (including spellings and paginations from the original documents), or else actually reproduces the documents themselves. The result is a sometimes bewildering variety of typography, but an invaluable reference tool. Much of the material in Lumpkin's anthology is also available in a slightly older volume, which also includes some unique material.

McGlothlin, William J., ed. *Baptist Confessions of Faith*. Philadelphia: American Baptist Publication Society, 1911.

Many of the English Baptist confessions were collected in a still earlier work. The advantage of this book is that it also includes other early Baptist documents besides confessions of faith, such as open letters, petitions, and explanations to governmental authorities, and apologies for Baptist principles. All of these documents illustrate important aspects of Baptist thought.

Underhill, Edward Bean, ed. *Confessions of Faith, and Other Public Documents, Illustrative of the History of the Baptist Churches of England in the 17th Century*. London: Hanserd Knollys Society / Haddon Brothers, 1854.

In America, Baptist polity developed along two lines. The South was dominated by the associational model as envisioned by Luther Rice. The North followed the pattern of service organizations as championed by Francis Wayland. The North did continue to make use of associations, but (until 1907) restricted their use to the local and state level. During this period, many fine statements of Baptist polity were produced, but one has stood out above all others.

> Hiscox, Edward T. *The New Directory for Baptist Churches*. Philadelphia: American Baptist Publication Society, 1894. Reprinted as *Principles and Practices for Baptist Churches*. Grand Rapids: Kregel Publications, 1970.

For years Hiscox's book has been used to teach Baptist polity in Bible colleges and seminaries. It has gone through several revisions, each of which, unfortunately, is weaker than the preceding. The original text, which is available through the Kregel reprint, belongs on the shelf of every Baptist pastor and deacon. The language is older and the plan of the book is sometimes confusing, but Hiscox deals with most of the major questions that arise from the structure of Baptist churches. Hiscox stood in the tradition of Francis Wayland, but much of his discussion applies to Baptists of any variety.

Hiscox was not the only northern Baptist who wrote on polity during this period. Indeed, the American Baptist Publication Society (a northern agency) released a large number of volumes dealing with Baptist distinctives. While the authors occasionally disagreed even among themselves, each made at least some contribution to Baptist self-understanding. Here are some of the books.

> Harvey, Hezekiah. *The Church: Its Polity and Ordinances*. Philadelphia: American Baptist Publication Society, 1879.
>
> Marsh, W. H. H. *The New Testament Church*. Philadelphia: American Baptist Publication Society, 1898.
>
> Pendleton, James M. *Distinctive Principles of Baptists*. Philadelphia: American Baptist Publication Society, 1882.
>
> Weston, Henry G. *Constitution and Polity of the New Testament Church*. Philadelphia: American Baptist Publication Society, 1895.

In addition to the above sustained treatments, the American Baptist Publication Society also issued a couple of anthologies. The first is actually a compilation of smaller publications that the Society had already issued. In this volume, each publication retains its own pagination. The second is a collection of lectures or sermons delivered by leading Baptist pastors and educators to the Madison Avenue Baptist Church in New York at the request of its pastor, Henry F. Weston.

> *The Baptist Manual: A Selection from the Series of Publications of the American Baptist Publication Society, Designed for the Use of Families; and as an Exposition of the Distinguishing Sentiments of the Denomination*. Philadelphia: American Baptist Publication Society, 1849.

The Madison Avenue Lectures. Philadelphia: American Baptist Publication Society, 1867.

Baptists of the South did a good bit of their own thinking about Baptist polity and distinctives. Several of their books have made enduring contributions. Interestingly enough, these were sometimes published through northern presses.

Broadus, John A. *The Duty of Baptists to Teach Their Distinctive Views.* Philadelphia: American Baptist Publication Society, [1881?].

Carroll, Benajah H. *Baptists and Their Doctrines: Sermons on Distinctive Baptist Principles.* New York: Fleming H. Revell, 1913.

Lyon, Ervin F. *Baptist Fundamentals.* Dallas: Baptist Standard, [1923?].

Mullins, Edgar Y. *Baptist Beliefs.* Louisville, KY: Baptist World, 1912.

In addition to their works on Baptist distinctives and church order, some Baptists have written full-scale systematic theologies. These typically include a section on ecclesiology, which can incorporate certain elements of church order. Three works are especially worth mentioning. The first is a reprint of an old work by an English Baptist. The second is a nineteenth century work by a Southern Baptist. The third is a volume by a prominent northern Baptist from the early twentieth century.

Gill, John. *Body of Divinity*, 3rd ed. 1839. Reprint, Atlanta: Turner Lassetter, 1965.

Dagg, John L. *Manual of Theology, Second Part: A Treatise on Church Order.* Charleston, SC: Southern Baptist Publication Society, 1859.

Strong, Augustus Hopkins. *Systematic Theology.* Valley Forge, PA: Judson Press, 1907.

The Regular Baptist movement represents Baptists who left the Northern Baptist Convention over theological liberalism. Many Baptist principles were threatened by theological liberalism, and Regular Baptists found it necessary to articulate these principles afresh. One of the leaders of the General Association of Regular Baptist Churches authored a volume that was useful for many years in communicating Baptist distinctives and polity. It can still be found occasionally in used book stores, and is worth reading.

Jackson, Paul R. *The Doctrine and Administration of the Church.* Schaumburg, IL: Regular Baptist Press, 1968.

Apart from principles of church polity, Regular Baptists have also been concerned with effective church organization. Churches are not businesses, but they must perform many businesslike functions: banking, keeping financial records, caring for personnel needs, and, in some cases, incorporating and qualifying for tax exemptions. All of these matters are addressed well in a volume that belongs on the shelf of every pastor and deacon.

Nolan, Michael. *The Business Side of Ministry.* Schaumburg, IL: Regular Baptist Press, 2011.

Not many good books have been written about planting Baptist churches. One slim volume has proven significantly helpful to many church planters. Copies can be ordered from Baptist Mid-Missions in Cleveland, Ohio.

Reese, J. Irving. *A Guide for Organizing and Conducting a Baptist Church*. 5th ed. Elyria, OH: Baptist Mission of North America, 1989.

Southern Baptists have seen a resurgence of conservative theology during the past decades. That resurgence has been accompanied by a renewed interest in church health on the part of key leaders. Mark Dever has been especially influential in articulating Baptist principles through his 9Marks ministry. Anything that Dever writes is worth reading, but the following are especially germane.

Dever, Mark. *Nine Marks of a Healthy Church*. 2nd ed. Wheaton, IL: Crossway Books, 2004.

_____. *What Is a Healthy Church?* Wheaton, IL: Crossway Books, 2007.

Dever, Mark and Paul Alexander. *The Deliberate Church: Building Your Ministry on the Gospel*. Wheaton: IL: Crossway Books, 2005.

As recently as a decade ago, finding all of these sources would have required contact with libraries all across the country. Some of the older works would have been nearly impossible for a non-scholar to access. Now, however, virtually all of the older books (1923 and earlier) in this list are available as PDF files that can be downloaded from the Internet. In fact, the availability of electronic files is one of the criteria that I have used in listing these works. While PDF files are a bit bulky, they have the advantage of reproducing entire books in photo-quality scans. The places to look are Google Books or the Internet Archive Text Archive.

Scripture Index

Subject Index